PUBLISHED by
PARABLES
Earthly Stories with a Heavenly Meaning

Anthony Ritthaler

Roaring at the Enemy

A Book Of Boldness, Anointing And Power

PUBLISHED by PARABLES
Earthly Stories with a Heavenly Meaning

ANTHONY RITTHALER

Pathways To The Past

Each volume stands alone as an Individual Book
Each volume stands together with others
to enhance the value of your collection

Build your Personal, Pastoral or Church Library
Pathways To The Past contains an ever-expanding list of
Christendom's most influencial authors

Augustine of Hippo
Athanasius
E. M. Bounds
John Bunyan
Brother Lawrence
Jessie Penn-Lewis
Bernard of Clairvaux
Andrew Murray
Watchman Nee
Arthur W. Pink
Hannah Whitall Smith
R. A. Torrey
A. W. Tozer
Jean-Pierre de Caussade
Thomas Watson
And many, many more.

Title: Walking On The Water With Jesus (Volume 1)
Anthony Ritthaler
Rights: All Rights Reserved
ISBN 978-1-945698-22-4
Doctrinal theology, Inspiration
Salvation, Meditation
Other books by this author include: Walking On The Water With Jesus (Volume 1 & 2), Soaring With Eagles (Volume 1 & 2), A Devil From The Beginning and Roaring With The Enemy.

Anthony Ritthaler

Roaring at the Enemy

A Book Of Boldness, Anointing And Power

PUBLISHED by PARABLES
Earthly Stories with a Heavenly Meaning

They Were Stronger Than Lions

There is a major thing missing in our churches all across America and that major thing is strong Christians. Christians all across this country are afraid of government, leadership, what others think, some man, some inward fear, and of course Satan himself. The Bible still says in II Timothy 1:7 that "God hath not given us the spirit of fear; but of power, and of love, and of a sound mind". Where are the Christians with backbones like a telephone pole, who have guts, courage, and boldness in the face of evil?

Anyone who has made a real difference in this world had to have the quality of boldness and had to go against the grain in order to change the world for the Glory of God. In the Book of II Samuel 1:23, as David reflected back on Jonathan and Saul's life, the two things he wanted to highlight was the fact that they were swifter than eagles, and stronger than lions. The government, our schools, and sadly our churches have trained their followers to never question any decision made, even if it's wrong and out of line with the constitution and the Bible. These are fear tactics that have produced weak citizens, uneducated students, and powerless Christians. When Adolf Hitler had his reign of terror untold millions lost their lives because they just went along with the crowd and refused to stand up to evil. When the three Hebrew children took a stand for righteousness, they faced amazing pressure, the king's commands, and the fiery furnace. Although they were greatly outnumbered, they knew that they had a God that would deliver them from the face of the enemy. We need more Christians with courage, faith, and honor like these men who forgot about the views of others and roared in the Devil's face.

Paul mentioned the importance of boldness often in the New Testament, but sadly Christians of our day are terrified of the brethren, and they want to be everyone's buddy. The Bible declares in Acts 4:13 that people noticed something different about Peter and John; that something they noticed was boldness and it made all the difference. When David stood before the giant in the Book of Samuel, many whispered under their breath. They said he was disobedient, rebellious, stubborn, crazy, and nuts, but the real problem was that they were chickens. For 40 long days thousands of people looked at this God-denying heathen and allowed him to mock the God of Israel and were very upset that David stepped out and made them look bad. We all understand that David was a man after God's own heart, so he was not the problem. The problem was leadership lacked the vision, drive, and guts to step up to the giant and slay him through the power of God. If David was alive today, I guarantee you that he would be kicked out of most churches today because he would stand for what's right and make others look bad through his spirit-filled life.

The great George Whitfield once said "The reason we don't have revival is because dead pastors are ministering to dead people and life cannot come from death. David was being hunted like a deer all because of one reason; jealousy. So many preachers use the bully pulpit, mind games, fear tactics, lies, and manipulation, all because of a jealous spirit. When Joseph became bold with his dreams, his brothers couldn't take it and they threw him in a pit to silence him. Some of the best Christians I know have been silenced because of bitter leadership who see the touch of God on a person and through a guilty conscience feel the need to discourage them. Anytime you have God's touch of approval, enemies will spring up to destroy you through lies, hurt, silly games, and clicks. We as the Body of Christ should be a unified, powerful, strong army who lock arms together to oppose fear on the Devil. We need to stop shooting our own and start attacking the forces of darkness. We all need to be bold, strong, wise, powerful, and faithful if we want to make a difference. We need a group of people to raise up, win battles, scare the Devil, charge Hell with a squirt gun, and obey God rather than man. God help this generation of timid, weak, frail, faithless, cowardly, cold, carnal, scared Christians who shake at the thought of taking a stand for God. The Devil has the upper hand because God's people refuse to battle him and claim the victory that is promised to them. It's getting harder and harder to find Christians that are stronger than lions in these last days and it breaks God's heart. The Devil never goes to sleep and when we do, he is plotting ways to destroy us. Folks, if we will dive into the blessed word, get on our knees again in prayer, and surrender it all to God we will gain the ability to scare the Devil with our roar. The Bible says in Matthew 16:18 "And I say also unto thee, that thou art Peter, and upon this rock I will build my church; and the gates of Hell shall not prevail against it". Christians in days gone by seemed to have the ability to shake the gates of Hell through their prayer life, their faith, their boldness, and their example and it made a huge difference. Today, Satan walks to and fro in this earth and literally laughs at the weakness of Christians.

As we close out this chapter, I want to bring your attention to a Christian that literally made Satan shake. In Daniel Ch. 6, we read about a man who struck fear in the heart of Satan. The man's name is Daniel and his anointing was from another world. On a daily basis, Daniel walked with the Lord and one day the Devil couldn't stand it anymore. We find through scripture that men were raised up who falsely accused Daniel and used his integrity against him. Through the decree of the king, Daniel was thrown into the hungry den of lions seemingly never to be seen again. As Daniel stared in the faces of the lions, a picture of the Devil, God showed up in a supernatural way and shut up the mouth of the lions. This story expresses the great importance of operating through the power of God and allowing Him to win battles for us. The Bible goes on to say that Daniel was not harmed in any way but his accusers were not so fortunate. All Daniel's accusers alone with their wives, and their children, were cast into the den of lions and all their bones were broken before they touched the ground. Daniel was the type of Christian that roared at Satan and sent him shaking in fear.

If you want to be great, you will have to follow God and have the strength of a lion. Sometimes you may have to go against the king, the government, leadership, the crowd, and the Devil to accomplish greatness for God. Walk in faith, trust in God, and fight Satan through the Lord, Jesus Christ. Remind yourself of the hundreds of scriptures about victory in Christ, the power of faith, and the strength of our Lord and you too can defeat Satan. Wake up every morning full armored and ready to fight against the powers of darkness. Have faith, have confidence, and punch the Devil in his mouth for God's glory. The Bible says this in Romans 16:20 "And the God of peace shall bruise Satan under your feet shortly". Christians: walk in victory, roar at the Devil, and allow God to fight your battles for you. Let's close with this verse from Romans 8:31 "If God be for us, who can be against us?" Amen for that verse.

Scriptures

II Timothy 1:7 "For God hath not given us the spirit of fear; but of power, and of love, and of a sound mind."

II Samuel 1:23 "Saul and Jonathan were lovely and pleasant in their lives, and in their death they were not divided: they were swifter than eagles, they were stronger than lions."

Acts 4:13 "Now when they saw the boldness of Peter and John, and perceived that they were unlearned and ignorant men, they marveled, and they took knowledge of them, that they had been with Jesus."

Matthew 16:18 "And I say also unto thee, that thou art Peter, and upon this rock I will build my church; and the gates of Hell shall not prevail against it."

Romans 8:31 "What shall we then say to these things? If God be for us, who can be against us?"

I Shall Bear You On Eagle's Wings

For so many around this world, becoming famous is their main goal. For other people, gaining popularity is at the top of their list. Some set out on a journey to build an empire, while others use and abuse others to become rich and to make a name for themselves. I've watched countless people strive after more land, endless fun, and new thrills. But joy and peace seem to be absent from their life. If people wish to live like this, that's their choice but things of this nature have never excited me. My mindset has always been to keep things simple, put God first, and watch God bless. The blessings from above are far greater than any treasure we can find down here. To feel His power, and to feel God's favor is the greatest achievement one could ever achieve and I strive to reach that goal every day. The journey to attain God's power will cause pain, lack of friends, suffering, giving, and holiness, and so many refuse to take these steps that lead to God's throne. Most care more about comfort, friends, family, and good times, and they know nothing about a touch from another world. When God Almighty puts His favor and arrival on your life, you will reach a different level and things of this life will mean nothing to you. To soar with God is my ultimate goal and if I have to be alone to do it, so be it. We need more Christians that aim to please God, not man. The next story will highlight the importance of walking with the Master and gaining the desires of our heart through a life pleasing to Him. Allow God to bless you through this powerful story.

Not long ago, God convicted me very strongly about writing a book called Soaring with Eagles. Once I surrendered to His will, the power of God controlled my hand and allowed me to write this book in 12 hours. Upon finishing this book, I remember looking at my wife and saying "I don't know how to explain it, but this book has God's approval and it will bless the world". Around two weeks later, while sitting with my family eating dinner I made another statement that was led by God. I remember looking at my wife and saying "Honey, wouldn't it be wonderful if God would send eagles our way to put His approval on this book", and what happened next is amazing. Around a month later while driving down the road, my wife looked over and saw a nest that was gigantic, about a quarter mile from our house. We pulled over and discovered that there were two huge eagle nests in plain view for the world to see. My neighbor said that in 55 years of living in our area she had never seen an eagle one time before. Folks, God sent these majestic eagles my way to encourage me in my writing ministry and it has meant the world to me. Every day people come from far and wide to view these eagles in flight and we have so many wonderful pictures that are priceless to me. God really knows how to bless His children and watching these eagles sent from God is a humbling experience.

Let's close this chapter with two verses and a closing statement. The Bible says in Psalm 103:5 "Who satisfieth thy mouth with good things; so that thy youth is renewed like the eagles". The Bible also says this in Exodus 19:4 "Ye have seen what I did unto the Egyptians, and how I bare you on eagles' wings, and brought you unto myself". Strive and hunger to be like the eagle and you will see things others will not and you will never regret it one time.

Amen and Amen.

Scriptures

Psalm 103:5 "Who satisfieth thy mouth with good things; so that thy youth is renewed like the eagles."

Exodus 19:4 "Ye have seen what I did unto the Egyptians, and how I bare you on eagles' wings, and brought you unto myself."

The Impact Of This Ministry

This chapter will give you a small glimpse into a heaven-sent ministry. It's been a real honor to watch God move on countless people, and all the glory goes directly to the great God of Heaven. The impact has been vast and the lives touched has been overwhelming. Every day people from around the country and the world tell me how this ministry changed their life. People from all religions, races, and backgrounds have been touched by Almighty God. We have been on 20 radio shows, spoke to millions, and seen God give hope to the hopeless more times than I can count. So often people come to me crying and expressing that they would not be here without this ministry. Drug addicts have gained victory, atheists' belief, church members' faith, the lost hope, and pastors' revival. One man read my first book 19 times, and a child said it changed her world. Everyday lives are changed and transformed and God is doing a marvelous work.

Please allow me to give you direct quotes from people that have read my books and now are on fire for God. These quotes will be from all different people from all walks of life.

Some famous, some not so famous. Some rich, and some poor. Some religious, and some who didn't go to church, but now do. These quotes touch my heart and I pray they touch yours. Here are just a handful of quotes from people that have been changed by this ministry.

From a singer from West Virginia: "Bro Tony, I got your book at a time when Satan was attacking me. The Devil tried to kill me with a 19 day depression and I was hanging on by a thread. I picked up your book, started to read and my chains of depression fell off and my joy returned. Now I'm writing music again and it's because of your book. I'm now about to sign a contract singing Gospel music and it wouldn't be possible without your book. Thank you."

From an 89 year old man who lost his wife off 66 years: "Tony, when my wife died I felt very lonely. One day I started reading your book and I haven't stopped. It's been three years now and I have read it every day. Thank you for writing it."

From a president of a radio show: "Tony, I interview over 350 authors a year and your book is the best I've ever read. It did so much for me."

From a little 7 year old girl at a revival meeting: "Tony, I read your book three times and now I want to be a Christian author when I grow up."

From an atheist at my work:
"Tony, I was an atheist, but after reading your books I now believe there is a God."

From a kind man who is a blessing to me:
"Bro Tony, I must admit every time I sat down to read your book I cried, over and over again God brought me to a place of brokenness."

From a man ready to kill himself:
"Bro Tony, I was so close to ending my life, but when I read your book God gave me hope again. Now I love God again and I am doing my best to serve Him."

From a firefighter: "Bro Tony, your book changed my life and I give it an 11 out of 10; it was that powerful."

From a missionary of 19 years: "It's like nothing I ever read, it was beautiful and encouraging."

From a cold Christian: "Bro Tony, I want to buy 12 books from you because your book lit a fire inside me that has not gone out. My day now consists of reading the Bible, praying, witnessing, and loving God. Thanks to your book, I surrendered everything to God."

From a Buddhist woman: "Tony, it's an excellent book and I learned a great deal about your God."

From a Deacon of a Baptist church: "Bro Tony, I must say your book was life-changing for me; it touched me so much as I read it."

From a sweet Methodist lady: "Tony, I learned more in one week with your book than I have in 70 years in church."

From a Christian out in sin: "I'm texting you tonight because I'm on chapter 17 of your book and God has struck me with tears and I'm calling out for mercy. Your book has touched my soul."

Finally, a dear brother with 8 kids: "My friend, I was struggling away from God but after getting your book I'm hungry for God again and I would like 125 books please."

My friends, these are just a handful of quotes and I literally could give more just like it for days. It's so wonderful to watch God move like in days of old and we give Him the praise for it. Thanks for all your love, prayers, and support because it's making a huge difference to others around us. May we all have ministries that shake the very foundations of Hell. I hope you enjoyed a small glimpse into my ministry and I thank you for helping me to help others. I'll close this chapter with this verse of scripture: Jude Ch. 22 "And of some having compassion, making a difference".

Scriptures

Jude 22 "And of some have compassion, making a difference."

ANTHONY RITTHALER

PUBLISHED by
PARABLES
Earthly Stories with a Heavenly Meaning

Anthony Ritthaler

Walking On The Water With Jesus
Volume One

A Book Of Hope Peace, Joy, And Faith

PUBLISHED by PARABLES
Earthly Stories with a Heavenly Meaning

ANTHONY RITTHALER

Pathways To The Past

Each volume stands alone as an Individual Book
Each volume stands together with others
to enhance the value of your collection

Build your Personal, Pastoral or Church Library
Pathways To The Past contains an ever-expanding list of
Christendom's most influencial authors

Augustine of Hippo
Athanasius
E. M. Bounds
John Bunyan
Brother Lawrence
Jessie Penn-Lewis
Bernard of Clairvaux
Andrew Murray
Watchman Nee
Arthur W. Pink
Hannah Whitall Smith
R. A. Torrey
A. W. Tozer
Jean-Pierre de Caussade
Thomas Watson
And many, many more.

Title: Walking On The Water With Jesus (Volume 1)
Anthony Ritthaler
Rights: All Rights Reserved
ISBN   xxxxxxxxxx
Doctrinal theology, Inspiration
Salvation, Meditation
Other books by this author include: Walking On The Water With Jesus (Volume 1) and A Devil From The Beginning.

Anthony Ritthaler

Walking On The Water With Jesus
Book One

A Book Of Hope Peace, Joy, And Faith

PUBLISHED by PARABLES
Earthly Stories with a Heavenly Meaning

Table of Contents

1. Introduction
2. The Night God Opened a Door for Me
3. Lighting Striking Twice in the Same Year
4. The Powerful Gospel Truth
5. Blaspheming the Holy Spirit
6. Give and Ye Shall Receive
7. The Great Blessings that Come with Helping the Poor
8. Proof that God Gives Us the Desires of Our Hearts (The Hersey Bar Story)
9. The Day God Sent an Angel My Way
10. The Lord Listens to Your Cry for Help
11. God Moving on My Behalf
12. Hearing God's Voice
13. The Amazing Tootsie Roll Story
14. A Sad Story That Still Breaks My Heart
15. God's Faithfulness in My Life
16. Special Delivery, Special Delivery
17. Walking by Faith Not By Sight

18. God Sending Us A Name for Our First Child
19. The Power of Prayer Can Change Everything
20. The Awful Mistake of Mocking God's Man
21. The Lord Touching Little Hope's Body
22. If That Isn't Love
23. Home Sweet Home
24. Great Services That I have Been in Over the Years
25. Crossing the Line With God
26. God Blessing Me With Mcmanna On a Hot Summer Day
27. God Speaking to a Man's Heart Before I Could
28. Feeling God's Power at Home One Day
29. Feeling Gods Power at Work
30. Feeling Gods Power at Church
31. God Can Be Clearly Seen When You Choose to Look for Him
32. Conclusion

Special Thanks

First and foremost, above anything or anyone else, I want to thank my Savior, the Lord Jesus Christ for all the blessings and gifts He has bestowed upon me and my family. The Lord is my strength, my help, my joy, my friend, and my life, and without Him none of this is possible. His influence on this book is very clear and with a grateful heart I want to thank the Lord for helping me write this book. Thanks Lord for your help, your wisdom, your grace, and your guidance through the years and thanks for redeeming my soul. Without you, Lord, I would be a drifting ship and I praise you from the depths of my heart.

Next, I would like to thank my parents for their support, advice, and labor to make this ministry possible. The lessons you have taught me as a young man have become a main-stay in my everyday life as an adult and I hold them dear to my heart. Thank you for always being there for me with a heart of love, compassion, and faith to witness the impossible along with me. Without your impact on my life, this ministry would not be where it is today. Thanks Mom and Dad for always caring for the spiritual well-being of your children.

Another group of important people I would love to thank is all the ministers of the Gospel that have influenced my life in a Godly way. Without spirit-filled preaching through out my life, I have no clue where I would be. Whenever I get a chance, I find myself craving after preaching and it has helped me so much. The old song says "Thank God for the preacher who told me of Jesus", and I want to personally say thanks to any preacher who has played a role in shaping my walk with God. God bless you all and thank you so much.

Last but not least I want to thank all of my supporters who have kept this ministry going. Without your prayers, and financial support, so many that needed hope would still be broken as I'm writing this today. To see revival it takes faith, belief, prayer, giving, and a vision to reach the world with the message of Jesus Christ. Thank God through your assistance we have seen thousands touched, hundreds renewed, and many changed.

As a writer I do not take this lightly and I understand without support all ministries would die. May God richly bless all those who have joined hands with me, and may many rewards be added to your account. Please enjoy the book and thank you very much for helping me bring light to a dark world.

Introduction

The book you are about to read will grab your attention in a remarkable way. I'm convinced that as you read God's spirit will hover over you and do things in your soul that very few books can do. This book is filled with amazing stories that will convict the sinner, convince the doubter, strengthen the weary, and revive the Saint. For far too long Christians have allowed Satan to intimidate them with his roar and it's high time that God's people roar back. God expects us and enables us to defeat the Devil through the power of His spirit. Through reading this book your faith will grow, your knowledge will increase, and your confidence will return in a victorious new way.

Always remember: the Devil can only tempt you but he cannot force you to do anything. We have a choice every day to walk with God and resist the Devil or we can listen to this great deceiver and live in misery. The book that lies in front of you can encourage you, ignite you, and even transform you by God's amazing grace. Folks, let's get our roar back and let's give Satan a black eye for the Glory of God. May the Lord use this book to make us strong Christians who accomplish amazing things through His spirit. God bless you as you read.

Chapter 1
The Night God Opened a Door for Me

The Bible teaches in Revelations 3:8 that God has set before us an open door which no man shutteth, and no man openeth. In John 10:7 Jesus declares that I am the door. In other words God has the ability to open or close any door he chooses by the authority of the word of God. The story that I will now tell you is a real account which happened at my parents house a few years ago. I am glad to report that Jesus is the same yesterday, today, and forever and He is still doing miracles today. Allow me to tell you a true story that is shocking to anyone who has ever heard it.

My wife and I decided to take a trip to my parent's house to pay them a visit on a Saturday night. It is always a joy to be around such godly people, who are always trying to grow in the things of God. I seem to learn something new when I'm in their presence and I have nothing but respect for my mom and dad. While we were fellowshipping and enjoying each other's company I looked at the clock and realized that it was already 12:30 a.m. I still had to put my Sunday School lesson on paper for my teen class at church. I told my wife that I would get things ready and warm up the car. When I started the car I closed the door without noticing that the keys were inside and I accidentally hit the power lock button by mistake. Immediately I went to all four doors to check if they were all locked. Once I knew this was true I checked them for a second time hoping one would be opened. Reality then sunk in that I had made a foolish mistake, and now I must break the news to my wife.

As I walked in the house I couldn't believe what had just happened. I then walked into the living room to find that my family was all ready to leave. At this point all hope seemed gone and I figured this would be a long night. I then looked at my wife and told her the bad news. She couldn't believe it, and her response to me was, "You better find a way to get it open." When she made that remark I wondered just how this would happen.

As I went back outside the example about Peter in prison entered my mind. The Bible declares, in Acts 12: 6-7 that God sent an angel and opened the prison for Peter, and I was praying He would do something for me. My first thought was go to the driver's side and check both doors to see if they were unlocked. After that didn't work I went to my daughter's door and I found that a miracle took place. Her door had opened and God helped me that night. I remember dancing for joy and running in the house at around 1:00 a.m. I told my wife that through prayer, God had opened Hopes door and we can go home now. Isn't it wonderful that we have a friend that sticketh closer than a brother? Glory to His name.

Scriptures Chapter 1

Revelations 3: 8: I know thy works: behold, I have set before thee an open door, and no man can shut it: for thou hast a little strength, and hast kept my word, and hast not denied my name.

John 10: 7: Then said Jesus unto them again, Verily, verily, I say unto you, I am the door of the sheep.

Acts 12: 6: And when Herod would have brought him forth, the same night Peter was sleeping between two soldiers, bound with two chains: and the keepers before the door kept the prison. 7: And, behold, the angel of the Lord came upon him, and a light shined in the prison: and he smote Peter on the side, and raised him up, saying, Arise up quickly. And his chains fell off from his hands.

Chapter 2
Lightening Striking Twice in the Same Year

If this chapter doesn't prove God watches over our lives, then nothing will. When people hear these two stories it causes them to do some soul searching like never before. What I'm about to tell you seems impossible but it is true. It happened while at work one day, God opened the eyes of one of my co-workers in an outstanding way. Let me tell you what took place.

I work at Poco Inc., a company that supplies signs, barrels, barricades, and other equipment to companies around Michigan to help fix the roads. That day I was loading a barrel trailer for my company that was heading for Ann Arbor to repair a road in the area. While I was working I accidentally forgot that I put my keys on the side of the trailer. Without my noticing, the truck and trailer took off with my keys on the side of it. What's stunning about this is that the step on the side of the trailer is very small and there was nothing to hold my keys on it. When I finally was made aware that my keys were missing I began to look around the yard but I could not find them. I then notified my boss that my keys were lost and I may have left them on the trailer. My boss called Mark, the driver of the truck, and asked him to check if my keys were still on the trailer. At this point in the story, he had already been driving for over forty minutes on the highway going up and down hills and driving at speeds of 70 mph on his way to Ann Arbor. When he stopped the vehicle and looked he found my keys were still on the trailer where I left them. I still remember when Mark returned to the shop with my keys in his hand. He had a look on his face that was one of amazement. He dropped the keys on my Bible and said to me, "Either I am a good driver or you're living right." I then replied, " It's probably a little bit of both." He walked away shaking his head and I thanked God for His goodness that day.

About six months later, lightening struck again, on a Sunday night. After church that night I strapped my little daughter, Hope, in her car seat for the ride home. However, I totally forgot that my Bible was still on the trunk where I put it while I was putting Hope in her seat. My wife has a 2008 Chevy Cobalt with a trunk lid about the width of my Bible. The car has no spoiler or anything that would hold my Bible in place and it was pretty windy that night as we headed for the house. We drove about thirty minutes home and twenty of it was highway driving. I can still remember that at one point we were up to 80 mph and I quickly reduced my speed. When we arrived at our home in Canton, Michigan I went to get Hope out of her car seat and discovered my Bible was still on the trunk, where I left it. The pages were blowing in the wind but it never moved an inch and nothing blew out of my Bible. I'm still using that Bible today.

God proves to me every day that without Him I can do nothing. The Lord always has His ever seeing eye open for His saints and these two stories prove it. What a wonderful God we serve!

Scriptures Chapter 2

Mark 4:39 "And he arose, and rebuked the wind, and said unto the sea, Peace, be still. And the wind ceased, and there was a great calm."

Joshua 10:14 "And there was no day like that before it or after it, that the Lord hearkened unto the voice of a man: for the Lord fought for Israel."

James 5:17 "Elijah was a man subject to like passions as we are, and he prayed earnestly that it might not rain: and it rained not on the earth by the space of three years and six months."

Hebrews 13:8 "Jesus Christ the same yesterday, and to-day, and forever."

Hebrews 11:6 "But without Faith it is impossible to please him:"

Chapter 3
The Powerful Gospel Truth

This story, above any in this book, is my personal favorite because it involves the Word of God. Through the years, I have seen God's word do the unthinkable. Growing up with godly parents, with scriptures on the walls of their house, and God in their hearts, it is safe to say the Bible has always been a big part of my life.

The Bible, to me, is alive, vibrant, powerful, life changing, supernatural, and glorious all in one. The gospel story can still transform the lowest, darkest, vilest sinner and put him on a completely different path. My family and I have witnessed, first hand, just how far God's grace can reach. We have seen total drunks changed in a moment of time, drug addicts made brand new, and gang members choose a whole different path. There is no limit to the love of God, or the mercy that he is able to extend. It spoke to my heart, at a young age, and did something that nothing else has ever been able to do. It sliced and diced me to pieces, and saved me from the many heartaches that life throws at me. I still remember a story about God's word that will stir your heart about the gospel and reveal what it is capable of doing.

A teenager, who was listening to a preacher live on the internet from Israel, got under deep conviction of God about his soul while he was dangling his feet in the Jordan River. He told his parents that the Lord was dealing with his heart and his parents got on a plane with him and flew 9,000 miles to Tennessee, rented a car, drove one hour to where the preaching was taking place, and he cried out to God for mercy. The church rejoiced and was shocked that the gospel affected that young man so much. The Bible teaches in Ephesians 3:20 that God is able to do exceeding abundantly above all that we ask or think. It is an unstoppable force that convicts people's hearts and changes their future. Thank God for His Word that guides us through the pitfalls of life. Allow me to give you a story that still touches my heart to this day.

Around two years ago God began to deal with me about doing something special for a true man of God. It became very important to me, and I wanted to make sure the gift was perfect. Many of my ideas were good, but none were giving me peace about the situation. My dad then made a suggestion that finally gave me the peace I was praying about. He mentioned that 2011 was the 400th Anniversary of the first printing of the King James 1611 AD Bible and they were selling exact replicas on the Internet. It was all I needed to hear because there could not be a better gift, on planet earth, than that.

Although I desired that Bible I promised my wife that

we would not buy it unless we had the extra money. Sad to say, we didn't at the time, but I believed God was going to provide it, somehow. Three days later a miracle took place in the form of $1,048 dollars that dropped out of the sky. My wife's first words were to go ahead and get that Bible you want. Joy overwhelmed my soul, and I was extremely grateful what God had done for me.

Without delay we ordered that Bible and it cost $380 dollars. It weighed around 40 pounds and it was beyond explanation. Before I gave it to the man of God I wanted to take it around the country and find the best of the best Christians to sign it for him. Needless to say it involved much travel and deep thought but it was well worth it. These are some of the names I was able to capture; the great Squire Parsons, Doctor Lawrence Mendez, and Steve and Mary Earlywine missionaries to Mexico.

Brother Earlywine once told me that when he was in Mexico he went door to door on visitation for five hours a day, for nine years straight. Every person that signed this Bible is very special in their own way. Some were amazing preachers, some were faithful missionaries, others were outstanding givers and the rest were examples that all could follow. I can still remember the reaction on people's faces when they saw that Bible for the first time. My dad, for example, asked me if he could look at it for a while and he had a look of complete amazement, as he went through each page.

Brother Martin Cooke, of The Inspirations, had a response that I will never forget. Brother Cooke is the founder and pianist for the very famous Inspiration Quartet. Words cannot describe how faithful and precious he really is. For over 38 years The Inspirations have had a song that has made it to number one in the country, in the field of gospel music. As I asked Brother Martin Cooke if he would sign that Bible he got very emotional. He then took the Bible to a spot away from the crowd so he could view it for himself. After he was done signing the Bible he thanked me and said that this Bible is the most beautiful thing he had ever seen. Others wept and all had respect for God's glorious word. When I asked these wonderful people to sign the Bible, I also had them write their favorite Bible verses. Nearly everyone who signed the Bible signed different verses from one another. The majority of the verses were from Psalms and Proverbs, but many also came from all over the Word of God.

One night, while at a Bob Evans Restaurant in Ohio, God swept over my soul in a special way. I leaned over and told my mother something that she and I will never forget. I told her that I was thinking of asking someone, in our church, to sign the Bible and if he did I believe he would sign Hebrews 4:12. To this day I can't explain why I said it but I knew God spoke to my heart that night. The next morning was a Sunday morning and this is the gospel truth. I approached the man who I was looking for, and he agreed to sign the Bible for me. This man is very humble, quiet, and godly. Never, up to that point, had I ever seen him sign anything before but he did that day. As he took the pen and signed his name, I stood in amazement as he wrote Hebrews 4:12 as his verse.

After everyone signed the Bible, he remained the only person to sign this verse. When I told my mom the story of how he signed the verse I said he would, she just couldn't believe it.

In the King James Bible there are over 30, 600 verses contained in its pages. This man picked the exact verse I thought he would, and it still blows me away to this day. This will forever be a story that I can pass on for generations to come. The Bible can be defined as Basic Instruction Before Leaving Earth. The Bible still works just as good today, as it ever has. This personal example moves my heart every time I tell it.

Scriptures Chapter 3

Ephesians 3:20: Now unto him that is able to do exceeding abundantly above all that we ask or think, according to the power that worketh in us

Hebrews 4:12: For the word of God is quick, and powerful, and sharper than any two-edged sword, piercing even to the dividing asunder of soul and spirit, and of the joints and marrow, and is a discerner of the thoughts and intents of the heart.

Chapter 4
Blaspheming the Holy Spirit

The most dangerous and damnable subject in this entire universe is the subject we are covering in this chapter. Many will debate you, disagree with you, or even laugh at you when this subject is discussed in a public setting. Most Christians do not like to consider this subject so they would rather explain it away. I have heard people go to vast extremes to erase this biblical reality from people's minds. They do this through false teaching and human reasoning.

Years ago, in the fundamental movement, many preachers would warn sinners of the dangers of stepping over the line and blaspheming God's Holy Spirit. As a result, silence would fill the auditorium and the lost would run to the altar under Holy Ghost conviction. Many verses in the Bible describe how God will destroy those who disrespect God's word. In the book of Proverbs alone there are multiple references that deal with disaster, sudden destruction, people's lamps being put out, and immediate death. Remember in 2 Kings 2: 23 where

Elisha just received a double portion of the Spirit of God from Elijah. The Bible records how little children met Elisha as he was going to Mt. Carmel from Bethel and decided that they were going to have fun at the man of God's expense. This decision proved to be fatal as Elisha cursed them in the name of the Lord. The word of God goes on to tell us that two she bears came out of the woods and killed forty-two of them for mocking the man of God. If I were to take you through God's Holy Word I would show you multiple times where God's anger was kindled against the lost for blaspheming His Holy Spirit.

In Matthew 12: 31-32: Jesus made a statement that should strike a dart of fear in an unbeliever's heart like nothing else can. His soul stirring words come at a point in His ministry when the crowds were thronging Him like never before. The Lord's fame was beyond belief and His miracles were beyond compare. Like the children in Elisha's day, the Pharisees in Jesus day made a foolish decision that grieved the Holy Spirit of God like nothing else in His three and a half year earthly ministry.

While Jesus was preaching and His Spirit was moving they accused the Lord of casting out devils by Beelzebub the prince of the devils. Their statement halted all the progress and wonderful blessings that others were witnessing at that present time. This caused the Lord to declare a statement that was stunning and earth shaking to those who were in attendance that day. Jesus turned to the Pharisees and uttered these fearful words. Matthew 31 "Wherefore I say unto you, All manner of sin and blasphemy shall be forgiven unto men: but the blasphemy against the Holy Ghost shall not be forgiven unto men. 32 And whosoever speaketh a word against the Son of man, it shall be forgiven him: but whosoever speaketh against the Holy Ghost, it shall not be forgiven him, neither in this world, neither in the world to come".

In the book of Mark 3:29 the Bible proclaims, "but he that shall blaspheme against the Holy Ghost hath never forgiveness, but is in danger of eternal damnation." Notice Jesus said, at any given time, if a man speaks against the Son or the Father, he may be forgiven, but if a man speaks against His Spirit his chance of forgiveness is forever over. May I submit to you that John the Baptist was filled with the Holy Ghost from his mother's womb. David was a man after God's own heart and walked in the Spirit most of his life. Paul preached with power and thousands were touched through his amazing life. Jonah preached to Ninevah and the whole nation, even the beasts, repented and feared his message from God. Peter preached on the day of Pentecost and three thousand were saved. Jesus gave his Apostles power to turn the world upside down in Acts 17: 6. As a result people feared and respected God's men and God's word.

Jesus teaches us in His Holy Book that His Word and His Spirit are two things that should never be disrespected or taken lightly. God is very long suffering in all of our lives according to 2 Peter 3: 9 "The Lord is not slack concerning his promise, as some men count slackness; but is longsuffering to us-ward, not willing that any should perish, but that all should come to repentance". However, His long suffering becomes exhausted when the Lord's Spirit or His Word is blasphemed to a certain point.

Please allow me to explain what I mean. Dr. J

Harold Smith, the great preacher who effected multitudes for the Savior, has one message that all should listen to. Dr. Smith preached a famous message entitled, "God's three deadlines." It is estimated that through that one message alone, over 1.4 million people have been converted to Christ. Dr. Smith describes, in great detail, this subject of blaspheming God's Holy Spirit. He said, in this message, that twenty-one times in is ministry he witnessed people blaspheming God's Spirit and God in return ended their lives within twenty-four hours; everytime. Dr. Smith lived as close to God as very few ever have. He would wake up at three in the morning, every day, and write a personal love letter to Jesus.

Dr. Smith lived so close to Jesus he knew nine years ahead of time the day he was going to die and he wrote it in his personal journal. Nine years later, the day he said he was going to die, was the day he went to heaven. Dr. Smith preached around seventy years reaching multitudes upon multitudes for Jesus. He preached live on radio and was faithful to his calling. In other words, he was a reliable source and someone you could take seriously.

God uses His word, preached by His men, filled with His Spirit to reach the lost. Where the Spirit of the Lord is, there is liberty, but when His Spirit is blasphemed, there is sudden destruction. Be very careful how you act when His Spirit is moving, because it could prove deadly in your life. God's Spirit is taken for granted in this generation, and as a result God will laugh at their calamity on judgement day.

The great Benjamin Franklin admitted that even though he was unconverted to Christ, he still had respect for George

Whitfield. Mr. Whitfield, along with other men of that time, were responsible for something called The Great Awakening that can be found in your history books. During this short period of time, in America and other parts of the world, thousands upon thousands were saved through the efforts of the Mr. Whitfield. Strong conviction filled the land, and many lost people couldn't eat due to the fear of dropping off into hell. Mr. Franklin confessed that watching Whitfield preach was like nothing he had ever seen before. He calculated that one night, after leaving Mr. Whitfield's service and walking home, that this man of God could be heard from some three quarters of a mile away. Mr. Whitfield did not have the benefit of amplified sound, like we do, only God's Holy Spirit. When God's Spirit is present in the church it makes all the difference in the world.

  Please allow me to give you an example from my life of someone who blasphemed God's Spirit and his life was abruptly ended. To this day I still tremble and shake whenever I think back on this incident, but I was there when it happened, so I guess I ought to know. I am humbled by the fact that before I left my twenties I witnessed this take place four times, with all of them people dying shortly after. I saw this take place four times in less than five years. God's Spirit is nothing to play around with and this account, when I was only twenty-six years old, is proof of that. Allow me to show you the severity of blaspheming God's Holy Spirit.

  One day, while at work around five and a half years ago, I received word that my business had hired three new workers. My routine, at that time as it is now, was to welcome my new co-workers and ask if I could help them in anyway. I can honestly say, with my heart pure before God, that I have never judged anyone else that I have ever worked with because of their appearance or their bad habits. Who am I to judge anyone? Within my own heart lies the potential to be just as bad or worse than anyone I will ever meet. Jesus said in John 15:5 "I am the vine, ye are the branches: He that abideth in me, and I in him, the same bringeth forth much fruit: for without me ye can do nothing." When I look at my own life, in light of the scriptures, I see a total mess without the grace and mercy of Almighty God.

With that being understood, for the first time in my life without knowing anything about a new man that started, God's Spirit told me to keep my distance from him. Never before or never again has that ever happened to me, but I wanted to obey the Lord. Whenever he needed help I tried my best to help him, but I didn't go out of my way to seek him out like I did with everyone else. We later found out that he was stealing from everyone he could at work and buying drugs with it. He would tell us his daughter had cancer and needed help; while all the time using it for his own ungodly habit. I noticed that when he got around me he would want to talk about God, but everything he said seemed wrong in my soul. I found out later that when he was around others he would make fun of God and mock the Bible.

One afternoon at work, a conversation took place between a fellow worker and myself that would prove fatal for this man. As I was working with a man named Jason something came out of my mouth that shocked both of us. At the time I knew very little about this man God told me to stay away from, but apparently the Spirit of God knew everything that I didn't know. I mentioned to Jason that I believe that this man I knew little about was going to die before the year was over and I don't know why. Jason said, "Why would you say that?" I said, "I don't know why but he will not live long." This man was quickly laid off from work and a few months went by without anyone hearing from him.

One day, while sitting in the break room talking to the guys, the Spirit of God swept over me and told me to open the Bible immediately and at around 12:40 p.m. I opened my Bible directly to Matthew 12, without turning anywhere else. My eyes then fell on verses 31 and 32 where Jesus referred to blaspheming the Holy Ghost. I read both verses twice and closed my Bible. A sudden quietness fell over me and I knew something was very wrong. For the next fifteen minutes I never said another word and people were asking if I was alright. I would just nod my head. My friend Tom Brown came to me, after lunch was over, and asked me if I remember this man who two months earlier I said would die. I responded that I did remember him and asked Tom, "What time did he die." Tom was in shock and he said, "How did you know he died?" I responded that God already told me around fifteen minutes ago.

Later in this book I will tell you a few more stories that relate to this topic and I pray that it will stir you like this one, no doubt, did. Please don't be an example, like this in someone else's book, respect the Lord for you are fearfully and wonderfully made. Psalms 139:14 says, "I will praise thee; for I am fearfully and wonderfully made: marvelous are thy works; and that my soul knoweth right well". Always be careful how you live your life, the things you say or do can haunt you. A lost sinner once told a man of God, and I quote, "In life I wanted Him not, and in death He wants me not." Your tongue can liberate you or condemn you along life's road. It all depends on how you use it.

Scriptures Chapter 4

2 Kings 2: 23: And he went up from thence unto Bethel: and as he was going up by the way, there came forth little children out of the city, and mocked him, and said unto him, Go up, thou bald head; go up, thou bald head. 24: And he turned back, and looked on them, and cursed them in the name of the LORD. And there came forth two she bears out of the wood, and tare forty and two children of them

Matthew 12: 31: Wherefore I say unto you, All manner of sin and blasphemy shall be forgiven unto men: but the blasphemy against the Holy Ghost shall not be forgiven unto men. 32: And whosoever speaketh a word against the Son of man, it shall be forgiven him: but whosoever speaketh against the Holy Ghost, it shall not be forgiven him, neither in this world, neither in the world to come

Mark 3: 29: But he that shall blaspheme against the Holy Ghost hath never forgiveness, but is in danger of eternal damnation:

Acts 17: 6: And when they found them not, they drew Jason and certain brethren unto the rulers of the city, crying, These that have turned the world upside down are come hither also;

2 Peter 3: 9: The Lord is not slack concerning his promise, as some men count slackness; but is longsuffering to us-ward, not willing that any should perish, but that all should come to repentance

Proverbs 1:26: I also will laugh at your calamity; I will mock when your fear cometh;

John 15: 5: I am the vine, ye are the branches: He that abideth in me, and I in him, the same bringeth forth much fruit: for without me ye can do nothing

Psalms 139:14: I will praise thee; for I am fearfully and wonderfully made: marvelous are thy works; and that my soul knoweth right well

CHAPTER 5
GIVE AND
YE SHALL RECEIVE

There is a secret within the blessed old book that few believe and claim as a promise in their own personal life. Whenever God makes a promise to us from His word it is a guarantee that it will come to pass. The Bible says that "God cannot lie and that heaven and earth shall pass away, but my words shall not pass away". The Bible also says, "Let God be true and every man a liar". The Bible goes on to tell us that God is a debtor to no man and that God shall supply all our need. In other words we can put full confidence in His word at all times.

In the Book of Luke 6:38, God makes a promise that if we give we shall receive. People all around the country doubt that this is true! They refuse to trust God with their funds and they limit the Holy One of Israel. Money has become a God to people and it has become a problem in the United States of America. If I took time to show you all the times God blessed me for giving by faith, and proved to me that Luke 6:38 was true, we would be literally using hundreds of examples. Please allow me to show you what I mean.

A young man got saved in our church and I could tell from the start that he was special. The Lord burned it in my heart to help him early and often. We attended a meeting in Detroit, Michigan one night and I had the joy of driving him to the inner city. As we began to talk I made it my goal that night to talk to him about this blessed subject. We talked about giving and receiving and the levels that it can take you with God. Many examples were given and the Spirit of God was moving in that car. I told him if he wanted to accomplish great things for the Lord he would have to help others along life's road. I then turned to the young man and made a statement that changed his life. I told him that if he determined to help others; God in return would do something special in his life. He told me he would do it and I knew he was telling the truth. Two weeks later, while working at Walmart, a fellow employee gave him a car for free. Things like that rarely happen but it did for him that day. What joy filled my heart when I heard the Good News.

Around a year later I had the joy of taking another young man under my wing. I tried to teach him the same truth. This man had a desire to do what was right and he became serious about giving. I made him the same promise and he took my advice. Around 2 days later he told me he helped just one person and a day later someone gave him a car that he is still driving today. Little is much when God is in it.

We have many examples in God's word that proves this is true. Remember how the lad gave Jesus his small lunch and Jesus took it and blessed it and fed 5,000 men, plus women and children. His disciples then took up 12 full baskets for themselves. Jesus proved that little is much when God is in it. I could go into many other examples from the Bible with you but time would not allow it.

I stand amazed how God always gives back more than what we give out. Jesus knows my heart, and it is a heart of thankfulness for his mercy on me. I remember when God told me to give my 2000 Chevy S-10 pickup to a man of God one day while I was at my parent's house. I felt burdened about this thought and I was a little hesitant because I just recently paid my truck off. I was finally sitting good financially with no truck payment. When I made the decision to follow the Lord, and step out by faith, The Devil tried everything in his power to stop that from happening. The Devil had a plan but God had a bigger plan. The Lord allowed me to sell my truck for $4,000 dollars and immediately I went and got a cashier's check and sent it to Mississippi to the man of God. What I remember most about that experience was the moment I held that big check in my hand. The Devil quickly jumped on my Shoulder and whispered in my ear, "Do you really want to do that?" I realized, at that point, that $4,000 dollars is the most money I ever held in my hand at one time in my life. The Bible teaches that we must trust God's word and not our feelings, and that is what I did.

It was a special feeling when that check left my hand and entered God's hand. At that time I had no back-up plan for another car, only God's promises. After a few days had past, God did something remarkable for me. While at my parent's house the Lord directed me to an ad in the paper displaying a 2005 Ford Mustang show car with only a few thousand miles on it. Basically, I was just looking because I knew I could never afford it. What's amazing about this is God reduced the price on that Mustang $4000 dollars which was the same amount I sold my truck for. God has everything thing under control in our lives if we can only follow his leadership. The preacher later told me that he had a special need at the time and his need was for $4,000 dollars to the penny.

The Mustang became a blessing to me and it was definitely an enjoyable ride. Every-where I went people gave me compliments on my beautiful car. A few years later God wanted to test my faith again, but this time it was with the Mustang. When the Lord spoke to my heart about giving my Mustang away to another preacher, I didn't know how to break the news to my wife. I told my wife that we needed to talk and she knew I was serious. The burden was heavy and my heart was over whelmed with joy as I told her what God put on my heart. She said OK it's your car and if God told you to do it then you should do it. Immediately after talking to my wife we talked to the preacher in private. He was almost speechless as he asked us to give him a day or two to talk with his wife about the situation. Two days later he made us a deal. He told us that the only way he would take the Mustang was if I took his car in return. We quickly agreed to that offer. The good Lord has blessed this move in a powerful way. Since that has happened, my mother offered me another car for free, the preacher gave me an expensive book for free and I no longer have a car payment.

Ever since we made this move in our lives, the windows of heaven have opened and on a daily basis God sends something our way. It has been remarkable to witness and it has been a joy to behold. Give and ye shall receive is more than a cute phrase, it is a biblical reality.

When giving is a part of your life, receiving will be as well. The first time I gave to the Lord it was hard for me, but as the years go by it has become easier and easier. Galations 6: 7 tells us that sowing and reaping is the eternal law of the harvest. If you sow good seed you will reap life eternal, but if you sow bad seed you will surely reap corruption in you life. It is really that simple!

Scriptures Chapter 5

Mt:24:35: Heaven and earth shall pass away, but my words shall not pass away.

Rom:3:4: God forbid: yea, let God be true, but every man a liar; as it is written, That thou mightest be justified in thy sayings, and mightest overcome when thou art judged.

Phil:4:19: But my God shall supply all your need according to his riches in glory by Christ Jesus.

Galations 6: 7: Be not deceived; God is not mocked: for whatsoever a man soweth, that shall he also reap.
8: For he that soweth to his flesh shall of the flesh reap corruption; but he that soweth to the Spirit shall of the Spirit reap life everlasting.

Chapter 6
The Great Blessings that Come with Helping the Poor

There is a special place in the heart of God for the man or woman who will reach out for the less fortunate. There are many verses in the Bible about helping the poor and needy. I believe the Lord is touched with the feelings of our infirmities and weeps over the pain we endure in our lives. Jesus' three and a half year ministry was full of examples of Him caring for the halt, lame, blind and the handicapped.

The Bible declares, in 2 Corinthians 8: 9 that Jesus became poor that we may become rich. Jesus traveled from place to place, in his three and a half year earthly ministry without a home to call his own. He suffered hunger, thirst, felt pain, experienced hard times and He dealt with sorrow, just like we do. He always went after those who other people despised. He went after the woman at the well, the maniac of Gadara, and the demon possessed Mary. Jesus had a soft spot in His heart for the down and out of society and commands us to also care for sinners, no matter how bad they might be. Beyond all the tattoos, the scars, the bad history, and the past people carry around with them is a soul Jesus died for. I believe people miss out on major blessings, in their life, when they ignore the poor and pass up opportunities to be a help to someone in need. Every time you help a needy person through life God writes it down and remembers it in your future.

When I think of helping the poor and being blessed, my mind thinks about William Booth. Mr. Booth loved all mankind, but especially the poor. He gave his life to preach to the lost and bless the needy. God allowed him to start something called the Salvation Army. This outreach has spread worldwide and has helped millions through the years. Proverbs 29:18 says where there is no vision the people perish. How you bless others will determine how much you will be blessed in the days to come.

My mind flashes back years ago when I had the joy of helping a very poor woman in buying her a car. This car was instrumental in bringing her family to church for around 7 years. It brought joy to my heart that this world can not give. I felt like I made a real difference that day and God blessed me for it. The very next day after I bought that woman a car, my boss told me that I would have a pay increase on my next check. God always blesses those who help the poor. I'm going to tell you two stories of how beneficial it is to help the poor and Lord willing it will motivate you to do it. I Timothy 6: 7 tells us that we brought nothing into this world and it is certain we can carry nothing out. The only thing that's going to matter, when we die, is what we did for Jesus. Let these two stories speak to your heart as you read them.

There was a famous preacher that decided one day to help a very troubled and needy child that had come to his church. The boy had a rough past and not even his parents showed interest in his future. He had no friends to speak of and no one that loved him. The preacher's heart ached for that boy and he was the only person on earth that was willing to offer any help towards him. He took the boy under his wing and started to see progress as the young man was growing. One day the pastor went to check on him and found that the young man had vanished from his place and ran away. The pastor searched for the boy but he could not be found. Many years later, on a Sunday morning, a visitor showed up in a new suit, a new tie, and brand new shoes. When the offering was given this man calmly dropped a check in the plate for one million dollars and addressed it, "For the Preacher." After service the Pastor went to the man and thanked him for such a kind offering that day. When the Pastor got a closer look at the man he realized that it was the boy he loved when nobody else would. He became a millionaire and he wanted to repay the love that the preacher showed him when he was a little boy.

Sometimes, when you help the poor, God will bless you in a way that is staggering years down the road. Psalms 41:1 says "blessed is he that considereth the poor; the Lord will deliver him in time of trouble".

The second story that I pray will speak to your heart is one from my own life at a gas station a few years ago. Nearly every chance I get, and God knows my heart, I try to extend a hand of mercy to the poor. On the other hand I really try my best to use wisdom in each and every situation I encounter. The word of God says that if a man don't work he shouldn't eat. Fully capable, healthy people that refuse to work have no reason, according to the Bible, to beg from those who work. God says in Proverbs 20:4 that the sluggard will not plow by reason of the cold; therefore shall he beg in harvest and have nothing. God always condemns laziness and has ordained that we work with our hands and provide for ourselves. The Lord tells us in I Timothy 5:8 but if any provide not for his own, and especially for those of his own house, he hath denied the faith, and is worse than an infidel. There are people out there that are smooth talkers and quick thinkers when it comes to stealing your hard-earned money, and you need to be careful. A man approached me one day and said he knew me and needed some money. He told me that he worked with me but couldn't remember my name. I found out later that he told the owner of the store I was at that he was his next door neighbor in Livonia, Michigan but the owner never lived in Livonia. People will go to any extreme necessary to trick you so they can fulfil their ungodly agenda. Every situation requires discernment and wisdom on our part because there are thousands of people that really do need help.

    Let me tell you this story and I hope it helps you. One day, late at night, I pulled into a gas station and I saw a man digging in the garbage can for bottles. As I watched this man for a moment something told me to help him in any way I could. I reached behind my seat and found a pop bottle and gave it to the man. He thanked me over and over for that one pop bottle and I could tell he meant it. Verses about helping the poor raced through my mind and as he walked away my heart broke. I remember chasing him down and giving him another bottle and the only two dollars in my wallet. A tear came to his eye and my heart was instantly healed. The next day, at work, they asked me to go on the road and help close a freeway. I rarely get a chance to go on the road and make state wages but after I helped that poor man God gave me an extra $200.00 that day. I am convinced it is because I helped the poor the day before.

The Bible teaches us in Ephesians 4: 32 that we ought to be tenderhearted forgiving one another even as God for Christ sake hath forgiven you. Ask yourself, when was the last time I helped someone in need. You may find that the answer will surprise you. The Bible still teaches whoso stoppeth his ears at the cry of the poor; he also shall cry himself but shall not be heard. (Proverbs 21:13)

Scriptures Chapter 6

2 Corinthians 8: 9: For ye know the grace of our Lord Jesus Christ, that, though he was rich, yet for your sakes he became poor, that ye through his poverty might be rich.

Proverbs 29:18 where there is no vision, the people perish: but he that keepeth the law, happy is he. Says where there is no vision the people perish

I Timothy 6: 7 for we brought nothing into this world, and it is certain we can carry nothing out.

Psalms 41:1 blessed is he that considereth the poor: the LORD will deliver him in time of trouble.

Proverbs 20: 4: The sluggard will not plow by reason of the cold; therefore shall he beg in harvest, and have nothing.

I Timothy 5: 8: But if any provide not for his own, and especially for those of his own house, he hath denied the faith, and is worse than an infidel.

Ephesians 4: 32: And be ye kind one to another, tenderhearted, forgiving one another, even as God for Christ's sake hath forgiven you.

Proverbs 21:13 whoso stoppeth his ears at the cry of the poor, he also shall cry himself but shall not be heard

Chapter 7
Proof that God Gives Us the Desires of Our Hearts (The Hershey Bar Story)

This story, in particular, shocks more people than any other story that I will tell in this book. The detail and the amazement of this story puzzles people to this day. When I describe this event in my life, I still find it hard to believe. The Bible says in Romans 8: 28 "And we know that all things work together for good to them that love God, to them who are the called according to his purpose." When you walk by faith and not by sight anything is possible with the Lord. Jesus said in Matthew 17: 20 "If ye have faith as a grain of mustard seed, ye shall say unto this mountain, remove hence to yonder place; and it shall remove; and nothing shall be impossible unto you."

The average Christian spends the majority of their time doubting God and therefore miracles are only things they read about, but it is not a reality in their everyday walk with God.

The Bible says in 1 John 5:14-15 "And this is the confidence that we have in him that, if we ask any thing according to his will, he heareth us." 15: "And if we know that he hear us, whatsoever we ask, we know that we have the petitions that we desired of him." When you pray you must believe God will answer you according to His will. The great George Mueller had around 30,000 answers to prayer throughout his life and they were all in private. Let me tell you this amazing story that has become a reality for me.

Around a year ago, in the summer time, God put something unusual on my heart that I wanted to get a preacher. It was so unusual that I really had to make sure it was God's will and not my own thoughts. After a few days of making it a matter of prayer I told my wife that I believe God was going to put it in someone's heart to buy me a five-pound Hershey bar to give to a preacher. Her first reaction was like Sarah when she found out that she would have a baby at ninety years of age. My wife thought it was crazy, to be honest, I did too, but I was sure God spoke to my heart. Week after week passed and still no sign of a five-pound Hershey bar. As time passed on my faith never wavered because I was confident God spoke to me.

One day, while reading the Bible at work, a young man named Steve shouted across the breakroom, in my direction, and from then on a glorious conversation took place. He said," Tony, do you know what I'm going to get you when I get some money?" I said," What's that Steve?" He said," A five pound Hershey bar; have you ever seen one?" My heart skipped a beat as I replied," I sure have." Little did he know that I had been praying about that for months. God is a faithful God that answers our requests like in days of old. When you think about how rare that was it almost seems like the stars were aligned at exactly the right time for that to happen. You see, His thoughts are not our thoughts, neither is His ways our ways. God works in a totally different way than we do. Jesus knows the beginning from the end and the hairs on our head are all numbered. When God did that for me it strengthened my faith and blessed my soul.

Do you know that ever since that day two other people also offered me a five pound Hershey bar and a teenager bought me a one pound Hershey bar for Christmas. Also, since that day God has put it on the heart of people that I work with to buy bulk candy with small Hershey bars in it. They tell me everyday to help myself. If anyone can explain how God did that, please let me know. Mark 6: 6: And he marveled because of their unbelief. And he went round about the villages, teaching. How much do we believe God, and how much more could He possibly do to convince us.

Scriptures Chapter 7

Romans 8: 28: And we know that all things work together for good to them that love God, to them who are the called according to his purpose.

Matthew 17: 20: And Jesus said unto them, Because of your unbelief: for verily I say unto you, If ye have faith as a grain of mustard seed, ye shall say unto this mountain, Remove hence to yonder place; and it shall remove; and nothing shall be impossible unto you.

I John 5:14: And this is the confidence that we have in him, that, if we ask any thing according to his will, he heareth us: 15: And if we know that he hear us, whatsoever we ask, we know that we have the petitions that we desired of him

Mark 6: 6: And he marveled because of their unbelief. And he went round about the villages, teaching.

Chapter 8
The Day God Sent an Angel My Way

As I read through the word of God I quickly realize that angels cover the pages of the Holy Scriptures. Hebrews 12:22 tells us that there are an innumerable company of angels. Psalms 34:7 talks about how the angels of God encampeth around them that fear Him. Remember how Gabriel appeared before Zacharias showing him that his wife Elizabeth would soon have John the Baptist who would be great in the sight of God. Or recall when an angel of the Lord appeared unto Samson's mother to announce that she would conceive and give birth to a man child that would judge Israel for twenty years.

I often think about how Jesus told the world, in Matthew 26:53 that He had the ability to call twelve legions of angels to deliver Him from the cross if need be. The Bible also says that they excel in strength according to Psalms 103:20. The Bible teaches that they protect his saints in the book of Daniel 6:22. Angels have many different abilities and purposes found in the Bible. If I expounded on them it would surely take up the rest of this book.

In my thirty years of being in church and hearing hundreds of good men of God preach, I have never once heard a preacher cover this topic in a service. My thoughts on why I never have are probably because many people are afraid to teach on the spirit world because it is somewhat unknown. People are unsure on the subject of demons and angels so they deny it all together. With that being said it does not change the reality of the battle between light and darkness as we know it. I refuse to lie to myself about angels and dare not change the truth of God's written word. The story I'm about to tell you is as real as the paper that I am writing on, and it should make your heart skip a beat.

Many years ago, while at work, something happened that sticks with me until this very day. That morning it was very busy and fast pace. I remember working at an incredible rate and going up to receive another order to complete when all of the sudden I was approached by a total stranger. When I asked him if he needed help with anything he responded in an unusual way. He called me by my first name. I was shocked that he knew my name seeing that we had never met before. He went on to ask me if I knew where the verse was, in the Bible, about strength. Not really understanding the importance of what was taking place I told him the verse he was looking for was Philippians 4:13. That verse tells the believer that we can do all things through Christ which strengtheneth me. He then responded by saying, "Thank you Tony" and walked away. To this day I never caught his name, but he sure knew mine.

When looking back on this incident I stand amazed that the Savior would send an angel my way. This moment in time changed my mindset concerning angels. Thanks be unto God for his watch care over us.

Many other times throughout my life I have felt the presence of angels and unknown forces keeping me safe. The Lord knows I am humbled for his hand of safety on my life. When we get to heaven and God gives us perfect understanding, only then will we comprehend His love toward us. When you study God's word, notice how many times it refers to His love and protection towards the Christian. You will then have a new found respect for God's mercy like never before. Angels are all around us, at all times. If we keep that in mind, it will help us walk the strait and narrow way for the Master.

Scriptures Chapter 8

Hebrews 12:22 But ye are come unto mount Sion, and unto the city of the living God, the heavenly Jerusalem, and to an innumerable company of angels,

Psalms 34:7 The angel of the LORD encampeth round about them that fear him, and delivereth them.

Matthew 26:53 Thinkest thou that I cannot now pray to my Father, and he shall presently give me more than twelve legions of angels?

Psalms 103:20 Bless the LORD, ye his angels, that excel in strength, that do his commandments, hearkening unto the voice of his word.

Daniel 6:22 My God hath sent his angel, and hath shut the lions' mouths, that they have not hurt me: forasmuch as before him innocency was found in me; and also before thee, O king, have I done no hurt

Philippians 4:13 I can do all things through Christ which strengtheneth me.

Chapter 9
The Lord Listens to Our Cry for Help

The great Dr. Phil Kidd has a saying and I quote, "When hope is all gone; help is on the way." God has a way of showing up when life has reached its lowest possible level. The Bible teaches, in Hebrews 7:25, that God is able to save them to the uttermost that come to him. No matter how sinful a man or woman lives the blood of Jesus can cover any transgression ever committed. Story after story throughout the pages of time reveal the fact that God came to seek and to save that which was lost (Luke 19:10) Sometimes the Lord must bring a man to his breaking point before he will seek the help that he so badly needs. From Charlotte Elliot, who wrote Just As I Am to William Cowper, who wrote There Is A Fountain Filled With Blood God has a way of getting one's attention and drawing them by His wonderful grace.

    In this chapter I will give you two stories from my life where God showed up, in gloomy situations, to answer a few cries for help. Both situations are different, but both are powerful in their own way. I trust that God will help you through these two stories and prove to you that he is still on His throne and He still answers prayer.

One day, as I was spending time with my family, the phone rang and a woman was on the other end of the phone begging for prayer. She told me that she was desperately in need of a job and she hadn't worked in eight months. This woman went on to say that she had put in fifty applications without one single response. She asked me to pray for her about a certain job that she desired and I promised her I would. The very next day the same lady called me with a joy that was not there the day before. She told me that the very next morning, after we talked, a company called her about a job. After eight months of searching it only took one night of prayer to get her a job. She also told me that out of the fifty job applications she applied for she got the certain job that we prayed about. The Bible tells us, in Psalms 86:10, "For thou art great, and doest wondrous things: thou art God alone." It is such a blessing to know that God hears the prayers of His saints and moves on our behalf.

The second story I wish to share with you is a little more serious and is very amazing. One night, at church about 7:10 p.m., a woman I work with suddenly came to my mind and my soul was troubled for her. It seemed like she needed help and God wanted me to put her on the church's prayer list immediately. My heart became burdened for her that night and I remember loosing a little sleep thinking about if she was O.K. The next morning at work this same woman approached me with a broken spirit and tears running down her face. She told me that she tried to find my number but couldn't and at around 7:10 p.m. she almost took her life, but something stopped her from doing it. I told her that it was God who stopped her, and that I was praying for her at that exact moment. After we talked for a minute or two the Spirit of God spoke to my heart about giving her a preaching CD that could help her if she would listen to it. Although I have hundreds of preaching CD's, God told me to give her one entitled, Manifestations of Demonic Activities. It is a CD about the crazy man from Mark chapter 5. This man was crying and cutting himself with stones and lived day and night in spiritual bondage. The Bible tells us that no one was willing to help him because he was seemingly a hopeless case. The community would just pass by him everytime. Often he tried to end it all and felt, within himself, that no one cared for his soul. When his life was at its lowest possible point and no one seemed to show interest in this man, thank God Jesus showed up at the perfect time to offer him hope.

Mark chapter 5 also tells us that this crazy man ran to Jesus and found the peace that he was looking for his whole life. My prayer in giving her this CD was that she would listen to it, fall under conviction, and run to Jesus for help like the crazy man did in Mark chapter 5. The Lord answered my prayer and the floodgates opened in this young lady's life. The next day, after I said that prayer, she told me that she listened to that CD I gave her 4 times. She promised to be at church Sunday to hear the gospel story. My heart was overwhelmed with excitement and I could see the spirit of God working on this young lady. The following Sunday she kept her promise and attended the house of God. She sat in the back that morning but God turned the altar into a magnet and brought her to the front at invitation time. Out of all the subjects that the preacher could have preached from that day he chose to preach from Mark chapter 5. My mother helped lead her to Christ that morning and our church shouted the victory.

God is still in the soul saving business and burdens can still be lifted at Calvary. Run to Christ while He is passing by and you too can be seated, clothed and in your right mind all the days of your life.

Scriptures Chapter 9

Hebrews 7:25 Wherefore he is able also to save them to the uttermost that come unto God by him, seeing he ever liveth to make intercession for them,

Luke 19:10: For the Son of man is come to seek and to save that which was lost.

Psalms 86:10: For thou art great, and doest wondrous things: thou art God alone.

Chapter 10
God Moving on My Behalf

When I think about the opportunity we have to help others, it really touches my heart in a special way. God says in II Corinthians 9:7 "Every man according as he purposeth in his heart, so let him give, not grudgingly, or of necessity: for God loveth a cheerful giver." He loveth a cheerful giver and He wants us to be a servant to others. The book of Jude verse 22: says, "and of some have compassion, making a difference".. When we help others I am convinced that God smiles and is happy with that decision.

The word of God teaches that we should become a living sacrifice, (Romans 12:1) on a daily basis, if we want His blessings in our lives. Sad to say that a very small percentage of Christians take that verse of scripture to heart and it stops them from many blessings they could enjoy. Every day of my life I've determined to help others because that's what it's all about. I believe that sowing good seed, throughout your life, will produce a harvest of positive things on a daily basis. When you give, with a pure heart, God in heaven will remember and reward that act of kindness in due time. Let me give you a story, from my life, that proves this is true.

Something that makes me very proud, in my life, is the decision I made years ago about helping at least one person every day. For eleven years, without fail, the good Lord has used me to help someone every day. This glorious decision in my life has produced a joy that this world could never give. For years and years I would give and it seemed like people would never give back. For around seven years this trend continued until one wonderful day God showed up when I needed him most. It was a long, hot summer day with the heat reaching dangerous levels at work. I was on the verge of passing out and to say I was thirsty was an under statement. We were not allowed to leave, after lunch was over, to go to the store and I was out of money. I remember saying a quick prayer to God asking Him for a drink of some sort. Within ten seconds my boss came through the door and said, "Tony, can I buy you a drink today?" I replied, "Yes, Sir!; and thank you very much." It was awesome how quick God answered that prayer. About thirty seconds after my prayer was answered another man came in the building and asked me if he could buy me a drink because something told him he should. I told him, "No thanks, someone just did but I appreciate the gesture." Before that day, I could not recall one time where someone offered me one thing at work but that day two people did in less than a minute.

It is a great feeling to know that God is with us when we need Him the most. Never stop helping others because that will be the day when God stops helping you. You will find that in life if you put Jesus first, others second and yourself last it will always produce JOY in your walk with God.

Scriptures Chapter 10

II Corinthians 9:7 Every man according as he purposeth in his heart, so let him give; not grudgingly, or of necessity: for God loveth a cheerful giver.

Jude VS 22: says, "and of some have compassion, making a difference".

Romans 12:1 I beseech you therefore, brethren, by the mercies of God, that ye present your bodies a living sacrifice, holy, acceptable unto God, which is your reasonable service

Chapter 11
Hearing God's Voice

The biggest problem facing Christians in this day and age is their inability to get alone with God. The average Christian surrounds himself with loud music, large crowds, dark atmospheres and bad influences. This produces much confusion, no peace, and bad choices in their lives. The ability to hear God in all this madness disappears and this results in sinful acts that destroy their future for God.

Christians today get caught up with this fast pace society and adapt the habits of a godless world. Between television, Internet, cell phones, work, school and raising a family, people's time is completely consumed and the Lord is forgotten. Christians have replaced songs like "Softly and Tenderly" with Christian rock and Christian rap. Their life is controlled by activities, fun time, stress and selfishness. Most people spend more time brushing their teeth and letting the dog out than they do thinking about God.

In I Kings 19:12 God spoke to Elijah with a still, small voice and Elijah had the ability to hear it. Most Christians today wouldn't have heard the voice because they live such a carnal, wicked, and uncommitted life. God longs to have fellowship with his children but we hinder Him through our life style and are unable to hear Him speak to our hearts. Often, in the Bible, Jesus went into the mountains all night praying to the Father. Daniel prayed three times a day and John the Baptist was alone learning from God. John the Beloved wrote the Book of Revelation while he was alone on the Isle of Patmos. Jesus wants us to be swift to hear, slow to speak and slow to wrath (James 1:19).

We must have "alone time" with God so we can be in a position to hear His voice when He speaks to our hearts. Ever since I was a child I have tried my best to stay unspotted by the world and to get alone with Jesus. Never, in my life, have I consumed alcohol or smoked cigarettes. I have never been at a party or ran with the wrong crowd. Never have I listened to loud music or attended fun night at school. Like David, I hate sin and anything that resembles it. Though I fail God, I'm sorry when I make mistakes and listen to as much preaching as possible. These decisions, in my life, have allowed me to stay in a position to hear God's voice when he speaks to my soul. This has produced great joy and unbelievable blessings that only come when God is directing our lives.

One of the best decisions I ever made in my life was when I decided to purchase one hundred and forty preaching tapes at Christmas one year. During a two-month period I listened to all one hundred and forty preaching tapes and never said one word. God gave me much knowledge through that experience and helped me grow as a Christian.

In my opinion, hearing others, without interjecting

our own beliefs, is a gift from God. The Lord gave us two ears and one mouth for a reason. We must train ourselves to learn from others every chance we get. Romans 10:17 says that faith cometh by hearing and hearing by the word of God. Proverbs 1:5 says a wise man will hear and increase learning. When we get to the point where we feel we have arrived, and disregard others wisdom, we will stop growing as a Christian. II Peter 3:18 says "But grow in grace, and in the knowledge of our Lord and Saviour Jesus Christ." We need to find time to get alone with God multiple times each day.

In this chapter we will look at a few times when God spoke to my heart, in a clear way, and used me to bless others. Through these examples you will see how important it is to hear God's voice and follow His leadership. These examples will prove that God still speaks to hearts today and I pray they will motivate you to get closer to God each and every day.

Many years ago, while sitting in my truck at work, God spoke to my heart in a way that was direct and clear. He told me to write a check for $1,500 dollars and give it to a man of God in Detroit. This pastor was dear to my heart but $1,500 dollars was a lot of money at that time for me to sign over. After a few minutes of thinking it over I remember taking my checkbook out and writing him that check. When I signed my name and put it in my Bible I felt a wonderful peace come over me and the Glory of God filled my truck. Words cannot express the feeling I had on the inside and I couldn't wait for church to arrive so I could give him that monster check. When I made it to church that following day, joy filled my soul as I gave him that check in private. As he looked at the check he asked me if I was sure I wanted to do this. I said in response that God spoke to my heart and told me to do it. He then pulled out a dentist bill that he had and said, "Look at the total on the bill." When I looked at the bill I saw that he had two teeth pulled and it cost him exactly $1,500 dollars. When God speaks to your heart, respond to Him with faith and assurance like I did that day and God will bless you.

The second story that comes to my mind happened a few years back at Hope Baptist Church. While sitting in church one day, listening to the message on a Sunday night, God told me to give a new couple in the church $100 dollars. After service I wrote a check for that amount and gave it to them in the parking lot before they left. When I told them God wanted me to give them that check for $100 dollars tears filled their eyes as they thanked me for the money. A few weeks later the man I helped told me that check was an answer to prayer and he wanted to tell me a story. He went on to say that before church that night he and his wife received a bill that day for $100 dollars and they didn't get paid until the next Friday. In the parking lot, before church that night, they asked God to send the money and help them in their time of need. God used me to meet their need and both the couple and I shouted the victory that day.

The third story I will share with you took place at work while I was reading my Bible at lunch. That particular day I packed a light lunch and I was hungry. Near the end of my reading, at around 12:50 p.m. in the afternoon, I came to Psalms 146:7 which says that God giveth food to the hungry. My eyes seemed to gaze on those words and I looked at that verse a number of times. God spoke to my heart at 12:55 p.m. and told me that He was going to prove that verse to me and give me some food that day. Within twenty minutes, of God speaking to my heart, three different people offered me food that day. I have learned over the years that God moves in mysterious ways, and that He can do the impossible if we will only hear His voice.

The final story I want to give you also took place at work and it will speak to your soul. As I was reading God's word one day the Lord told me to buy a candy bar and hand it out to someone. Immediately I rose from my seat and obeyed the voice of God. As I went to the machine to buy a Milky Way, a man came in the building and said, "What do you need, Tony?" I said to him, "What do you mean by that statement?" He said to me, "You must need something because something told me to come in here and give you some candy." He opened his bag and said, "Take anything you want." The Bible says in Luke 6:38 give and ye shall receive. God can give you anything you desire if you will listen to His voice and do what he commands you to do. Jesus said in John 10:27 "My sheep hear my voice, and I know them, and they follow me." The more you obey God's voice the more you will have life, and have it more abundantly.

God is searching for those who will make Him the center of their lives and communicate with Him on a regular basis. When is the last time you heard his voice in your life?

Scriptures Chapter 11

I Kings 19:12 And after the earthquake a fire; but the LORD was not in the fire: and after the fire a still small voice

James 1:19 Wherefore, my beloved brethren, let every

man be swift to hear, slow to speak, slow to wrath

Romans 10:17 So then faith cometh by hearing, and hearing by the word of God.

Proverbs 1: 5 A wise man will hear, and will increase learning; and a man of understanding shall attain unto wise counsels: says a wise man will hear and increase learning

II Peter 3: 18 But grow in grace, and in the knowledge of our Lord and Saviour Jesus Christ. To him be glory both now and for ever. Amen.

Psalms 146:7 Which executeth judgment for the oppressed: which giveth food to the hungry.

Luke 6: 38 Give, and it shall be given unto you; good measure, pressed down, and shaken together, and running over, shall men give into your bosom. For with the same measure that ye mete withal it shall be measured to you again

John 10: 27 My sheep hear my voice, and I know them, and they follow me:

Chapter 12
The Amazing Tootsie Roll Story

The story I'm about to tell you shocks and amazes everyone that hears it. When I think back on this story I must confess that it still staggers my thinking as well. The details and events that lead to this blessing are still hard to believe. Let me tell you the story and show you that the goodness of God will lead men to repentance.

When my daughter was around one year of age, we happened to be walking through Meijer around the time of Thanksgiving. The store was all decorated for the holidays and they had everything already setup. When you first walked into Meijer you would have certain displays that would instantly catch your eye. My daughter was fascinated with fish, at the time, and she kept pointing to the back of the store where they were located. On our way to the fish something caught my eye long before we got there.

Immediately, when I stepped into the store, I saw a large amount of rare candy that got my attention. You see,

I like candy, any kind of sweets. That display got a hold of me for the rest of the night. The first item I saw was a gigantic Reese Cup that must have been a half pound. I had seen it before so it wasn't a big deal to me. The second thing I saw was a five-pound Hershey Bar that seemed bigger than life and was simply awesome to behold; however I must admit that I had seen them in days gone by as well. The last item I looked at was something that was a first for me. It was to become a special part of my life. What I saw was the biggest Tootsie Roll that I had ever laid my eyes upon.

Something about that Tootsie Roll captured me because it was so unique. My first thought was that I may never see that again, and my second thought was that God could give that to me if I would just pray for it. My goal was to give it away to a preacher when God gave it to me. The Bible teaches in the book of Hebrews 11:6 that without faith it is impossible to please him; for he that cometh to God must believe that he is, and that he is a rewarder of them that diligently seek him. I told my wife that I was going to pray for that Tootsie Roll and trust God to give it to me. We never mentioned it to anyone at the church or to any family member but God was moving behind the scenes on my behalf.

It was two days later when I was asked to go on the road with a man named Randy Lawson. We loaded up the truck and hit the road. As we were driving to the jobsite I told him about the huge Tootsie Roll I had seen and that I was trusting God to give it to me. He had seen the Lord do amazing things in the past for me, and I felt like he believed it would happen someday or someway. What happened next stunned both of us. While we were getting on I-275 to hit the freeway I pointed up above us and both of our eyes looked at a Tootsie Roll semi-truck driving the other way. I can honestly say in my thirty years of living that was the very first time I had ever seen a Tootsie Roll semi-truck. Randy told me in twenty two years of driving and over forty four years of living that was his first encounter with a Tootsie Roll semi-truck, as well. The very next day we had to go to the same jobsite to work. As we were getting on I-275 again, at the exact same spot, it happened again. The Tootsie Roll semi-truck past by for the second straight day! As the Tootsie Roll semi-truck drove by again, Randy looked at me and said, "I can't believe that just happened."

    The very next day was my birthday and the church had a surprise birthday party for me after services. We had cake and ice cream and I was very thankful for their kindness. After church was over, my in-laws invited me over to celebrate my birthday. I can still remember walking in the house and being approached by little Hunter. He had a present in his hand that he was eager to give me. I remember being extremely tired and totally exhausted. Hunter insisted that I open my gift before I did anything else. When I sat down and began opening my gift I discovered that God answered my prayer. My present was that Tootsie Roll that I had seen just a few days earlier. Thank God He is still on His throne and He really does care for His children.

Scriptures Chapter 12

    Hebrews 11: 6: But without faith it is impossible to please him: for he that cometh to God must believe that he is, and that he is a rewarder of them that diligently seek him.

Chapter 13
A Sad Story That Still Breaks My Heart

Often times, through life, things are bound to come our way that saddens our day and sometimes even tests our faith. Life can be like a roller coaster at times and it is how we handle each trial and tribulation that will determine whether we grow or die as a Christian. Job 1:21 says, "Naked came I out of my mother's womb, and naked shall I return thither: the LORD gave, and the LORD hath taken away; blessed be the name of the LORD". Life at times will be great, but at other times it feels like you can't take another step. Job was on top of the mountain one day and lost it all the next day. Sometimes the trial of your faith worketh patience and God is trying to build your strength in Him through sudden bad news that comes your way. I've learned through the years that God's word has every answer for every problem we will ever face in life. Never trust in your feelings but rather in God's unchanging promises.

Often in my life many pains, heartaches, tragedies, surprises, and sudden deaths have tried to derail me from the shining path. If it wasn't for God's word I would have more questions than answers. Thankfully I have always understood that God's hand can be seen in every triumph or tragedy that is sent my way. Although I could give you many different stories in my life that shocked me, one in particular stands out to me. This story breaks my heart and it is sobering to say the least. This is a true account that proves the severity of making fun of the word of God. Your heart will be enlarged with faith as you read this story from my past. To this day it troubles me and fills my soul with grief. Here is a story that will stick with you for years to come.

When I first started working at Poco, I was introduced to a man who was happy to test my faith in every way he could. He worked me harder and treated me worse than any other person at my job. Over the course of time, I began to earn his trust and prove to him that I was a true Christian. This man was a rough, tough and rugged individual who had a sinful past. We became pretty close to each other and he told me that I was the only person on earth he would talk to about God. Every once in a while he would ask me different questions about heaven and hell and I would do my best to answer him according to the Bible. He became precious to me and I developed a heavy burden for his soul. This man struggled with heart problems and health was a chief concern for him. After a few episodes with his heart, and many days of missing work, he sadly lost his job. My heart went out to him and I wondered how I could help him.

Around three weeks after he was fired, the Spirit of God strongly urged me to visit his home and offer him some aid in any possible way I could. As I followed God's leadership and drove to his house, something terrible was about to happen. To be honest, I expected a warm welcome by this man as I planned on giving him some money and a CD about hell. As I knocked on the door I was greeted by this man's wife who saw my Bible and cursed me off the porch. Her words were extremely blasphemous and dangerous. She talked to me like an animal rather than a human and made it clear that I never come back. As I left her porch and made it back to my car, the Holy Spirit pleaded with me to stay as long as it took. Sitting in my car that day and thinking about what just took place made me very uneasy and very worried for that lady. After about seven minutes of waiting the man I went to see came outside and apologized on his wife's behalf and invited me in with open arms. He told me that his wife answered because he was sleeping and was sorry for how she treated me.

We talked that day for around thirty-five minutes and many kind words were exchanged. At the end of our conversation I asked him if he would listen to a CD on hell because I may never see him again. He promised me he would and thanked me for my visit. The CD was called; Four Times Man Cannot Die. This CD was filled with examples of folks dying too soon and opening their eyes in the flames of hell.

This would indeed be the last time we spoke and the last time we seen each other again. Around a year later, while at work as I was walking through the shop, my boss called me into his office. He gave me the news that the man I visited only a year earlier had passed away. He was in his early fifties. The news stunned me and caused me to inquire how he died. My first thought was that he most likely had a heart attack and that was how he left this world. However, after further research, we found out that he killed himself by putting a gun in his mouth and blowing his head off.

After hearing this news it made me wonder if what that woman said to me that day on her porch caused her to lose her husband. The Bible says in Revelations 21:8 "But the fearful, and unbelieving, and the abominable, and murderers, and whoremongers, and sorcerers, and idolaters, and all liars, shall have their part in the lake which burneth with fire and brimstone: which is the second death". When people laugh at the word of God, and despise His Spirit, this will be the final state of man. According to Proverbs 6:15 "Therefore shall his calamity come suddenly; suddenly shall he be broken without remedy." I still miss my friend and I'm sure this woman will miss her husband. Life is but a vapor that appeareth for a little while then vanisheth away. (James 4:14) When you laugh and make light of the Spirit of God, your life will quickly take a turn for the worse. Don't force God to take drastic measures in your life by provoking Him to anger. Be careful what you say and who you say it to.

Scriptures Chapter 13

Job 1:21 And said, Naked came I out of my mother's womb, and naked shall I return thither: the LORD gave, and the LORD hath taken away; blessed be the name of the LORD

Revelations 21: 8: But the fearful, and unbelieving, and the abominable, and murderers, and whoremongers, and sorcerers, and idolaters, and all liars, shall have their part in the lake which burneth with fire and brimstone: which is the second death.

Proverbs 6:15 Therefore shall his calamity come suddenly; suddenly shall he be broken without remedy.

James 4:14 Whereas ye know not what shall be on the morrow. For what is your life? It is even a vapour, that appeareth for a little time, and then vanisheth away.

Chapter 14
God's Faithfulness in My Life

It is no secret, to those who know me, that the grand old hymns of the faith play a major role in my everyday life. One of my hobbies is to study each hymn's history, and the men and women who penned them down. Nearly every hymn that is found in your hymnal came from powerful Christians who were writing under the inspiration of the Holy Spirit. When you deeply study the people, who God used to pen these songs, you will find that their impact still reaches the world hundreds of years after their deaths.

One of my favorite songs ever written is a song entitled, "Great is Thy Faithfulness." It was penned by Mr. Thomas Chisholm. This song expresses the faithfulness of God in a way that is honest and true. This song has played a big part in my life and the lives of countless thousands through the years. Mr. Chisholm wanted to tell the world about the faithfulness of God in his own personal walk through this song. Many Christians, all across this country, could stand up and testify about the love, grace and faithfulness of God throughout the pages of their life. I Corinthians 10:13, tells us that God is faithful. Revelations 19:11 says that God is faithful and true. No man or woman that has ever walked with God has been able to describe just how faithful Jesus really is. He is just, Holy, Pure, Matchless, Glorious, and Lovely. Hundreds of verses describe His Faithfulness toward His saints and I aim to give you examples, in this chapter that will prove it even more. When you read these examples, I want it to dawn on you how good God really is to each and every one of us.

The Bible tells us in Psalms 40:5 "Many, O LORD my God, are thy wonderful works which thou hast done, and thy thoughts which are to us-ward; they cannot be reckoned up in order unto thee; if I would declare and speak of them, they are more than can be numbered." There have been many times, in my life, when I found that verse to be true and wonderful while serving Him. It is humbling to know that out of seven billion people that inhabit earth, God has the ability to think about us individually. Allow me to explain what I am talking about through a few amazing stories that have came to pass in my life.

A few years ago, on a Saturday morning, my wife went downstairs to cook breakfast and noticed that water was leaking through the ceiling. Upon further investigation we discovered that the floor was rotting out in the upstairs bathroom and needed to be fixed immediately. We got a bucket and placed it under the spot where the water was leaking and began trusting the Lord for the funds to repair it. My wife was worried, but I never was. As the problem got worse, and the situation became darker, I told my wife that God would meet our need shortly.

The Bible teaches, in Malachi 3:10-11 that if we give to His work, He in return will rebuke the devourer and provide all our needs. The next day God answered our prayer and sent two men to our house to fix our problem. They paid for all the parts, charging nothing for the labor and in less than twenty-four hours they had everything finished. This would have cost us over a thousand dollars and drained us financially. God proved to us that day He is faithful and we were extremely thankful for what He did for us.

The second example of God's faithfulness in my life happened around Christmas time a few years ago. My work hours were low that winter, and we were struggling to pay the bills. My wife asked me one day how we were going to pay for Christmas, and I couldn't give her an answer. I remember telling her that God is faithful and He would send the money somehow. As we went to church that following Wednesday an awesome man asked if he could speak to me in private. He told me that God put it on his heart to give my wife and me one hundred dollars for Christmas gifts. His gift overwhelmed me and blessed my heart in a special way. Two days later, at my company Christmas party, my boss gave me an extra bonus that I was not expecting. When I opened the envelope I saw a check for five hundred dollars for more Christmas gifts. The Bible teaches that the goodness of God will lead us to repentance. We had a beautiful Christmas that year and God proved, once again, His watchcare over our lives.

The third example of His faithfulness in my life took place just a short while ago. John the Baptist said, in Luke 3:11 that if we have two coats we should impart to him that hath none and God will bless you. God laid it on my heart to find two people that needed a coat and give them each one coat. Both coats were used but they were very nice. One coat was black leather with the American flag on the back and the other coat was tan leather. It was the coat that I wore everywhere I went. Both men loved the coats, but my decision of giving my coats away left me with none. A few months later, on a Sunday morning, a young man approached me and said he had a gift for me. We went to his car and he pulled out the gift. To my amazement it wasn't money, shoes, or a Bible, but it was a coat. He told me that God told him to get me a coat and make sure it was a nice one. The coat was made in England and was worth more than the other two coats combined. Once again God showed up in a timely way and attended to my need. Over and over, through out my life, God has been faithful to me, even though I have failed Him.

The next example that I'm going to share with you comes from a Sunday night service. God spoke to my heart about helping the pastor. As the man of God was preaching to his flock, God directed me to give him my golf clubs after the service that night. The clubs came from my dad, at Christmas one year, and were very much used. They were special to me and it was hard to give them away. After church that night my father-in-law asked my wife if I needed some golf clubs for any reason. I was amazed how quickly God replaced my clubs with other ones. After looking at the clubs I picked a couple of them that I would use and left the rest for someone else who may have needed them. About seven months later, at work one day, I received a call from my wife that ministered to my heart. She told me that her uncle called her and said he had a new set of golf clubs for me if I needed them. Some of the clubs were still in their factory wrappings and they were in great shape.

It truly is great how God uses people to meet our needs, and wants. I love the old Charles Gabriel song that says, "I stand amazed at the presence of Jesus the Nazarene and wonder how he could love me a sinner condemned unclean."

The last example that I pray will bless your heart is simple, yet profound concerning God's faithfulness. Not long ago, after teaching the teens on a Sunday morning, God performed a miracle that others saw with their own eyes. The Lord told me to help a few people, and if I did he would help me. I reached in my wallet and grabbed everything I had and gave it away. After I did this I looked at my wife, in front of four people, and said,"Someone will take us out today and you don't have to worry about cooking this afternoon." Immediately after this statement was made I walked towards the auditorium and through two sets of doors and was stopped by my Grandpa. He told me that after church he was going to take us out to eat at a restaurant called Baldos. My wife and the other four people were standing there when he told me the news, and I looked at my wife and said,"God sure is good; isn't He?"

Psalms 57:10 tells us God's mercy is great unto the heavens, and thy truth unto the clouds. The Lord has been so good to my family and me over the years, and has proved time and time again that He is faithful and true in my life. The Bible says it best in Psalms 62:8 "Trust in him at all times; ye people, pour out your heart before him: God is a refuge for us. Selah."

Scriptures Chapter 14

I Corinthians 10: 13: There hath no temptation taken you but such as is common to man: but God is faithful, who will not suffer you to be tempted above that ye are able; but will with the temptation also make a way to escape, that ye may be able to bear it.

Revelations 19: 11: And I saw heaven opened, and behold a white horse; and he that sat upon him was called Faithful and True, and in righteousness he doth judge and make war.

Psalms 40: 5: Many, O LORD my God, are thy wonderful works which thou hast done, and thy thoughts which are to us-ward: they cannot be reckoned up in order unto thee: if I would declare and speak of them, they are more than can be numbered.

Malachi 3: 10: Bring ye all the tithes into the storehouse, that there may be meat in mine house, and prove me now herewith, saith the LORD of hosts, if I will not open you the windows of heaven, and pour you out a blessing, that there shall not be room enough to receive it. 11: And I will rebuke the devourer for your sakes, and he shall not destroy the fruits of your ground; neither shall your vine cast her fruit before the time in the field, saith the LORD of hosts. That if we give to His work, He in return will rebuke the devourer and provide all our needs.

Luke 3: 11: He answereth and saith unto them, He that hath two coats, let him impart to him that hath none; and he that hath meat, let him do likewise.

Psalms 57: 10: For thy mercy is great unto the heavens, and thy truth unto the clouds

Psalms 62: 8: Trust in him at all times; ye people, pour out your heart before him: God is a refuge for us. Selah

Chapter 15
Special Delivery, Special Delivery

One of my all time favorite songs, as I was growing up, was a song entitled, "God Delivers Again." It is a song about how God, through a man named Moses, parted the Red Sea and brought the children of Israel through on dry ground. Every time God's people encountered impossible circumstances, God always showed up exactly at the right time, and delivered them out of every situation.

All throughout the Bible there is a rich history of God sending His people a "Special Delivery," when they least expected it. Jesus loves to give good gifts unto His children, and He does it on a daily basis. The word of God tells us in James 1:17 "Every good gift and every perfect gift cometh from above." God is always seeking opportunities to send a special delivery from His storehouse of love, but we hinder Him many times through our unbelief. According to Mark 6:6, the Bible teaches that Jesus wanted to bless His people in a marvelous way, but He couldn't because of their unbelief. We tend to doubt God rather than believe Him and that is why Christians have very few blessings in their everyday life. Hebrews 11:6 says, "That without faith it is impossible to please Him." God has never changed, and He is willing and able to send something special your way, but you first must believe that He can.

A story that has always touched and blessed my heart is found in I Kings chapter 17 with a man called Elijah. The Bible teaches in James 5:16 that Elijah was just as much human as you and I but Elijah exercised more faith than you and I do. One day this man of God told King Ahab that through his word God would not allow it to rain on earth for the space of three and a half years. God told Elijah to go to the brook Cherith, before Jordan, because He had a Special Delivery for him there. God not only allowed Elijah to drink of the brook, He also, commanded the ravens to bring him food every morning and every night. There will be times, in the child of God's life, when God commands His spiritual mail carrier to bring you a delivery that is first class and right on time. This Chapter will cover several examples, in my life, where God sent me a delivery that was unexpected, but overwhelming in my walk with Him. Let me share these examples that blessed my heart, and I hope they bless yours.

Many years ago, while sitting in the house of God, I remember having a burden on my heart that nobody else even knew about. It was not mentioned to anyone, not even my parents, my wife, or my pastor. God spoke to my heart that night about taking my burden to the Lord and leaving it there. The Bible says in James 1:6 "To ask the Lord in faith, nothing wavering and it will surely come to pass." My heart was broken over the prayer when I started, but when I finished the Spirit of God made it clear that the need would be met. As I rose to my feet, I was approached by a man, almost instantly, with a gift in his hand. He asked if he could speak to me and I said, "Sure." He told me that as I was praying, something told him to write me a check for $100 dollars. He then handed me the check and said I pray it will be a blessing to you. Praise the Lord, it was exactly what I needed and it still blesses my heart to this day.

Another special delivery from God, that blesses my heart, happened at work when I was twenty five years old. A man that worked with me, from time to time, said he needed to speak to me and that it was urgent. I remember meeting him in the parking lot, by his car, and I still remember his look of excitement; like it was yesterday. He told me he had a special gift that he wanted me to have. He then reached in his car and pulled out a beautiful CD holder and it was brand new. He then told me to look inside to see what it was. I opened it up and discovered that it was the entire Old and New Testament of the Bible on CD. It was so thoughtful and my heart melted within me when he handed it to me. That delivery from God still remains one of the greatest blessings that I have ever received.

Allow me to give you another delivery, from a preacher one day, that shook me while I was hitting golf balls at my parent's house. My mom came outside and handed me a letter and told me that I needed to read it. The letter was from a man of God that has given his all for the Lord, and he has always taken the time to help me in my journey with God. He told me, through this letter, that a special gift was being sent be way of FED-X and it would be at my house in about a week. The news stunned me and encouraged my heart as I waited for this delivery. Around two weeks later the gift arrived like he promised and my wife and I opened it together. The gift was extremely unique and very rare. My wife asked me what it was and I proudly and humbly told her that the gift was a copy of five signatures of some of the greatest Christians who have ever lived. Alongside their names were their own personal life verses that meant so much to them. The gift blessed me because it came at a time when I was a little down about life, and wondered if anyone cared about me. My friend, I'm glad to report that God cares for you, and longs to meet your every need when you serve Him with a pure heart.

Something else that comes to mind is a delivery that came to me while I was very tired, late on the road, one night. At the time I was working long hours and there was no time to take breaks at all. It was the dog days of summer and we were on the go all day. David said, in the book of Psalms 37:25 that in all his life he had never seen the righteous forsaken, nor His seed begging bread. My God promises us, through His word, that no matter how dark our situation looks He will take care of it for us if we can only trust Him. To say that I was hungry was putting it lightly. I remember my stomach growling while we were working that night. At that very moment, I remember asking the Lord for a miracle like he supplied in Matthew chapter 14 when He fed the five thousand with just five loaves and two fishes. To my amazement, less than five minutes later He did just that. I remember a man from M-DOT pulled up with a box of White Castle's sliders that fed about twenty people, including me. It came at a time when I felt weak and dizzy, and the timing was impeccable. God gave me strength the rest of the night. I thank and praise the Lord for His special delivery and answering my prayer. Don't ever give up on God, for He owns the cattle on a thousand hills and the clouds are nothing more than the dust off His feet.

Let me end this chapter with one more phenomenal story that will build up your faith in God. This story is a reminder of His provision in our life, and His constant watch care over us. A young man in our church accepted the Lord as his Savior and began to grow in the Knowledge of His Lord very fast. My heart's desire was to help him grow in any way I could, so I gave him something that was dear to me to help him grow. After I made the decision to help this young man I decided to call my mother and ask her opinion on this matter. She said if God spoke to you about it, then do it and he will bless you for it. I then thanked her and hung up the phone. Joy filled my heart after our conversation and my decision to help this young man was confirmed. Later that night, when church was over, as I was preparing to leave, the pastor's wife stopped me. She told me that there was a special delivery for me but it was a secret who it was from. She handed me a blank envelope and walked away. When we got to the car I opened up the envelope and there was $50 dollars inside. To this day I have no idea who gave it to me, but I thank God for it anyway. We serve a Holy God that takes special interest in every move we make, and every step we take. The last phrase in the song, God delivers again, reads as follows: Just when things look hopeless my God delivers again.

Scriptures Chapter 15

James 1: 17: Every good gift and every perfect gift is from above, and cometh down from the Father of lights, with whom is no variableness, neither shadow of turning.

Hebrews 11: 6: But without faith it is impossible to please him: for he that cometh to God must believe that he is, and that he is a rewarder of them that diligently seek him.

James 5: 16: Confess your faults one to another, and pray one for another, that ye may be healed. The effectual fervent prayer of a righteous man availeth much.

James 1: 6: But let him ask in faith, nothing wavering. For he that wavereth is like a wave of the sea driven with the wind and tossed.

Psalms 37: 25: I have been young, and now am old; yet have I not seen the righteous forsaken, nor his seed begging bread.

Chapter 16
Walking By Faith Not By Sight

To be honest, the concept of walking by faith and not by sight is easier said than done. When I look around this country I quickly discover that this idea is almost a thing of the past. The Fanny Crosby's and Ira Sankey's of the world do not exist anymore.

The great Fanny Crosby was blind six months after her birth. She refused to ever use that as an excuse because she felt as though she could see things spiritually that people could never see. She was forced to walk by faith everyday of her life. She went on to write around 9,000 songs that have touched millions of lives. She had most of the Bible memorized and she was a giving machine. Fanny Crosby sold around 1, 000,000 copies of her works with every penny going to the Lord. Mrs. Crosby's life puts us all to shame and she could not even see like you and me. Doing what she did took a lot of faith and a lot of trust. Our biggest problem, or struggle in life, is that we want to make it work, without trusting in the Lord. Sometimes we need to let go of our problems and let God take over.

While working one day, my wife called me at around 11:00 a.m. in the morning to notify me that we needed glasses. I told my wife to make an appointment. She then told me that we really didn't have the money. I then responded that sometimes, in life, God wants us to trust Him and so she made the appointment. When I arrived home later that afternoon I asked if we had received any mail. She said yes we did. I then ask, "Was there a check?" She said, "Yes there was." She then told me it was a check for three hundred eighty five dollars. We went to the appointment at America's Best and both of us bought new glasses, and some new contacts. Altogether the cost was three hundred sixty five dollars. After the appointment we went to dinner with the remaining twenty dollars.

There must be times, in our lives, when we rely on Him whether we understand it or not. It was about a month later, while I was on the Internet, a commercial came on for America's best when I was posting this story about the glasses. That commercial was a reminder of God's goodness.

We need more moments like this in our lives as we walk with God. These moments are when we can reflect on His blessings. Like the old hymn says, "Count your many blessings. Name them one by one. And it will surprise you what the Lord has done."

Scriptures Chapter 16

Psalm 37:4 "Delight thyself also in the Lord: and he shall give thee the desires of thine heart."

Psalm 21:2 "Thou hast given him his heart's desire, and hast not withholden the request of his lips. Selah."

Chapter 17
God Sending Us a Name for Our First Child

When my wife and I found out that we were going to have our first child, many thoughts ran through our minds. Naturally, at first, it was a shock that we were going to be parents. We also had the fear of the unknown and different emotions that we had never experienced before. The next feeling we had was joy like the Bible teaches in John 16:21. We then felt a bond like we have never known between us. We also thought about our future in a fashion like never before. Needless to say we were doing more thinking than ever before.

The Bible teaches us to trust in the Lord with all our heart and lean not upon our own understanding. In all thy ways acknowledge Him, and He shall direct thy paths. We had to learn more than ever whether we understood it or not, God was going to help us every step of the way. God has always been there for us and there is never any reason to doubt Him. Jesus said in Hebrews 13:5 that I will never leave thee nor forsake thee.

I can still remember when we had the ultrasound and found out we were having a little girl. Excitement filled our hearts and wonder did as well. At that point our minds began to shift to two things. Number one was having a healthy baby. That was such a concern that we had because I know story after story of people that had unhealthy children and the heartbreak that it can cause. One story always sticks out to me and it involves a great songwriter.

A mother once had the sorrow of losing eighteen children to death, and the nineteenth was sick also. She raised him for Christ and as a result he wrote over four hundred hymns and the famous song, OH HAPPY DAY! Can you imagine what that mother and father felt like as one child died after another. To be honest, we had a fear about the health of our little one, and was simply trusting Jesus to give us a healthy child.

Secondly, our next concern was baby names. Every name has a meaning and we were aware of that. Naomi, in the Bible, means beautiful, but Mara means bitter. There is a long study about names that will bless your heart, found throughout the pages of history if you study it out. As we prayed about the right name for our child, we must have gone through 700 to 800 names. We didn't have peace about any of them. After weeks of searching for the proper name, we came up with three possible choices. The first was Ella because we felt that was a unique name. Next was Melody, which is a good Bible name. Last, but not least, was Hope which is found all throughout the word of God. We wanted to consider all these names before making a final decision. After much thought and prayer God seemed to give us peace about the name Hope. Once God spoke to my heart, my wife and I agreed together that this was the name God gave us for our child. This was around five months before Hope's birth and we never questioned it again.

When the time came that my wife was to be delivered, we arrived at the hospital under the doctor's request. I felt like it was a mistake because the doctor was trying to speed up the process rather than letting it happen on God's timetable. For two days they tried to induce labor on my wife by using medications and other things but to no avail. My wife was then at her lowest point as we were sent home without a baby to hold in our arms. I assured my wife that God has a purpose for everything that happens in our lives and once it comes to pass we will then understand it. We returned to the hospital for another couple days of labor and pain. Praise the Lord at 2:15 a.m. the next morning, we held a beautiful, healthy little girl in our arms. Hope was born on August 24th 2010.

As we were packing up to leave the hospital, God told me to open my Bible and when I did it opened up to Romans 8:24 and as I was reading that verse God gave me assurance that He gave us her name. When looking at that verse it said, "for we are saved by hope: but hope that is seen is not hope: for what a man seeth, why doth he yet hope for?" That verse alone has the word hope in it more times than any verse in the Bible, and that's when Hope was born 8:24. God works in mysterious ways and I found out later that Hope is considered the greatest word in the English language.

Scriptures Chapter 17

John 16: 21 A woman when she is in travail hath sorrow,

because her hour is come: but as soon as she is delivered of the child, she remembereth no more the anguish, for joy that a man is born into the world.

Hebrews 13: 5 Let your conversation be without covetousness; and be content with such things as ye have: for he hath said, I will never leave thee, nor forsake thee

Romans 8: 24 For we are saved by hope: but hope that is seen is not hope: for what a man seeth, why doth he yet hope for?

Chapter 18
The Power of Prayer Can Change Everything

When I begin to think about the difference prayer has made in my life, it humbles me to the lowest degree. From the start of my life, to the place I am today, someone has always been praying for me. My Mom and Dad have always prayed for my safety, my future, and my soul. There have been many times throughout the course of my life when other's prayed and have rescued me from certain danger. Sometimes I feel His presence in a stronger fashion more than at other times, and I must conclude that others are praying for me.

My mother told me that when I was a baby I had a rare step in my spine that would eventually sever my nerves in the spinal column. That was a major physical problem for my future. She told me how Van Born Baptist Church prayed for days that God would heal my back. The doctors determined that only fifty people in America had this rare disorder and forty eight of them were paralyzed. The odds were stacked against me but God is a God that can do the impossible. When people are determined to intercede for others, God hears them. My mom told me that over night my back was healed and the doctors had no answer how it happened

The Bible is full of supernatural events that took place through the power of prayer. Remember Elijah prayed 63 words in I Kings 18:36-39 and the fire fell from heaven. Daniel prayed to the Lord and God sent an angel to stop the mouth of the lion. When a nation prays together, it will always stay together.

Mr. D. L. Moody and Ira Sankey, the great duo of some of the best revivals this world has ever seen, had a special request to the God of heaven. They made it a goal to pray for $20,000 dollars for Mr. Moody's College without anyone else knowing about it. They labored and toiled in prayer all that night. When the morning finally came, they found that every penny they were seeking was accounted for. When you open God's word and begin to read, that is God speaking to you. But when you fall on your knees and pray, that is you speaking to God. Please permit me to show you a few examples of just how powerful prayer can be if we will get plugged into its power.

There was a church in Alabama that desperately needed help from God concerning repairs on their building. They sought God's face through prayer and desired that He would meet their need of $30,000 dollars. We were on vacation, at the time, and we loved the pastor and his family very much. One day when were visiting folks in the neighborhood for visitation a miracle was sitting at the house of God, and we didn't even know it. When we arrived back at the church the pastor noticed an envelope on the front steps. I remember when he opened the envelope and discovered that it was a check for $30,000 dollars. God answered his prayer in a way that was special and unique.

My dad began to wonder how this happened, and who sent him the check. After much research my dad found out that a church in Michigan sold its building and was looking to help other churches for the cause of Christ. Somehow and someway God put it on that church's heart to send a portion of the money to Alabama to Pastor John Joiner and his congregation. Prayer can open doors of opportunity in our lives if we would just do it more often.

Another story that blesses my soul is the story of George Mueller. He ran an orphanage with around 180 needy children. Bro. Mueller ran out of food one day and his children were hungry. Many started to complain about the situation and question where the food would come from. Bro. Mueller saw this not as an obstacle but rather an opportunity for God to do something great. He went on with his normal routine of setting the table and making sure everything was ready for supper. When everything was in place he had the children bow their heads in prayer. As he prayed he thanked God for the food that was about to come. When his prayer was ended they heard a knock on the door. Bro. Mueller opened the door and found a man standing there with an answer to his prayer. The man told the story how he was heading to town with a wagon full of food when all of a sudden his ride broke down. All the food would spoil if it were not eaten within a day. He asked if Bro. Mueller needed it and he said yes I do and so do these children. He invited the man in for dinner and everyone was fed and they had food to spare. God is in the business of helping His children through prayer.

While working one day, a man that has always been a blessing to me was facing pain that was extremely intense. He was passing kidney stones and he said this was not something new. I could tell he was very uncomfortable and he needed help. He asked me to pray for him because the pain was almost unbearable. Three days later they disappeared and he has never had them appear again. Sometimes God likes to prove that He is still in control of all challenges that this world has to offer.

A preacher friend of mine had a tragedy strike his life that was sudden and heart breaking to put it kindly. His precious wife of over 40 years passed away with him holding her hand. They had a bond that was God given and she owned a good portion of his heart. Funds were tight for the man of God and the funeral was very costly. The preacher was at a loss for words and really didn't know how he would pay for the funeral. He began to pray earnestly about this need as his heart was broken. People began to give towards this need in a wonderful way. In just a matter of days a little over $17,000 dollars came in and it was just enough to cover all the costs. When I heard that story it blessed my heart and helped me to realize that anything is possible when prayer is involved.

Let me give you a personal story that will sum this all up for us. Around one year ago today something happened at my work that was beyond description. I was informed, immediately upon arrival, on a Monday morning that my friend Justin was in a horrible accident and they were unsure if he would make it. Upon hearing the news I was in shock! Justin has always been a help to me and the news filled my heart with sorrow. A few minutes later my boss asked me to get on the golf cart because he had more details about this horrible accident.

My boss told me that Justin was found in a ditch with life threatening injuries and his head was face down in a pool of blood. They rushed him to the hospital where he received emergency assistance. It seemed like a hopeless case and a tragic outcome. Justin was in a slight coma and in danger of dying or never being the same. My boss asked if I could say a quick prayer for Justin because he was in fatal condition. I can remember saying a very quick prayer for him and being at peace about the whole situation. Around twelve minutes later we got new reports that Justin sat up in his bed. He was texting friends and family that he was fine. Although he was sore and beat up, he was responding without the help of others. This news was amazing and I was praising the Lord for what He was doing. Everyone was speechless and filled with wonder with what they just witnessed.

Two short weeks later Justin came back to work and surprised us all. Within that day we had an unbelievable conversation that we will never forget. Justin's first question to me was, "Were you praying for me." Very quickly I said, "Yes." He said, "Thank you Tony, I really felt like you were. " I then told him that he was lucky to be alive. He then said, "I sure am." From this point in our conversation I switched gears and asked him if he believed in angels. Justin responded that he did now! My response to him was, "good because I feel like you will meet one in the near future, so be ready." The very next morning Justin told me a phenomenal story. Justin told me that when he went home, after our conversation, that he became very hungry and he craved pizza. He said he drove to the nearest pizza joint and he was approached by a stranger. This stranger walked directly up to Justin and said, "You really should be dead right now" and walked away without ever buying a pizza. Justin said it stunned him because he was covered that night and it would have been hard for anyone to know he was in a serious accident a few weeks prior to that.

Everyday I walk by him at work I see a walking miracle that proves prayer works. Without prayer where would we be!

Scriptures Chapter 18

Jude 22 "And of some have compassion, making a difference."

Psalm 145:8 "The Lord is gracious, and full of compassion; slow to anger, and of great mercy."

I Corinthians 13:2 "And though I have the gift of prophecy, and understand all mysteries, and all knowledge; and though I have all faith, so that I could remove mountains, and have not charity, I am nothing."

Acts 20:35 "It is more blessed to give than to receive."

Chapter 19
The Awful Mistake of Mocking God's Man

Many years ago, in the United States of America, the vast majority of sinners and saints alike had a reverence for a holy man of God. When preachers made public appearances in the market places and in the local businesses, people would often stop and show respect to the man of God. History books tell us that when the great Charles Finney would appear in the factories of his day, people would turn off the machines, get on their knees and beg for forgiveness at just the sight of him. Mr. Finney had such a powerful testimony that sinners would fall under conviction simply by his walking into their building. Ask yourself, when is the last time you have seen anyone, in this generation have respect for a man of God like that?

In the eyes of God, the greatest position a man can occupy in this world is that of a preacher. People today will laugh, disrespect, backtalk, murmur, curse, and blaspheme a preacher and never think twice about it. Sometimes I cringe when I hear the way people talk and act around a man of God. In 2 Peter 3: 3 the scriptures say, "Knowing this first, that there shall come in the last days scoffers, walking after their own lusts." In 2 Timothy 3: 8 the Bible tells us the following, "Now as Jannes and Jambres withstood Moses, so do these also resist the truth; men of corrupt minds, reprobate concerning the faith." The Bible says that there will be those who resist the truth and have corrupt minds. Proverbs 30: 12 teaches that there is a generation that is pure in their own eyes and yet is not washed from their filthiness. People all over this country have no filter on their language, their conduct or their actions. They treat the Bible like a comic book and God's men like Bozo the Clown. Many people, down through the years have suffered judgement, pain, torment and even death for disrespecting a man of God. Please be careful not to put your tongue on a man of God in any way, shape or form.

The ministers of the gospel of Jesus Christ are special in God's eyes and He will protect them at all costs. The worst decision that a man or woman, boy or girl, will ever make is to laugh, mock or mistreat a man of God. Everyone I have ever seen, at my work, who has laughed at me or the Bible are either fired, judged, or dead. We need an old fashioned moving of the judgement of God to sweep across this country like in days of old. In Judges 16:30, when the Philistines made fun of Samson, little did they know that it would be their last day of life before they opened their eyes in a Christless hell. In the book of Numbers 16:32, when Korah, Dathan and all the crowd rebelled against Moses, little did they know that God would open up the earth and drop them into the pit alive . This chapter will give you a few examples of the vengeance and wrath of God against those who have mocked God's men over the years. These accounts are sobering and heart stopping in there description and will make the hairs on your neck stand-up. Please consider these examples and allow them to minister to your heart.

Several years ago a young couple decided to have fun at a man of God's expense. This decision proved to be foolish and costly a few months later. Dr. Don Green was conducting a tent revival years ago and he was in the prime of his ministry at the time. Dr. Green has read through the Bible over 170 times and he prays for 5 hours a day. He has pastored Parker Memorial Baptist Church for around 60 years and he is without a doubt one of the best men of God in this country. One day, while the meeting was going on, the young couple, I alluded to, made fun of the way Dr. Green was raising money for the tent meeting that week in the privacy of their own home. The young couple was expecting a new healthy baby in a couple months and was planning a good future for their child. When it was finally time for the child to be delivered, they were devastated when they discovered that their child was missing multiple fingers on each hand. The Bible says in Numbers (32:23 "But if ye will not do so, behold, ye have sinned against the LORD: and be sure your sin will find you out." When you say things you ought not to say about a man of God expect a whirlwind of heartache to come your way.

Another story that comes to my mind involves an incident from the great Percy Ray. If you ever take the time to study this man of God's life you will quickly realize that he is one of the greatest men ever to live. The stories that surround his ministry are nothing short of amazing. Dr Percy Ray was very unusual, very holy and extremely unique. His walk with God was something to behold and everyone knew he was an old fashioned man of God. Although I could use many different examples that would blow your mind concerning the faith, one in particular fits this chapter perfectly. This story will open your eyes like very few stories you will ever read. Allow me to tell you this jaw dropping story that should keep us all in line with God.

One day, as Dr. Ray was shopping in a convenience store down south, a woman approached him with tears flowing down her cheeks. She tapped him on the shoulder and asked to speak to him immediately. Trembling and shaking, she told Dr. Ray that she had said something she shouldn't have and she wanted him to forgive her. Dr Ray looked at the woman and told her that God already told me what you said and God wants me to give you a message. He then told her that in nine days she would be dead and her husband would bury her in that blue dress that she loved so well. Nine days later that lady was laying in the funeral home; and her husband buried her in that blue dress that she loved so well. When you cross spiritual lines, with the Lord, and God signs your death warrant your as good as dead.

The last story in this chapter comes from my own life, around three years ago, when I was 28 years old. This is a sad story and it happened while I was eating dinner with my wife and my daughter after a Sunday morning service. Please listen as I tell you this real story that still hurts me to this day. One Saturday night God spoke to my heart about teaching to the teens about the dangers of mocking God. That night God's spirit was very strong in my house and after my lesson was complete fear gripped my heart over this subject. The next morning, when I arrived at church, I was all business and the atmosphere was pretty quiet in the little room where we teach the teens. God's spirit was real that day and the class went very good. We talked about many stories that proved the subject at hand and hearts were touched in that room.

After church that morning, as my wife and I were driving home, I remember being very tired and really hungry. The message that morning drained nearly all of my energy and I looked forward to eating a good meal and resting that afternoon. After arriving at our home and sitting down to eat lunch something shocking was about to take place. Shortly after praying over the meal my phone rang and it was someone I hadn't heard from in a while. When I answered the phone the voice on the other end was very vile and full of cursing. This man was calling from a Detroit Tigers game and I could tell he was drunk. He said some foolish things about God and about the Bible that I sure didn't appreciate. To make it worse, my family was sitting there and I was grieved in my spirit. As I hung up the phone, after this shocking phone call, I looked at my wife and told her that this man was in serious trouble for what he just did. It turns out that I was right because that night this man's wife was rushed to the hospital and stayed there for two weeks. They lost a great deal of their finances and his life has been down hill ever since.

God's word, God's spirit, and God's man are never meant to be messed with and when they are God will always get the final say. Isaiah 1:20 says "But if ye refuse and rebel, ye shall be devoured with the sword; for the mouth of the LORD hath spoken it." God promises that certain punishment is headed your way when you treat the things of God with a disrespectful attitude. God records every idle word that mankind speaks and records them in His eternal Book. If you live a life of sin and foolishness it will be shouted from the housetop one day.

Hopefully this chapter has shed a light on this subject like you have never seen before. Never be guilty of crossing a man of God all the days of your life and you will be much better off.

Scriptures Chapter 19

2 Peter 3: 3 Knowing this first, that there shall come in the last days scoffers, walking after their own lusts, tells us that in the last days there will be those who mock God and walk after their own lusts

2 Timothy 3: 8 Now as Jannes and Jambres withstood Moses, so do these also resist the truth: men of corrupt minds, reprobate concerning the faith. Says that there will be those who resist the truth and have corrupt minds.

Proverbs 30: 12 There is a generation that are pure in their own eyes, and yet is not washed from their filthiness. Teaches that there is a generation that are pure in their own eyes and yet is not washed from their filthiness.

judges 16: 30 And Samson said, Let me die with the Philistines. And he bowed himself with all his might; and the house fell upon the lords, and upon all the people that were therein. So the dead which he slew at his death were more than they which he slew in his life.

Numbers 16: 32 And the earth opened her mouth, and

swallowed them up, and their houses, and all the men that appertained unto Korah, and all their goods.

33: They, and all that appertained to them, went down alive into the pit, and the earth closed upon them: and they perished from among the congregation.

34: And all Israel that were round about them fled at the cry of them: for they said, Lest the earth swallow us up also.

35: And there came out a fire from the LORD, and consumed the two hundred and fifty men that offered incense.

Numbers 32: 23 But if ye will not do so, behold, ye have sinned against the LORD: and be sure your sin will find you out.

Isaiah 1: 20 says "But if ye refuse and rebel, ye shall be devoured with the sword: for the mouth of the LORD hath spoken it.

Chapter 20
The Lord Touching Little Hope's Body

My wife and I experienced a night that we will not soon forget. We were awakened at around 1:00 a.m. in the morning to find that our little girl, Hope, was lying in a pool of vomit. My wife rushed her into the bathroom and did her best to clean Hope up but it didn't last long. Hope quickly threw up again and again. We then were forced to take her to the hospital at around 1:45 a.m., where we remained for the rest of the night. Hope's fever began to rise and she threw up about every fifteen minutes on average. The car was a mess, we were a mess and more importantly, Hope was a total mess.

While at the hospital Hope got worse and worse as we began to worry about dehydration. When things kept getting worse, and we felt we were at our wits end, God was about to perform a miracle for us.

I remember reading my Bible and starting at Matthew chapter one, trusting God to answer our prayers. At around 3:00 a.m., I came to Matthew chapter 8, when Jesus began his many different miracles. Hope was in the middle of throwing up for the fifteenth time. Things looked dark, but God's light was about to shine through. While reading Matthew 8:14-15 God sweetly spoke peace to my soul. I saw in these verses how God touched Peter's Mother-in-law's, and immediately the fever left her. God seemed to speak to my heart that He had just did the same thing for Hope. I looked over at my wife and stroked my daughter's hair and said, "We can go home if you want because Jesus just healed little Hope." Many people heard me say those words and my wife said we probably should stay because we are here already. I replied okay but she is healed.

Proud to report that Jesus indeed healed little Hope and it was instant. Hope never again threw up that night and the fever left her. What first was a dark circumstance turned into a great blessing. We will always remember that miracle and we're forever thankful for it.

Sometimes like with the life of Lazarus, God may not show up when we want Him to, but rather in a time that is altogether perfect. God is always RIGHT ON TIME.

Scriptures Chapter 20

Matthew 8: 14: And when Jesus was come into Peter's house, he saw his wife's mother laid, and sick of a fever. 15: And he touched her hand, and the fever left her: and she arose, and ministered unto them.

Chapter 21
If That Isn't Love

Sometimes there are songs, with lyrics and phrases that are so good it causes you to sing them all day long. The Bible teaches, in Ephesians 5:19, that we should allow the Lord to speak to us through Psalms, hymns, and spiritual songs and make them a part of our daily routine. When your down in the dumps, remember a good old gospel song and a smile will return on your face.

In this chapter, I will give you the story of how God gave me the third verse of one of the best songs that has been penned in this generation. Every song has a unique story behind it and this will be no different. This story still makes me smile whenever I think about it. God sends blessings our way that encourage our hearts, and inspire us to tell others about His wonderful love. This story will stand out in your mind as a miracle, and will prove to you that God's love is real. If you are someone who has never experienced the love of Christ, then allow this simple story to convince you today.

A few years ago at my work, God overshadowed me in

a way that was beautiful and transparent. The only thing that seemed to race through my mind that day was a song by Dottie Rambo entitled, "If That Isn't love." This song expresses the love of God, like few songs can, and has always spoken to this sinner's heart. Over and over again I can remember singing that song and God's spirit growing sweeter, the more I dwelt on the words.

As I stepped outside, I recall singing the chorus of that song which says, "If that isn't love the Ocean is dry, there's no stars in the skies, and the sparrow can't fly." What's amazing about this is that a sparrow flew right in front of me when I was singing that song. God spoke to my heart in a glorious way and showed me that His love was real, and He sent a sparrow to prove it to me. Less than five minutes after this incident took place, God gave me the words to the third verse of this grand old song.

The words read like this, "Jesus in power has risen, forgiving you and me, and one day by grace I shall see Him, through the blood that He shed for me."

The following Sunday I sang that song and God's Spirit moved in a powerful way and many lives were touched. A Godly song is like water to a thirsty soul, and we need to drink from the Lord's fountain every day. Colossians 3:16 says, " let the word of Christ dwell in you richly in all wisdom; teaching and admonishing one another in Psalms and hymns and spiritual songs, singing with grace in your hearts to the Lord."

Scriptures Chapter 21

Ephesians 5: 19: Speaking to yourselves in psalms and hymns and spiritual songs, singing and making melody in your heart to the Lord;

Colossians 3: 16: Let the word of Christ dwell in you richly in all wisdom; teaching and admonishing one another in psalms and hymns and spiritual songs, singing with grace in your hearts to the Lord.

Chapter 22
Home Sweet Home

If I had only one message to give that would help this generation of teens, it would be a message found in Matthew 6:33, "But seek ye first the kingdom of God, and his righteousness; and all these things shall be added unto you." Jesus given us a promise in this verse that has never failed anybody in the past, nor will it ever fail anyone in the future. It was the single greatest verse that helped me through my teenage years and it saved me from many hard times and scars in my early years. The Bible clearly tells us, in this verse, to seek the kingdom of God and His righteousness above any other thing that life has to offer. If you do this, God in return will give you anything that you need. You must make Jesus first and foremost in your life if you want a bright future to come your way.

Far too many people plan on one day having a big house, a car, a boat load of money, fun times, and a wonderful family on their own abilities without the Lord as their foundation. This philosophy will lead to disappointment, sorrow, and many tears. Without the Lord, as the center of our life, we will have a future built on sinking sand and total disaster according to the word of God. People love to use God as the spare tire in their road of life, and only wish to reach out for Him after their lives are in a total ruin. This way of thinking is completely opposite of God's plan for our life and we wonder why things are not turning out right. The Bible plainly states that Jesus must be our first option, for every need we have in life, if we want His blessings in return. Allow me to explain both sides of life the best way I know how.

First, there is a blessed side of life that we can enjoy if we rely on God for everything, rather than ourselves. The Bible teaches in Psalms 23:6 that surely goodness and mercy shall follow me all the days of my life; and I will dwell in the house of the LORD forever. Notice how goodness and mercy shall follow you, all the days of your life. God promises to bring things into your life when you put Him first.

Proverbs 28:20, "A faithful man shall abound with blessings: but he that maketh haste to be rich shall not be innocent." Isaiah 40:31, "But they that wait upon the LORD shall renew their strength; they shall mount up with wings as eagles; they shall run, and not be weary; and they shall walk, and not faint." Malachi 3:10 teaches that on this blessed pathway God is able to open up the windows of heaven and pour out blessings every day.

When you journey through life in the blessed way; that doesn't mean you will never have problems, it just means you will never have problems by yourself. Proverbs 18:24, "A man that hath friends must shew himself friendly: and there is a friend that sticketh closer than a brother." Hebrews 13:5, "Let your conversation be without covetousness; and be content with such things as ye have: for he hath said, I will never leave thee, nor forsake thee."

When you walk with God on a daily basis, your path will be filled with light, joy, peace, safety, goodness, faith, love, meekness, treasures, shelter, grace, forgiveness, glory, assurance, and salvation. Simply put, your cup of blessings will be running over if you put Him first. In the blessed way, God will order your steps, and give you the desires of your heart. That is the right path that everyone should travel on, according to the scriptures.

Secondly however, I'm sad to say, there is another path that is available to you that the majority of mankind is finding themselves on. This path is a path of darkness, cursing, and self-righteousness that makes God unpleased. God is a jealous God, according to His word and He wants you to make Him first place in your life. Most teens, and adults alike, are on a broad path that is leading them to destruction, and they don't even realize it. The Bible says in Proverbs 14:12, 'There is a way which seemeth right unto a man, but the end thereof are the ways of death."

The Bible teaches that when man leaves God's plan for their life and tries to put their own life together, they are headed for danger. The Bible says in James 4:17, "Therefore to him that knoweth to do good, and doeth it not, to him it is sin." The Bible teaches us in 1 John 2:15 to love not the world, neither the things that are in the world. If any man love the world, the love of the Father is not in him. In Psalms 9: 17, "The wicked shall be turned into hell, and all the nations that forget God."

When something else is first in your life, it has become an idol and you will soon forget God. Once you forget God, and make other things your goal in life, this is when Satan steps in where God is supposed to be. When this starts to take place, trouble begins to come your way and hard times will multiple for you. The Bible teaches in Luke chapter 4 that Satan is the god of this world, and he will give you anything you desire as long as you forget about God. The Devil may seem like your friend, but the Bible teaches he is a liar, a murderer, a roaring lion, and a master deceiver. He seeks to destroy your life through hurtful lusts, sin, and pleasures that will never last. On this path the Bible teaches that it is slippery, dangerous, violent, punishing, and deadly. Proverbs 3:33, "The curse of the LORD is in the house of the wicked: but he blesseth the habitation of the just." The Bible teaches that everyone who travels this way is cursed.

Proverbs 4:19, "The way of the wicked is as darkness: they know not at what they stumble." The Bible tells us that the wicked constantly abide in darkness, and stumble through life. Proverbs 13:15 declares that life is hard for those on this path. Proverbs 13:21 says, "Evil pursueth sinners: but to the righteous good shall be repayed." The Bible teaches that evil pursueth after sinners, or in other words, follows those on this path. People often wonder why life is so hard, but they never serve God and make Him the pinnacle of their lives. The longer you stay on this path of selfishness, and self-dependence, the farther you get from God's will for your life. Many people who stay on this path become vain, greedy, covetous, and far to busy building their own empire. The Bible teaches in Luke 12:21, "So is he that layeth up treasure for himself, and is not rich toward God." It also states, in Mark 8:36, "For what shall it profit a man, if he shall gain the whole world, and lose his own soul?" Always remember that anything you hold in your hand down here you will surely leave to others.

When God is removed from your mind, you will make very foolish decisions and destroy your life forever. Psalms 14:1 says the fool hath said in his heart there is no God. Fools make a mock at sin and take the things of God lightly. Romans 6:23 says the wages of sin is death and the soul that sinneth shall die. When the Lord is not important in your life your chances of success disappears. Please be sure you avoid this path, at all costs! Follow the Lord with all your heart. I would venture to say that in my entire life I have only seen a handful of young people choose THE BLESSED PATH for their life. Sadly, in contrast, I have witnessed hundreds of people pick the cursed path and it has devastated their future with God.

For every Joseph, David, and Daniel, found in the will of God there are millions found in the will of the Devil. It is sad to see such a small percentage do what Jesus said in Matthew 6:33. We, as teachers and preachers, can only point people in the right direction, but we do not have the ability to live their lives for them. My goal and wish, through this chapter, is to cause someone to develop a hunger for God that has never been there before. My life has been a prime example of someone who has always tried to put God first, and could care less about achieving my own personal dreams. Never, in my childhood growing up or even in my teenage years, did I ever attend a party to fit in with others. Praise the Lord, I have never smoked a cigarette or touched alcohol in my life. I've tried to live clean and holy and if I would slip, in any way, I would repent very quickly.

Though my teenage years were rough at times, I never dropped out of church, and strived to stay faithful to the Savior. God has been so good to me, and has rewarded me for putting Him first. Although I never worried about a car, over time He gave me a Ford Mustang show car. Even though I didn't date a girl until I was twenty-five years old, God allowed me to meet my wife at church. Never did I even think about having a child, and God gave me a beautiful little girl later down the road. God has also given me a job that I love and too many blessings to number. The progress and advancement of my life is not due to planning but do to the Lord fulfilling His promise in Matthew 6:33. God cannot lie. Titus 1:2, "In hope of eternal life, which God, that cannot lie, promised before the world began; and my life is living proof of that."

Last year, nearly every day of the year, God used people to bless my family. With the remainder of this chapter please allow me to give you two stories that help prove that God will take care of you if you serve Him with ALL YOUR HEART.

The first story I want to give you is from one of the greatest Christians ever to breathe God's air. His name was Isaac Watts and his story is proof of God's provision in one's life. The second story will be how God worked things out to bless us with the home we enjoy now. I pray these two stories will speak to your heart and show you the importance of putting the Lord above anything and everything this world has to offer. Let me first start with Mr. Isaac Watts and show you the grace of God in his journey with Christ.

Isaac Watts was, without a doubt, one of the smartest, most gifted and spirit filled Christians that this world has ever seen. He is referred to as the Father of hymnology. Mr. Watts introduced his own personal hymns to his church, and the church embraced and supported them in a wonderful way. Mr. Watts went against the traditional thinking of how songs were sung in churches all across the world. Before Isaac Watts came along, only the Psalms were sung in church services and anything else was considered blasphemy.

Mr. Watts wrote biblical, uplifting and Christ honoring songs that became rapidly very popular and spread to other congregations across the world. Many different revivals, throughout the pages of time, can largely be attributed to the hymns that Mr. Watts wrote. He had already mastered four languages before the age of thirteen, and wrote many of his six hundred plus songs before the age of twenty. Mr. Watts wrote what many consider the greatest song in English history entitled, "When I survey the wondrous cross." Isaac Watts also wrote one of the greatest Christmas songs ever penned as well entitled, "Joy to the world." The Bible teaches in 1 Corinthians 3:6," I have planted, Apollos watered; but God gave the increase."

Music prepares the heart for preaching; and preaching helps draw people to Christ for salvation. Godly music and powerful preaching work together to speak to the lost and both, in their own way, can awaken a dead soul for Christ. Every soul that walks the aisle, through an Isaac Watts song, is fruit that is added to his account. It is widely known that Isaac Watts wrote a song entitled, "At the Cross." This song was one of the key factors in the great Fanny Crosby coming to Jesus in faith and repentance.

Mrs. Crosby wrote over nine thousand songs and walked with the Lord as close as any woman in the last thousand years. She won thousands upon thousands to the Lord through her own hymns and impacted this world like very few ever have. Every life touched and every soul reached for the Lord through her music can be traced back to Mr. Isaac Watts. The Bible teaches he gets credit for his influence of planting the seed in the case of Fanny Crosby.

Mr. Isaac Watts also wrote the song entitled, "Am I a soldier of the cross." This one song was the key component in starting one of the greatest teams in gospel history which was D.L.Moody and Ira Sankey. Through this song, and its impact on their partnership, it kick started some of the best revivals this world has ever known. Multitudes were saved from the fires of hell through these revivals and Mr. Isaac Watts was an influence on every one of them.

Mr. Watts also wrote a song that made a major difference in the life of an Olympic hero by the name of Eric Lindell. Brother Lindell won Olympic medals for his country and heavenly treasures for his Savior. Through one of the old hymns that Isaac Watts wrote, many years before Eric Lindell felt God tug at his heart, and it caused him to give the rest of his years as a missionary to China. The story is told that when he boarded the ship to sail to a foreign land, thousands gathered to bid him farewell that day. With tears in his eyes, he led the people in the Isaac Watts hymn that affected his own life so deeply. For nineteen years Lindell served in China, in submission to God, and Isaac Watts was a big reason why.

His songs have stood the test of time and it is safe to say that his legacy is beyond compare. He wrote many books including a children's book that sold 80,000 copies in the first year and is still selling today. Many other stories surround this man's life, but I want to give you a story that relates to this chapter.

Isaac Watts was a frail man in stature, but a giant in faith. He worked night and day to advance the kingdom of God, and he was rewarded in a very unique way. People say he was short, unattractive and physically very weak. A woman fell in love with him one day through his beautiful poetry and longed for a chance to meet him in person. The story is told that her wish was granted one day and she was extremely disappointed. She was completely turned off by his appearance and broke his heart by running away. Mr. Watts took this experience as a sign from God never to marry anyone, but rather give his life as a servant for His Master.

Between pastoring, writing books, producing hymns, and serving others his body gave out on him at only twenty-eight years old. Isaac Watts became a little worried about his future, and wanted to resign his role as the shepherd of his flock. When he addressed his people about his health, a wealthy family in his church refused the notion of him resigning, and offered that he stay at their home, until he figured things out. Isaac quickly agreed to their generous offer and continued his work for God. Isaac was only suppose to stay at this couples home for two weeks but he ended up staying for the next thirty-eight years.

God blessed Mr. Watts dedication and paid for every meal, sheltered him with a home he never paid for and let him live in comfort for the majority of his life. Isaac Watts' life proves that God is a debtor to no man and the fountain of blessings will flow in our lives if we will make Him the heartbeat of our future. Isaac Watts may have been unattractive to this world, but he is glorious in the world to come.

For the rest of this chapter I would like to share with you a similar story of how the precious Lord blessed us with our home in a special way. The Lord deserves all the credit in this story and I lift up holy hands in praise for what He has done.

When my wife and I were engaged to be married, the search for a home quickly became a top priority in our lives. We began to look at many houses, apartments, and other places and every situation seemed to offer hope but always fell through the cracks of possibility. Before we knew it, the time had come to be married and we were still unsure of where we were going to live.

After our honeymoon was over, we still had no place to live, and we were trusting God in a fashion we never had before. My parents offered us a place to sleep in their garage, for a few days, while we continued to look for a home. My uncle also allowed us to stay in his house while they went on vacation for a week and it seemed like the door of opportunity was closing for us. After a few more days of searching, we then looked at some apartments in Belleville, Michigan. We thought that any place is better than no place. After meeting with the manager in charge we signed a one-year agreement to live there. The apartment cost $625.00 a month and it was like putting our money in a bag with holes in it; like the word of God teaches. We were told to make a one hundred dollar deposit towards the apartment, but they gave us two weeks to get out of our lease if something better came along. The very next day God had wonderful news for us that would change everything.

My uncle told me that a Christian man from his church had a condo for sale in Canton, Michigan and that we really needed to look at it. When my uncle said that to me something in my soul told me to take his advice. The next day my wife and I traveled towards Canton to look at the condo. After meeting with the owners, and walking through their home, God gave me peace that this was the right place for us. God worked it out for us and blessed us through out the entire process of finding a home we could call our own.

The condo originally cost $89,000 dollars a few years prior, and we ended up paying $42,000 dollars for it. We also had a wonderful, godly real estate lady by the name of Pam Hicks, who helped us with the condo. She helped us every step of the way. She was great throughout the whole experience and was a blessing to my wife and me. Pam Hicks paid around $850 dollars that we didn't have, to help us get our condo. All in all, we saved around $50,000 dollars on our condo and God's handprints could be clearly seen. God placed us in a wonderful community, with awesome neighbors, and gave us a beautiful starter home. There is no way to explain why God was so gracious to us, but all I can say is faithfulness really pays off. Put God first and you will begin to see your life come together in a perfect way.

Scriptures Chapter 22

Matthew 6: 33 But seek ye first the kingdom of God, and his righteousness; and all these things shall be added unto you.

Psalms 23: 6 Surely goodness and mercy shall follow me all the days of my life: and I will dwell in the house of the LORD forever.

Proverbs 28: 20 A faithful man shall abound with blessings: but he that maketh haste to be rich shall not be innocent.

Isaiah 40:31 But they that wait upon the LORD shall renew their strength; they shall mount up with wings as eagles; they shall run, and not be weary; and they shall walk, and not faint.

Malachi 3:10 Bring ye all the tithes into the storehouse, that there may be meat in mine house, and prove me now herewith, saith the LORD of hosts, if I will not open you the windows of heaven, and pour you out a blessing, that there shall not be room enough to receive it.

Proverbs 18: 24 A man that hath friends must shew himself friendly: and there is a friend that sticketh closer than a brother.

Hebrews 13: 5 Let your conversation be without covetousness; and be content with such things as ye have: for he hath said, I will never leave thee, nor forsake thee.

Proverbs 14:12 There is a way which seemeth right unto a man, but the end thereof are the ways of death

James 4:17 Therefore to him that knoweth to do good, and doeth it not, to him it is sin.

1 John 2:15 Love not the world, neither the things that are in the world. If any man love the world, the love of the Father is not in him.

Psalms 9:17 The wicked shall be turned into hell, and all the nations that forget God.

Proverbs 3: 33 The curse of the LORD is in the house of the wicked: but he blesseth the habitation of the just.

Proverbs 4:19 The way of the wicked is as darkness: they know not at what they stumble.

Proverbs 13:15 Good understanding giveth favour: but the way of transgressors is hard. Declares that life is hard for those on this path.

Proverbs 13: 21 Evil pursueth sinners: but to the righteous good shall be repayed.

Luke 12: 21 So is he that layeth up treasure for himself, and is not rich toward God.

Mark 8: 36 For what shall it profit a man, if he shall gain the whole world, and lose his own soul?

Psalms 14:1 The fool hath said in his heart, There is no God. They are corrupt, they have done abominable works, there is none that doeth good.

Romans 6: 23 For the wages of sin is death; but the gift of God is eternal life through Jesus Christ our Lord

Titus 1:2 In hope of eternal life, which God, that cannot lie, promised before the world began

1 Corinthians 3: 6 I have planted, Apollos watered; but God gave the increase

Chapter 23
Great Services That I Have Been In Over The Years

    I have tried my best, over the years, to study some of the greatest revivals that have ever been recorded through the pages of time. Great men, through a greater God, have been instrumental in making a tremendous difference for Jesus. The apostle Peter preached on the day of Pentecost and 3,000 were born again. Jonah preached a message of repentance and all of Ninevah believed God from the greatest to the least of them. Spirit filled men of God like Charles and John Wesley saw thousands upon thousands converted to the Lord and totally transformed through a salvation experience. They said when Jonathan Edwards preached, during the great awakening, revival spread to multiple parts of the world and people were afraid of waking up in hell before the morning hit.

    Many stirring messages have been thundered throughout the ages with results that have stood the test of time. When God's presence can be felt in a service, lives will be touched, souls will be converted, and a real difference will be made.

Great services are almost a thing of the past and Christians all around this country long for the days of old when God seemed to move among his people. The purpose beyond this chapter is to prove that God is still in control, and that He is still in the soul saving business.

In this chapter I will share with you some of the very best services that I have ever been apart of. Lord willing, this will help you to realize that even though we are in the last days, God is still interested in changing lives and blessing His children. You will read a handful of powerful services that the good Lord has allowed me to be a part of through the years in this chapter. May God bless your heart as you read these stories.

Many years ago, at Open Door Baptist Church in Detroit, Michigan, God gave us an amazing service one day. I remember waking up on a Sunday and playing a gospel music tape while I was getting ready for church. God seemed to burn a particular song I was listening to in my heart and mind. The song was entitled, "Drifting to far from the shore" and that morning I listened to that song around fifteen times as I prepared myself for church. Peace came over my soul and I was absolutely positive God wanted me to sing that song, at church, that morning. Sure enough that Sunday morning, the pastor asked me to sing a song that was on my heart.

Before I sang my song, I gave a testimony of how God dealt with me about the song I was going to sing and I believe somebody needs to get right with God today. After my song was over I sat down to hear what the pastor was going to say. He stood up and said a statement that I will never forget. He told the congregation that he had a message that he studied for all week, that he really wanted to preach, but God would not allow him. Instead he told us how the Lord changed his message, in the middle of the night, to a message entitled, "Drifting to far from the shore." My song fit his message like a glove and the power of God filled the air. When the invitation was given that morning the altar was covered with people pouring their hearts out to God. A number of people were saved and many more were helped. It was a service from heaven and it's impact is still being felt to this day.

Another service that comes to mind is a service that took place in Lansing, Michigan a few years ago. This service was special to me, and to all that attended that night. Even before the service began, in the car ride there, we could sense something glorious would happen in the meeting that night. As we were going down the road, a song came on entitled, "He didn't through the clay away." For some reason, the words in this song jumped out that day like never before. A man I was riding with never heard the song before, and kept playing it over and over again as he wiped tears from his eyes. The song speaks of God" ability to forgive those who have made mistakes in their past. Only God has the power to forgive and forget mistakes we have made over the years. We can forgive, but we do not have the ability to forget things in our past. This song is very special and it sure did touch our hearts on our way to the house of God that night.

When we arrived in Lansing to hear the word of God, something amazing happened just prior to the preaching. A man stood up, who had been converted a couple of years before, and sang the same exact song we heard on the way to church that night. When he was singing that song, people shouted, cried, rejoiced, and glorified God. The pastor of that church announced to his people that this song did more for his spirit than any other song he had ever heard. The pastor asked him to sing it over and over again and the Spirit of God completely took over. As he sang, people ran to the altar, gave away money, and revival swept through the church.

After the song service was concluded, and it was time for preaching, the service was about to reach new heights as the man of God started his message. The man of God preached from Jeremiah 18:1 about the potter and the clay. He preached with total liberty that night and many lives were helped. The whole service flowed together in perfect harmony and they had a wonderful meeting that week. When God is in a meeting, it will always have the potential of being great. Let me give you two more services that I consider great over my years of walking with the Lord.

One night, at Midwestern Baptist College, I witnessed a scene that I will always remember. A friend of mine, who was actually the best man in my wedding, preached a life-changing message to those in attendance that evening. As he was delivering his sermon, to a crowd of around 700 that night, the power of God fell on him in a manner I had never seen before. In the white heat of preaching, under the influence of the Holy Ghost, this man jumped on the pulpit and was preaching from on top of the pulpit. This man is short in stature, but powerful in faith. Everyone in attendance wondered how he did that, and I must admit I did too. The service was indescribable and it spoke to many hearts. The Bible teaches in Romans 8:31, "What shall we then say to these things? If God be for us, who can be against us?" As I look back on that experience I believe God was with us that night and it felt like the gates of hell could not prevail against us.

The final great service I wish to bring to your attention was at Open Door Baptist Church's tent meeting in Detroit, Michigan. To this day it still remains one of the greatest services I have ever been a part of in my thirty one years on earth. The Spirit of God seemed to hover over the tent that night as the preacher opened the Bible. In the crowd were amazing servants of God, and also sinners that needed to hear from heaven. The preacher had unusual power resting on him that night as he started his message. I had never seen a group of people listen so well, and it felt like God's spirit was everywhere. His subject was,"How to have the power of God, on your life, and what it takes to get it."

There was a stillness to that service that was priceless and every soul looked to be touched. People filled the altar when he was finished and many gave their lives for the service of God. That one message helped me more than any other message that I have ever heard. It took me to a level with Christ that I had never known. Matthew 5:6, "Blessed are they which do hunger and thirst after righteousness: for they shall be filled." The Bible says that those who are hungry and thirsty for His righteousness shall be filled. As I got up from the altar, that night, I had a new desire to hunger after the Lord like never before.

In closing out this chapter, I will be the first to say that services around this country are just a shadow of what they once were, but they still do exist. The Bible does teach that in the last days there will be a great falling away [2 Thessalonians 2:3] and true men of God would be hard to find. After traveling to many churches around this country I must confess that what the Bible teaches concerning the end time is indeed true. I've asked myself, on many occasions, where is the Lord God of Elijah. I wondered, in my heart, if the church of the living God still remains in these last dark days. I'm glad to report that I have witnessed His wonders in churches over the years and have felt His power on several occasions. Although the majority of churches have turned from the truth, some still stand with the Lord. Our job, as Christians, is to support these ministries and help in any way possible as God directs us. When you sense revival, in a church, do whatever it takes to keep the fire going. We are the biggest problem why God is not moving in our churches anymore and there is no one to blame but ourselves. D.L.Moody once said that Christians are like the Dead Sea, they take in everything they can but they give nothing away. Christians are like spiritual sponges that take from the church and add nothing to it. Allow revival to begin in your own heart and it will surprise you how big of a difference you can make. God can still move like in days gone by if we will only allow Him to.

Scriptures Chapter 23

Jeremiah 18: 1: Thus saith the LORD, Go and get a potter's earthen bottle, and take of the ancients of the people, and of the ancients of the priests; 2: And go forth unto the valley of the son of Hinnom, which is by the entry of the east gate, and proclaim there the words that I shall tell thee, 3: And say, Hear ye the word of the LORD, O kings of Judah, and inhabitants of Jerusalem; Thus saith the LORD of hosts, the God of Israel; Behold, I will bring evil upon this place, the which whosoever heareth, his ears shall tingle. 4: Because they have forsaken me, and have estranged this place, and have burned incense in it unto other gods, whom neither they nor their fathers have known, nor the kings of Judah, and have filled this place with the blood of innocents; 5: They have built also the high places of Baal, to burn their sons with fire for burnt offerings unto Baal, which I commanded not, nor spake it, neither came it into my mind: 6: Therefore, behold, the days come, saith the LORD, that this place shall no more be called Tophet, nor The valley of the son of Hinnom, but The valley of slaughter.

Romans 8: 31: What shall we then say to these things? If God be for us, who can be against us?

Matthew 5: 6: Blessed are they which do hunger and thirst after righteousness: for they shall be filled. says that those who are hungry and thirsty for His righteousness shall be filled.

2 Thessalonians 2:3: Let no man deceive you by any means: for that day shall not come, except there come a falling away first, and that man of sin be revealed, the son of perdition

Chapter 24
Crossing the Line with God

When you study through the 66 books of the King James 1611 AD Bible, you will find many times where people crossed lines with God that proved to be deadly. We all understand the love and long suffering of a thrice Holy God through what Christ did on the cross. The sacrificial death on the cross still remains the greatest display of mercy and grace that has ever been known. The love of God is undeniable and it is the driving force of our faith, as we know it. The born again redeemed are trusting in nothing else than the death, burial and resurrection as our way to heaven. On the other hand, there is another side of God that is rarely expressed but is just as true.

The Bible gives us hundreds of verses about judgement, damnation and death. I could personally take my Bible and show you example after example of where God's patience ran out and people crossed an eternal line with God that suddenly ended their life. From Nabal disrespecting David, and God killing him, to Korah and his crowd going against Moses in Numbers 16:32-34; God will always get the final say in these matters. The word of God says in Proverbs 1:7, "The fear of the LORD is the beginning of knowledge: but fools despise wisdom and instruction." Basically, that verse is teaching us that you can never get past first base with God unless you learn how to fear Him.

The book of James 3:8 says, "But the tongue can no man tame; it is an unruly evil, full of deadly poison." Jesus said in Matthew 12:36, "But I say unto you, that every idle word that men shall speak, they shall give account thereof in the Day of Judgment." In verse 37, "For by thy words thou shalt be justified, and by thy words thou shalt be condemned" and in Luke 12:5, "But I will forewarn you whom ye shall fear: Fear him, which after he hath killed hath power to cast into hell; yea, I say unto you, Fear him". In Proverbs 29:1 we see He that being often reproved (or warned) hardeneth his neck, shall suddenly be destroyed, and that without remedy. In other words, God takes His Word very seriously whether we do or not. My Dad always taught me how to fear and respect God in my everyday life. His "life verse" is found in Hebrews 10:31, "It is a fearful thing to fall into the hands of the living God". It is a powerful verse of scripture that stuck with me through my life growing up. This verse will be important with the story I am about to tell. After this story is finished I pray that you will have a new found respect for God.

One night, as we were visiting people in Detroit inviting folks out to church, something serious happened that is troubling to say the least. My Father and I were on Gilbert St. trying to witness for our Blessed Savior. We didn't know it, but to our surprise gang members lived in the majority of those houses on that street. That really didn't matter to either one of us because we had a heavy burden to reach the lost. As we began to knock doors on this street, we said a quick prayer for safety before we got started. I remember the third house we came to God opened the door for a great witness that I will never forget. Two young women, who obviously had problems, were listening very intently as the Gospel was going forth. My Dad was doing all the talking and I was doing all the praying.

As the witness was advancing and hearts were being touched, something tragic was about to happen that would change everything. I remember seeing a man, from a gang's house across the street, and he was approaching us at a rapid pace. Before we knew it he had engaged in our conversation in an abrupt way. He interrupted my Dad and began to mock the Bible and the Lord Jesus Christ. He cursed God with the foulest language I've ever heard. My Dad tried to calm him down the best he could, but nothing seemed to work. Finally, in the heat of the moment, my Dad said to him this statement. "If God is not real, go get a gun and blow your head off and we will see if He is real." The man, in anger, retaliated by saying, "I'll get a gun and blow your head off." As the man left to get his gun, my Dad continued on like nothing ever happened. The two young ladies were in shock and assured us that he was crazy. My Dad then responded that he was not afraid of that man, but he would leave if they were uncomfortable. However, before he left he quoted the famous verse in Galatians 6:7, "Be not deceived; God is not mocked: for whatsoever a man soweth, that shall he also reap." When my Dad said that verse something turned on in my soul and I knew that man was in serious trouble for what he had done.

Two days later, after church was over while we

were dropping someone off, something caught my eye. On the telephone pole was a picture of a man that looked all too familiar to my Dad and I. As we looked closer we discovered that a man had died a day earlier and it happened to be the man that interrupted us. The police also were at that gang house. A number of the gang members, with their hands handcuffed behind their backs, were being arrested. The Bible tells us in Psalms 7:11 God judgeth the righteous, and God is angry with the wicked every day. Please be careful what you say, and when you say it because God's ears are open at all times.

Scriptures Chapter 24

Numbers 16: 2: And the earth opened her mouth, and swallowed them up, and their houses, and all the men that appertained unto Korah, and all their goods. 33: They, and all that appertained to them, went down alive into the pit, and the earth closed upon them: and they perished from among the congregation. 34: And all Israel that were round about them fled at the cry of them: for they said, Lest the earth swallow us up also.

Proverbs 1: 7: The fear of the LORD is the beginning of knowledge: but fools despise wisdom and instruction.

James 3:8: But the tongue can no man tame; it is an unruly evil, full of deadly poison.

Matthew 12: 36: But I say unto you, That every idle word that men shall speak, they shall give account thereof in the Day of Judgment. 37: For by thy words thou shalt be justified, and by thy words thou shalt be condemned

Luke 12: 5: But I will forewarn you whom ye shall fear: Fear him, which after he hath killed hath power to cast into hell; yea, I say unto you, Fear him.

Proverbs 29: 1 He, that being often reproved hardeneth his neck, shall suddenly be destroyed, and that without remedy.

Hebrews 10: 31: It is a fearful thing to fall into the hands of the living God.

Galatians 6: 7: Be not deceived; God is not mocked: for whatsoever a man soweth, that shall he also reap.

Psalms 7: 11: God judgeth the righteous, and God is angry with the wicked every day.

Chapter 25
God Blessing Me with McManna on a Hot Summer Day

Often, throughout the course of life, many people lack in thanking God for his blessings; no matter how small they seem to be. Paul said in I Thessalonians 5:18, "In every thing give thanks: for this is the will of God in Christ Jesus concerning you." It is the will of God for us to be thankful for everything we receive. The next time you read through your Bible I challenge you to take notice of just how many times people are unthankful for God's grace in their lives.

One example, of people being unthankful in the Bible, is when Jesus healed the ten lepers in Luke 17:12-19, only one of them even said thank you. Paul said in the last days, that people would become unthankful. 2 Timothy 3:2 says. "For men shall be lovers of their own selves, covetous, boasters, proud, blasphemers, disobedient to parents, unthankful, unholy," Matthew 24:12 says, "And because iniquity shall abound, the love of many shall wax cold." I can still remember, very vividly, when God laid it on my heart to give a man $1,000 dollars for

Christmas one year. After I worked hard for the money and gave him the check, this man barely said thank you, and went on his merry way. I determined, from that moment on, never to take things I receive from others lightly and act like that man did with the blessings that may come my way. Whether it is a suit coat or a candy bar, I want to be sure they know I appreciate them thinking about me. Every blessing I receive, from the hands of others, I either write it down on a piece of paper or store it in my memory banks because I never want to forget it. Sometimes God puts it on people's hearts to be a blessing to me, and sometimes He takes it upon Himself to bless me.

The story I'm about to tell you blesses my heart fresh and new everytime I tell it and I will never forget this beautiful story as long you as He gives me breath. Allow me to share with you a story that seems small but it definitely cheered my heart.

One day, in the summer time, I received word that I would be hitting the road, and the driver was ready to go. Whenever my work makes that statement it basically means there is no time to grab anything, just go. The temperature that day exceeded 90 degrees and the weather channel warned that it was dangerous conditions. I was thirsty, hungry and getting very dizzy because of my lack of food intake that day. I still remember almost passing out, due to the heat and I was praying for a miracle.

We were working on Southfield freeway that day picking up barrels. As I became weaker and weaker, I asked the driver if I could have a minute because dehydration was hitting my body. After a few minutes had passed we continued working and I was trusting God all the way. During that time, McDonalds had something called The Monopoly Game going on where you could win free food. This game was about to prove critical to me, and God was about to bless me in an unusual way. I had no food or money but thankfully I had God.

After about five minutes of work I looked on the ground and saw a McDonald's cup. To my surprise, the cup still had the two Monopoly pieces still on it. As I peeled the pieces off the cup, one of the pieces happened to be a free quarter pounder with cheese. My first thought was this is a one in a million situation and rarely ever do people throw away one of those Monopoly cups without checking the pieces first. It was without a doubt a blessing from God. We went back to work and I had renewed energy that wasn't there before. It was still hot and I was still weak but I was very excited.

As we went down the road a little bit farther God was about to perform a second miracle that day. To my amazement, I looked and found a second McDonalds cup, and that too had the Monopoly pieces on it. I was in total shock at this point. As I peeled off the pieces I found that one of the pieces was a large fry. After our work was over, we went to McDonalds and cashed in my pieces. It was an amazing day and I still stand in awe of what happened. Psalms 115:3 says, "But our God is in the heavens: he hath done whatsoever he hath pleased." Although I will never understand how it came to pass that day, I must conclude that it was God who did it. I will end the chapter with this verse that seems fitting. Psalms 68:9, "Blessed be the Lord, who daily loadeth us with benefits, even the God of our salvation. Selah."

Scriptures Chapter 25

I Thessalonians 5: 18: In every thing give thanks: for this is the will of God in Christ Jesus concerning you.

Luke 17:12: And as he entered into a certain village, there met him ten men that were lepers, which stood afar off: 13: And they lifted up their voices, and said, Jesus, Master, have mercy on us. 14: And when he saw them, he said unto them, Go shew yourselves unto the priests. And it came to pass, that, as they went, they were cleansed.

15: And one of them, when he saw that he was healed, turned back, and with a loud voice glorified God, 16: And fell down on his face at his feet, giving him thanks: and he was a Samaritan. 17: And Jesus answering said, "Were there not ten cleansed? but where are the nine? 18: There are not found that returned to give glory to God, save this stranger.

19: And he said unto him, Arise, go thy way: thy faith hath made thee whole"

2 Timothy 3:2: For men shall be lovers of their own selves, covetous, boasters, proud, blasphemers, disobedient to parents, unthankful, unholy,

Matthew 24:12: And because iniquity shall abound, the love of many shall wax cold.

Psalms 115: 3: But our God is in the heavens: he hath done whatsoever he hath pleased.

Psalms 68:9: Blessed be the Lord, who daily loadeth us with benefits, even the God of our salvation. Selah.

Chapter 26
God Speaking to a Man's Heart Before I Could, at Work

The Bible often tells us, in great detail, the dangers of walking away from the Lord and running from His perfect will in our life. Jonah is a good example of someone who tried to flee from the presence of God and found himself in a horrible circumstance. God will never send judgement before He first sends a warning.

Many times, according to the book of Hebrews 12:5-8 God chastens those that are His, but that chastening can reach a point of something more drastic over time. If God's children refuse to repent and get right with God, over a space of time, the Bible teaches that God will turn to other forms of punishment. Paul always had a fear, in 1 Corinthians 9:27, of getting away from God and becoming a castaway. In the book of 1 Samuel 18:10 Saul got away from God so bad that God gave him an evil spirit until the day he died. Saul went to heaven, but he was judged for his attitude towards King David.

In Psalms 78:49 we see how God can send people evil angels to afflict and torment those who rebel against His plan for their lives. God punished a man with leprosy, in the Old Testament, for knowingly sinning against the man of God. Whether it is Achan, who stole from God and was stoned, or Samson that had his eyes plucked out by the Philistines, God will use any means necessary to grab one's attention. God is longsuffering and very patient with His children, but there is a time and place where He must send judgement to the backslider in order to get His divine message across.

The final step, according to Acts chapter 5, 1 John 5:16 and Proverbs 29:1 is a premature death only after all other warnings are unheeded. Many times throughout the Bible, and history for that matter, are examples of this divine judgement-taking place in the believer's life. I personally know four times when this has taken place, and every story is very tragic. Revelations 3:16 tells us that the lukewarm Christian makes God sick, and can be spewed (or vomited) out of His mouth. When people leave their first love, and forsake God's will like Demas did in 2 Timothy 4:10, you are surely headed for a whirlwind of destruction.

Please allow me to describe what I'm talking about through a real story that happened, at my work, years ago. This story will open up your eyes to the reality that God is a God of judgement and it should cause you to live more seriously in your walk with the Lord. I'm still in shock that this took place, but it did and I will never forget it. Let me tell you this story and allow the Holy Ghost to minister to your heart in a powerful way.

There was a man, at my work, that I loved as a brother from the first day I met him. Although he had a rough past something about this man was special to me, and I tried my best to help him every chance I got. One day, after witnessing to this man, he fell under deep conviction of God about his sin. For over three nights this man lost sleep, and was shaking in his condition. Joy filled my heart one-day as he attended a Sunday morning service. All the prayers for this man yielded fruit as he walked the aisle and accepted Jesus Christ as his personal Savior. The church shouted the victory and there was a brand new creature standing among us that day. This man instantly volunteered to be baptized and his desire was to help others almost immediately.

For around three months I watched this man serve the Lord and try his absolute best to walk the straight and narrow way for Christ. After three months were over, this man made a common mistake that many Christians make, he started to resort back to bad habits of his past. I watched his life literally being sucked out of him by old friends and old sins that he wasn't willing to forsake. My heart sank as he started drifting away from the Lord and separating himself from me. For months and months he completely left the Lord, and served his flesh. Over and over I would reach out to this man but with no success. I loved him like a brother, and attempted to be a blessing to him, but he ignored all blessings and all warnings that were sent his way. This man became totally entangled in his sin, and was in chains of heaviness that restricted him in serving the Master.

One day, as I drove into work, something very strange took place in my spirit that had never taken place before. From out of nowhere this brother, who I haven't talked with for two months, came to my mind. The Lord would not allow me to get out of the car and begin work until I delivered a certain message to this man. The Lord told me to tell him that if he didn't get right with God, very quickly, danger was headed his way, and God was going to make him a castaway like the Bible teaches.

I can still remember sitting in my car, for around ten minutes, trying to figure out how I was going to do it. I determined to tell him in private; away from the crowd. As I walked up to the building to deliver this serious message, it was almost like silence filled the air. My soul and spirit was troubled, but I was ready to give this man the bad news. As I walked into the building, to start my workday, a man approached me weeping in a way that was unforgettable. His cheeks were red and sorrow filled his face. In front of everyone, he poured out his heart to me that morning. He told me that God spoke to him and warned him about his spiritual state and he needed to get right with God. He asked me to pray with him, and he told me he would be at church on Sunday. This man seemed very honest and concerned and he kept his word and showed up on Sunday, like he said.

What's amazing about this story is that it wasn't just any man that approached me that day, it was the man who God wanted me to convey the message to. Before I could speak to him, he came searching for me. It's amazing how God deals with His children when we stray away from the fold, but in love and compassion He will leave the ninety and nine and go after that one lost sheep. The great old song, that has touched thousands for Christ, tells the world that "I've wondered far away from God, but now I'm coming home." When you come back to the Father with a broken heart, He will gladly welcome you back with arms wide open, with grace that is able to help in your time of need. Psalms 25:11 says, "For thy name's sake, O LORD, pardon mine iniquity; for it is great." Isaiah 55:7 tells the sinner that if he will forsake his own way, and return unto the Lord, then God will show him mercy and he will abundantly pardon. Thank God we serve a God of love and mercy, and He will always be a God of a second chance to those who will turn to Him.

Scriptures Chapter 26

Hebrews 12: 5: And she brought forth a man-child, who was to rule all nations with a rod of iron: and her child was caught up unto God, and to his throne.

6: And the woman fled into the wilderness, where she hath a place prepared of God, that they should feed her there a thousand two hundred and threescore days. 7: And there was war in heaven: Michael and his angels fought against the dragon; and the dragon fought and his angels, 8: And prevailed not; neither was their place found any more in heaven

1 Corinthians 9: 27: But I keep under my body, and bring it into subjection: lest that by any means, when I have preached to others, I myself should be a castaway

1 Samuel 18 10 And Saul sought to smite David even to the wall with the javelin; but he slipped away out of Saul's presence, and he smote the javelin into the wall: and David fled, and escaped that night.

Psalms 78: 49 He cast upon them the fierceness of his anger, wrath, and indignation, and trouble, by sending evil angels among them.

1 John 5:16 If any man see his brother sin a sin which is not unto death, he shall ask, and he shall give him life for them that sin not unto death. There is a sin unto death: I do not say that he shall pray for it.

Proverbs 29: 1: He, that being often reproved hardeneth his neck, shall suddenly be destroyed, and that without remedy.

Revelations 3: 16 So then because thou art lukewarm, and neither cold nor hot, I will spew thee out of my mouth.

2 Timothy 4:10 For Demas hath forsaken me, having loved this present world, and is departed unto Thessalonica; Crescens to Galatia, Titus unto Dalmatia,

Psalms 25:1 For thy name's sake, O LORD, pardon mine iniquity; for it is great.
Isaiah 55: 7 Let the wicked forsake his way, and the unrighteous man his thoughts: and let him return unto the LORD, and he will have mercy upon him; and to our God, for he will abundantly pardon.

Chapter 27
Feeling God's Power At Home One Day

When I was growing up, as a child and even as a young man, I found that the majority of churches I attended frowned upon rejoicing, praising God, saying amen, and of coarse shouting. My mom and dad could tell you that this belief didn't bother me much at the time because in those days I was very quiet and extremely shy. Many times I could go through multiple services without saying anything, but still enjoying the singing and preaching. I did not like attention and would rather be in the shadows in every service I would attend.

The good Lord has always installed in me a deep admiration and respect for God's man, God's people, and God's word. My mom and I have driven five and a half hours, one way, to hear preaching that only lasted one hour while renting a hotel room, and giving that preacher a large love offering to help him along the way.

God knows my heart when I confess to you that I've always struggled with praising the Lord, in the house of God because I do not want to offend people. On the other hand I also do not want to grieve God's Spirit either. Ephesians 4:30 tells us not to grieve His Spirit in church and holding in our praise that God deserves, and holding it back DOES JUST THAT. When you read the book of Psalms you will find hundreds of verses that tell the Christian to praise the Lord for His goodness in the church. Peter said we aught to obey God rather than man. I Thessalonians 4:16 says the Lord shall descend with a shout. Psalms 150:6 says let everything that hath breath praise the Lord. Praise ye the Lord. When Christians refuse to praise the Lord for His blessings, they are grieving the Holy Spirit in the church, and His power can not flow like it could if they would only praise Him.

Over the years God has taught me that praising the Lord, in church, is what God wants you to do. I will praise Him whether others are doing it or not. When I think about how good God has been to me in my life, I can't help but give Him the entire honor He deserves. Everyday of my life, whether it be at church, on the job or even at home, I try to worship the Lord in spirit and in truth. When you love God, others and life your feelings will begin to change concerning shouting and worshiping God. I feel it is a shame that men and women, boys and girls, grandpas and grandmas can go to sporting events and shout till they can't shout anymore, but go to church and just sit there when services are taking place. There is something wrong with that. If we have the victory, then why aren't we excited about it? This once shy boy shouts everywhere he goes and is proud of it.

Let me tell you a true story that took place, in my home one day, a few years back. When I tell you the story think how amazing this is. One day at lunch, God put it on my heart to go home and study in peace for about thirty minutes away from the crowds. When I arrived at my house it was indeed peaceful as my condominium looked like a ghost town. I remember sitting down and opening my Bible to Ephesians chapter 3 and reading that great chapter. When I arrived at verse 19 and 20 of that chapter, God got a hold of my heart in a powerful way. I read the phrase, "that ye might be filled with all the fullness of God," and something turned on in my soul.

The glory of God filled my house and before I knew it I was shouting in praise to the Lord. I called my boss and when he answered I shouted at the top of my lungs for the joy that was in my heart. The impact of that shout was so powerful that an object, in my house, fell over from about 10 feet away. He asked if I had neighbors and I said, "Yes." He said if they were sleeping they are awake now. After we ended our conversation I stood up the object that had fell over and thanked God for his power and blessings on my life. Jesus said in Matthew 5:16 let your light shine before men, and that's what we all should try to do. The Bible says that the Lord hath done great things for us; whereof we are glad.

Scriptures Chapter 27

Ephesians 4: 30: And grieve not the Holy Spirit of God, whereby ye are sealed unto the day of redemption.

I Thessalonians 4: 16: For the Lord himself shall descend from heaven with a shout, with the voice of the archangel, and with the trump of God: and the dead in Christ shall rise first:

Psalms 150: 6: Let every thing that hath breath praise the LORD. Praise ye the LORD.

Matthew 5: 16: Let your light so shine before men, that they may see your good works, and glorify your Father which is in heaven.

Chapter 28
Feeling God's Power at Work

Many times, over the years at work, I have felt an overflowing of God's power. Many miracles have been seen, many have been saved, and all have heard about the Lord. My co-workers are precious to me and I love them with all my heart. Many of them are like family and I would go to any extreme to help them.

Often, through the years, I have shouted for joy, sang hymns in their presence, and talked about Jesus whenever a door opens for me. Sometimes I feel like I'm the only hope they have and I must point them to Jesus. I'm not afraid to stand up for the Lord, and I'm definitely not afraid to praise His Holy name.

For many years I worked by myself and others would hear me shout from far distances away. One day I was in the yard by myself and it was one of the coldest days of winter. While people were getting warm inside, my heart was being warmed outside as I was thinking about the love of God. As I remember correctly God's Spirit overshadowed me one day and I lifted up my voice in praise to the Father. When I shouted I was about 1,300 feet from the building and the bay door was closed. In just a moment I looked and the bay door was opening and sure enough here comes the boss on the golf cart. When he finally came to where I was he asked me if everything was all right. I said, "Life couldn't be better, sir." He heard me all the way in the building through the big bay door.

There have been times, at work, when His glory fell upon me and I would work as if I was five people instead of one. God would empower, strengthen, and use me for His honor and praise. Without His Spirit working in our souls we would live defeated lives but thanks be to God that giveth us the victory (I Corinthians 15:57). Many amazing stories can be told about encounters from God at my work but let me tell you one that sticks out concerning praising the Lord.

One day, at my work, as I was putting an order together with another co-worker, God filled me with His Spirit. This moving of God promoted me to shout like never before. It seemed like time stood still for a second as praise left my lips. I still remember going back to work as though nothing ever happened. Over the span of about forty minutes nature took its course and I had to use the restroom. When I made it to the building it felt like every radio was blaring at a very high level. As I walked through the shop I noticed that a man named Ed Harris was smiling at me. I asked him, why he was smiling at me? He gave me a response that I really couldn't believe. He said I'm smiling because I heard you from inside the shop over these radios that are playing and I just shook my head and smiled. There were five radios playing, machines running, and other noises going on at the same time. When I shouted to the Lord, I was around 1,200 feet from the building and all the doors were shut. Psalms 93:4 says that the Lord on high is mightier than the noise of many waters, yea than the mighty waves of the sea. When we lift up our voices unto Him, God will be pleased, and we will be blessed.

Scriptures Chapter 28

I Corinthians 15: 57: But thanks be to God, which giveth us the victory through our Lord Jesus Christ.

Psalms 93: 4: The LORD on high is mightier than the noise of many waters, yea, than the mighty waves of the sea.

Chapter 29
Feeling God's Power at Church

My wife and I made plans one weekend to take a three-day vacation and travel up to her grandmothers's house in Hillsdale, Michigan. I was very weary, fatigued and physically drained due to work, church, and the pressures of life. Over the years I have learned that sometimes it is good to come apart and rest a while like Jesus told His disciples. When my wife and I travel to Hillsdale, we always make it a habit to visit a friend of ours that Pastor's in Jonesville, Michigan and try to encourage him in some way. The Pastors name is Tom McCue and his church is Fellowship Baptist Church.

Pastor McCue is one of my ten favorite preachers, and he is unique in every way. He stands six foot seven inches tall and weighs about four hundred pounds. He has bad feet but preaches with power from on high. Whenever I am blessed, to hear Pastor McCue preach the word of God it always encourages my heart and ignites my soul. The story I'm about to tell happened at Pastor McCue's church and it will never lose its power, in my heart, and Lord willing in your heart as well. In all my years in church I have never seen a story like this before and I may never see one like it again. Let me tell you this story and allow God to speak to your heart.

One Sunday morning, my family and I attended Fellowship Baptist Church in hopes of being a blessing to the man of God, and his ministry. We were greeted with friendly handshakes and warm words as we took our seat in the front. The crowd was pretty small that day, the service had no energy, and seemingly no life during the song service. When Pastor McCue mounted the pulpit he welcomed the visitors and opened to the book of Joshua. Joy bells were ringing in my soul as Pastor McCue began his sermon.

As I normally do, when preaching is being brought forth, I shouted "AMEN" in praise and thankfulness for God's word being thundered by God's man. As the sermon went longer and longer, I realized that I was the only person in the whole church that was supporting the Pastor and his message. His members failed to notice that their leader was pouring his heart out that day with little or no appreciation in return.

After the service was over my heart was heavy for the man of God. As I went back to my wife's grandmother's house I felt for my friend and thought about him for much of the afternoon. I decided to return to Fellowship Baptist for the evening service to hear the Assistant Pastor preach. As I was shaking hands, something happened that stunned me. In the middle of talking to a very nice lady, from that church, an elderly lady was determined to give me a piece of her mind. This elderly lady was probably in her eighties and struggled to even make it to her seat. She looked me right in my eyes and without hesitation said, "Young man, when you shout and carry on that really annoys me, and I wish you would stop." Her statement was very direct and very bold. I responded by saying, "I'm sorry if I offended you, but the scriptures are full of verses where God encourages us to shout and I am just trying to help God's man."

As the young preacher stood up to preach I tried my best to ignore what had just happened. However, her words kept ringing in my ears all night long. In my heart I knew if she did not repent quickly for what she said to me, trouble was headed her way. The preacher preached a wonderful message that night that spoke to hearts within the congregation. When the invitation was given I went to the altar to thank God for the message I heard that night and for His goodness towards me. As I was praying something happened that totally surprised me. That elderly lady that could hardly move ran to the altar like an Olympic sprinter and begged for forgiveness because of her rude words towards me. That was the first time, in my life, I have ever seen a lady of her age admit she was wrong and apologize to someone of my age.

God's fear gripped her heart that night as she cried out to God. She sought me out after the service and asked me to forgive her for what she did. God's Spirit was grieved that day but thank God she got things right. I still wonder what would have happened if she would not have repented that day. This story reminds me of that old song we teach our kids in Sunday school while they are young entitled, "Oh be careful little mouth what you say." As I drove back home that night I was reminded of the awesome judgement of an Almighty God.

The next time you see someone praising God, you may want to think before you speak.

Scriptures Chapter 29

1 Peter 1:8 "Whom having not seen, ye love; in whom, though now ye see him not, yet believing, ye rejoice with joy unspeakable and full of glory."

Psalm 34:7 "The angel of the Lord encampeth round about them that fear him, and delivereth them."

Daniel 3:25 "He answered and said, Lo, I see four men loose, walking in the midst of the fire, and they have no hurt; and the form of the fourth is like the Son of God."

Chapter 30
God can be Clearly Seen when You Choose to Look for Him

In this world we live in today many people claim that they are atheists, and that God is not real. They will go to great extremes to deny the Bible, and instead go about to establish their own righteousness. They reject that the Bible is inspired and they have no faith in a supernatural God that spoke the world into existence. To argue with this type of person is pointless, and the Bible teaches that they are willingly ignorant (2 Peter 3:5).

The word of God teaches, in Romans 1:20 for the invisible things of him from the creation of the world are clearly seen, being understood by the things that are made, even his eternal power and Godhead; so that they are without excuse. Hebrews 11:1 says, "Now faith is the substance of things hoped for, the evidence of things not seen." In other words, God teaches us, through His word, that in every person's life there are certain times and places when God reveals His truth to mankind.

Salvation of the soul, according to Jonah, is of the Lord, and it comes and goes like the wind; found in John 3:8. God will enlighten a man or woman's pathway in a fashion that is real and eye opening. During these rare and special encounters mankind is forced to make a spiritual decision that will change their future, forever. According to Isaiah 55:6 we must do it on God's timetable, not our timetable. This decision, that you must make, could either be the greatest of your life or the worst of your life.

Many people make the decision to reject the Light, and as a result they forever abide in the dark. Romans 1:21 teaches, "Because that, when they knew God, they glorified him not as God, neither were thankful; but became vain in their imaginations, and their foolish heart was darkened." Once darkness overtakes a person and they refuse the Savior, God, according to Romans 1:28 refuses them and gives them something called a reprobate mind. Once this process takes place in a person's heart and mind there is no hope of reaching that person with the glorious Light again. The next step, in their lives, is total foolishness, wickedness, unrighteousness, disobedience, inventors of evil things, corrupt minds, proud, boasters, haters of God and so on and so forth. When you accept the Lord, and become a child of the King, everything is clearly seen. On the other hand when you refuse the Light, everything is blurry and impossible for you to see.

Titus 1: 15 teaches that, "Unto the pure all things are pure: but unto them that are defiled and unbelieving is nothing pure; but even their mind and conscience is defiled." Once, God makes you a reprobate and turns you over to Satan, your understanding of spiritual matters will be eternally gone. In

2 Corinthians 4: 3 the Bible says, "but if our gospel be hid, it is hid to them that are lost," verse 4 "In whom the god of this world hath blinded the minds of them, which believe not, lest the light of the glorious gospel of Christ, who is the image of God, should shine unto them. Those verses say the Gospel is hid to them that are lost. God's word tells us that the God of this world hath blinded the minds of them, which believe not. 1 Timothy 4:2 says, "Speaking lies in hypocrisy; having their conscience seared with a hot iron." The scriptures say, God sears people's consciences with a hot iron. In other words, it's not a question if God is real, but it is a question of what you have done with the Light that God has already tried to give you.

Jesus said, "I am the light of the world: he that followeth me shall not walk in darkness, but shall have the Light of Life." (John: 8:12) In 1 John 1:7 says, "But if we walk in the light, as he is in the light, we have fellowship one with another, and the blood of Jesus Christ his Son cleanseth us from all sin." God is the only one, in this world, that has the power to give Light to a fallen sinner and raise them from a dead state according to Ephesians 2:1. Even though a sinner takes this spiritual calling for granted, God takes it very seriously. Jesus said, in John 12:35, yet a little while is the light with you. Walk while ye have the light, lest darkness come upon you: for he that walketh in darkness knoweth not whither he goeth.

The Bible says in Romans 3:4 God forbid: yea, let God be true, but every man a liar; as it is written, that thou mightest be justified in thy sayings, and mightest overcome when thou art judged. Psalms 19: 7 the law of the LORD is perfect, converting the soul: the testimony of the LORD is sure, making wise the simple. Matthew 24 35: Heaven and earth shall pass away, but my words shall not pass away. May I submit to you that people that claim they are atheists are people who rejected Christ at some point in their lives and God rejected them. God's word is perfect but man's opinions are wrong. According to God's Holy word, the book of Titus 2: 11 says, "For the grace of God that bringeth salvation hath appeared to all men." That includes all of those who claim to be atheists. Either God is lying when he said that His grace has appeared to all men, or the atheist is lying!

The Bible says in Titus 1:2 "In hope of eternal life, which God, that cannot lie, promised before the world began." Hebrews 6:18 says, "That by two immutable things, in which it was impossible for God to lie, we might have a strong consolation, who have fled for refuge to lay hold upon the hope set before us." However, in the book of Psalms 116: 11 the Bible says, "I said in my haste, All men are liars." God is a God of truth and righteousness and His word teaches in Psalms 8: 4: What is man, that thou art mindful of him? And the son of man, that thou visitest him?

Atheists ignore obvious proofs that God is real, on a daily basis, and allow the Devil to blind their eyes, while truth passes them by. Everytime the sun rises in the morning and the moon shines at night, God is reminding us that He exists, found in Psalms 19:1-2. Everytime a baby is born, something in our spirit reminds us there is a God found in Psalms 139:13-18. Everytime a rainbow appears in the sky, God reminds us that there is a God according to Genesis 9:12-16. Everytime a volcano erupts it reminds mankind that there is a fire in hell found in Job 28: 5. Everywhere we turn and anywhere we look the footprints of the Nazarene can clearly be seen. For the rest of this chapter I am going to give you examples that will prove to you the realness of God from my own personal experiences. Although I will only list a few examples to prove to you God is real, the truth is I could give you many more but time will not allow me. I hope you enjoy these powerful and timely experiences that I have had and I pray they will change your mind forever.

The Bible teaches us in Psalms 118: 24: This is the day which the LORD hath made; we will rejoice and be glad in it. Everyday of my life I realize that each day is different than the next, and God has something new for me if I will only look for it. As I work, shop, travel or worship my eyes are always searching for something from the Lord that is fresh and new. We that understand Psalms 139: 7-10, know that everywhere we go in life God goes with us. Sometimes we miss His presence and things He sends our way because our minds are occupied with everything else. A good example of this would be a sign that I see often while driving down the road working construction. The sign simply says, "Prepare to meet thy God Amos" 4: 12: It seems like everytime we drive by that sign it jumps out at me, and it speaks to me. With that being said, there are thousands that will pass that same sign, in their own travels each day, and will fail to notice that it even exists.

God's presence surrounds mankind and can easily be seen if we will only look for it. Isaiah (45: 22. Look unto me, and be ye saved, all the ends of the earth: for I am God, and there is none else. Sometimes God sends things our way when we are hurting to remind us that He loves us. Psalms 147:5, "Great is our Lord, and of great power: his understanding is infinite."

Many times when we feel at our lowest state in life, God shows up to encourage us to go another mile for Him.

I can still remember a few years ago when God showed up, in a special way for my family, in a tough time in our lives. My Grandfather just died and he was very dear to us. It is never easy losing a loved one, but it makes it much better when you know they are in heaven upon leaving this life. Many people gave testimonies about his life at the funeral, and most wept while doing so. We sang his favorite hymns, and preached to my family that day. We could definitely feel God's spirit that day and it was hard to say goodbye.

After the services were concluded I felt the need to ride with my mom over to the cemetery and offer support in anyway I could. We talked for a minute and shared verses with one another as my dad drove. About five minutes into our drive I told my mom to look over to her left, for God had a message for her that day. As my mom looked to her left there was a sign that said, "I am the Resurrection and the Life. It reminded us of the fact that even though we were burying her dad, and my grandfather, we would see him again through Jesus and the power of His resurrection. God has a way of showing up when you need Him most. There have been times, in my walk with God, when His presence has been so strong that others around me could not deny it either. Many times at church, at home, at work, or on the road, silence has overshadowed the area, and God has showed up when we least expected it.

This last example I want to give you will change your life, if you will allow the Holy Spirit to speak to your heart. This example is powerful and revealing, and is stunning in every single way. Allow me to tell you a true story that happened while driving with a man at my work.

One day, at around 1:30 p.m., my boss notified me that I was going on a long ride and I would not be back until late that night. I grabbed my lunch and headed out on the ride with a man whom I have so much respect for. This man always treats me well and we help each other nearly everyday. This man is not a Christian, but he has values and respects those who are Christians. I remember going on a two-hour drive that day and finding myself in an area that was secluded and barren. It seemed like we kept driving deeper and deeper into the woods, and human life was nowhere to be found. As we were talking his phone rang and the man answered and got some bad news. He found out that his father-in-law had passed away. He became very sad. He told me the news and my heart broke for him. I tried to comfort him the best I could.

God opened a door for me that day and we began to talk about life and death and the importance of knowing Christ before we die. As we began to talk about death, the Spirit of God told me to point to a tree in the middle of nowhere. Believe it or not, there was a sign on the tree that had the famous verse that says, "For the wages of sin is death; but the gift of God is eternal life through Jesus Christ our Lord."[Romans (6:23] The timing was perfect and silence filled the truck for over a minute, as we were speechless.

God showed up in the backwoods that day and His presence was real. Around two months later I was with the same man, but this time in Detroit, Michigan. As we were driving, the subject about heaven and hell came up again. God's Spirit started to move in that truck. I shared some verses with him and told him how much God loved him. After a few minutes the conversation got serious, and I made a statement that we will never forget. I remember looking at the man and telling him that one verse of scripture applies to his life, more than any other, in the entire Bible. He asked me what verse I was referring to. I told him that the verse I was thinking about was Hebrews 9: 27. After I told him that verse the conversation ended and for about five minutes nothing was said. I can remember, as we were arriving at our destination, I happened to look to my right and I couldn't believe my eyes. I asked the man to read what the sign said that I was looking at. He said the sign says, " Hebrews 9:27 And as it is appointed unto men once to die, but after this the judgment." Again silence filled that truck because he and I both knew that God was real that day.

When you wake up to the reality that God is real, your eyes will begin to see things that they have never seen before. The Bible says in Psalms 14:1: The fool hath said in his heart, there is no God, they are corrupt, they have done abominable works, there is none that doeth good. I pray that through this chapter it has dawned on you that God really does exist and He ever liveth to make intercession for us (Romans 8:26.) The scriptures also says, in 2 Peter 3: 9 The Lord is not slack concerning his promise, as some men count slackness; but is longsuffering to us-ward, not willing that any should perish, but that all should come to repentance. Come to Christ today and find out what life is all about.

Scriptures Chapter 30

2 Peter 3: 5 For this they willingly are ignorant of, that by the word of God the heavens were of old, and the earth standing out of the water and in the water

Romans 1: 20 For the invisible things of him from the creation of the world are clearly seen, being understood by the things that are made, even his eternal power and Godhead; so that they are without excuse

Hebrews 11: 1 Now faith is the substance of things hoped for, the evidence of things not seen.

John 3: 8 The wind bloweth where it listeth, and thou hearest the sound thereof, but canst not tell whence it cometh, and whither it goeth: so is every one that is born of the Spirit.

Isaiah 55: 6 Seek ye the LORD while he may be found, call ye upon him while he is near.

Romans 1: 21 Because that, when they knew God, they glorified him not as God, neither were thankful; but became vain in their imaginations, and their foolish heart was darkened

Romans 1: 28 And even as they did not like to retain God in their knowledge, God gave them over to a reprobate mind, to do those things which are not convenient;

Titus 1: 15 Unto the pure all things are pure: but unto them that are defiled and unbelieving is nothing pure; but even their mind and conscience is defiled.

2 Corinthians 4 3 But if our gospel be hid, it is hid to them that are lost:4: In whom the god of this world hath blinded the minds of them which believe not, lest the light of the glorious gospel of Christ, who is the image of God, should shine unto them. It says the Gospel is hid to them that are lost.

1 Timothy 4: 2 Speaking lies in hypocrisy; having their conscience seared with a hot iron; says God sears peoples consciences with a hot iron.

John: 8:12 Then spake Jesus again unto them, saying, I am the light of the world: he that followeth me shall not walk in darkness, but shall have the light of life.

1 John 1:7 But if we walk in the light, as he is in the light, we have fellowship one with another, and the blood of Jesus Christ his Son cleanseth us from all sin.

Ephesians 2: 1 And you hath he quickened, who were dead in trespasses and sins

John 12: 35 Then Jesus said unto them, Yet a little while is the light with you. Walk while ye have the light, lest darkness come upon you: for he that walketh in darkness knoweth not whither he goeth.

Romans 3:4 God forbid: yea, let God be true, but every man a liar; as it is written, That thou mightest be justified in thy sayings, and mightest overcome when thou art judged.

Psalms 19: 7 The law of the LORD is perfect, converting the soul: the testimony of the LORD is sure, making wise the simple.

Matthew 24 35: Heaven and earth shall pass away, but my words shall not pass away.

Titus 2: 11 For the grace of God that bringeth salvation hath appeared to all men.

Titus 1: 2 In hope of eternal life, which God, that cannot lie, promised before the world began

Hebrews 6:18 That by two immutable things, in which it was impossible for God to lie, we might have a strong consolation, who have fled for refuge to lay hold upon the hope set before us.

Psalms 116: 11 I said in my haste, All men are liars.

Psalms 8: 4: What is man, that thou art mindful of him? and the son of man, that thou visitest him?

Psalms 19:1 The heavens declare the glory of God; and the firmament sheweth his handywork.2: Day unto day uttereth speech, and night unto night sheweth knowledge.

Psalms 139: 13: For thou hast possessed my reins: thou hast covered me in my mother's womb. 14: I will praise thee; for I am fearfully and wonderfully made: marvellous are thy works; and that my soul knoweth right well. 15: My substance was not hid from thee, when I was made in secret, and curiously wrought in the lowest parts of the earth. 16: Thine eyes did see my substance, yet being unperfect; and in thy book all my members were written, which in continuance were fashioned, when as yet there was none of them. 17: How precious also are thy thoughts unto me, O God! how great is the sum of them! 18: If I should count them, they are more in number than the sand: when I awake, I am still with thee

Genesis 9: 12 And God said, This is the token of the covenant which I make between me and you and every living creature that is with you, for perpetual generations: 13: I do set my bow in the cloud, and it shall be for a token of a covenant between me and the earth. 14: And it shall come to pass, when I bring a cloud over the earth, that the bow shall be seen in the cloud: 15: And I will remember my covenant, which is between me and you and every living creature of all flesh; and the waters shall no more become a flood to destroy all flesh. 16: And the bow shall be in the cloud; and I will look upon it, that I may remember the everlasting covenant between God and every living creature of all flesh that is upon the earth.

Job 28: 5 As for the earth, out of it cometh bread: and under it is turned up as it were fire.

Psalms 118: 24: This is the day which the LORD hath made; we will rejoice and be glad in it.

Psalms 139: 7 Whither shall I go from thy spirit? or whither shall I flee from thy presence? 8: If I ascend up into heaven, thou art there: if I make my bed in hell, behold, thou art there. 9: If I take the wings of the morning, and dwell in the uttermost parts of the sea; 10: Even there shall thy hand lead me, and thy right hand shall hold me.

Amos 4: 12: Therefore thus will I do unto thee, O Israel: and because I will do this unto thee, prepare to meet thy God, O Israel

Isaiah 45: 22. Look unto me, and be ye saved, all the ends of the earth: for I am God, and there is none else

Psalms (147: 5. Great is our Lord, and of great power: his understanding is infinite.

Romans 6:23 For the wages of sin is death; but the gift of God is eternal life through Jesus Christ our Lord

Hebrews 9:27 And as it is appointed unto men once to die, but after this the judgment:

Psalms 14:1: The fool hath said in his heart, There is no God. They are corrupt, they have done abominable works, there is none that doeth good

Romans 8:26 Likewise the Spirit also helpeth our infirmities: for we know not what we should pray for as we ought: but the Spirit itself maketh intercession for us with groanings which cannot be uttered

2 Peter 3: 9 The Lord is not slack concerning his promise, as some men count slackness; but is longsuffering to us-ward, not willing that any should perish, but that all should come to repentance.

Conclusion

As we close out this book, I trust the Lord Almighty blessed you in various ways. My goal in writing this book was to build you up in the most holy faith and open your eyes to the fact that we are on the winning side. Hopefully the Lord has blessed you through these stories and filled you with His power in the process.

I'm praying that as we conclude this book you have now gained the tools and confidence to win battles over Satan on a regular basis. If you are still trapped in his prison, come to Jesus who has the ability to set you free. Refuse to allow Satan to defeat you any longer. Get up, dust yourself off, and be a victor through the blood of God's son. Understand that through the blood and the spirit-filled life Satan must run for cover. Satan is looking for the weak, the scared, and the shattered to attack, but he wants no part of the mighty. Be a strong Christian, go on the offensive, and put fear in the Devil through a life empowered by God. Don't be a victim any longer, but a victor; be a lion and impose fear on the enemy all the days of your life. If God is for us, who can be against us?

Thanks for reading this book and I pray you have found

revival through this effort. Roar at the enemy and go on for His glory.

With Love
Bro Tony
II Samuel 1:23

tScriptures Chapter ~ Conclusion

John 10:10 "I am come that they might have life, and that they might have it more abundantly."

Hebrews 2:9 "That he by the grace of God should taste death for every man."

John 3:16 "For God so loved the world, that he gave his only begotton Son, that whosoever believeth in him should not perish, but have everlasting life."

John 1:12 "But as many as received him, to them gave he power to become the sons of God, even to them that believe on his name."

Romans 10:13 "For whosoever shall call upon the name of the Lord shall be saved."

Ephesians 1:7 "In whom we have redemption through his blood, the forgiveness of sins, according to the riches of his grace."

Hebrews 9:27 "And as it is appointed unto a man once to die, but after this the judgment."

Isaiah 55:6 "Seek ye the Lord while he may be found, call ye upon him while is near."

Published By Parables

OUR MISSION

The primary mission of Published By Parables, a Christian publisher, is to publish Contemporary and Classic Christian books from an evangelical perspective that honors Christ and promotes the values and virtues of His Kingdom.

Are You An Aspiring Christian Author?

We fulfill our mission best by providing Christian authors and writers publishing options that are uniquely Christian, quick, affordable and easy to understand -- in an effort to please Christ who has called us to a writing ministry. We know the challenges of getting published, especially if you're a first-time author. God, who called you to write your book, will provide the grace sufficient to the task of getting it published.

We understand the value of a dollar; know the importance of producing a quality product; and publish what we publish for the glory of God.

Surf and Explore our site --
then use our easy-to-use "Tell Us" button
to tell us about yourself and about your book.

We're a one-stop, full-service Christian publisher.
We know our limits. We know our capabilities.
You won't be disappointed.

www.PublishedByParables.com

ANTHONY RITTHALER

PUBLISHED by PARABLES
Earthly Stories with a Heavenly Meaning

PUBLISHED by
PARABLES
Earthly Stories with a Heavenly Meaning

Anthony Ritthaler

Walking On The Water With Jesus
Volume Two

A Book Of Hope Peace, Joy, And Faith

Published by PARABLES
Earthly Stories with a Heavenly Meaning

ANTHONY RITTHALER

Pathways To The Past

Each volume stands alone as an Individual Book
Each volume stands together with others
to enhance the value of your collection

Build your Personal, Pastoral or Church Library
Pathways To The Past contains an ever-expanding list of
Christendom's most influencial authors

Augustine of Hippo
Athanasius
E. M. Bounds
John Bunyan
Brother Lawrence
Jessie Penn-Lewis
Bernard of Clairvaux
Andrew Murray
Watchman Nee
Arthur W. Pink
Hannah Whitall Smith
R. A. Torrey
A. W. Tozer
Jean-Pierre de Caussade
Thomas Watson
And many, many more.

Title: Walking On The Water With Jesus (Volume 2)
 Anthony Ritthaler
Rights: All Rights Reserved
ISBN 978-1-945698-01-9
Doctrinal theology, Inspiration
Salvation, Meditation
Other books by this author include: Walking On The Water With Jesus (Volume 1 & 2), Soaring With Eagles (Volume 1 & 2) and A Devil From The Beginning.

Anthony Ritthaler

Walking On The Water With Jesus
Book Two

A Book Of Hope Peace, Joy, And Faith

PUBLISHED by PARABLES
Earthly Stories with a Heavenly Meaning

Table of Contents

About the Author
Introduction
1. God's Golden Rule
2. Holding off the rain
3. There is rest in Christ
4. Hearing a sweet voice on a Monday morning
5. A service I will never forget
6. My grace is sufficient for thee
7. A sudden change in the air
8. O taste and see that the Lord is good
9. Divine protection from above
10. The Almighty Judgment of God
11. The overshadowing of the Holy Ghost
12. Behold the Messiah
13. A man's best friend
14. Where is the Lord God of Elijah
15. What a great God we serve
16. A super blessing

17. My help cometh from the Lord
18. God is always pleased with compassion
19. Tis so sweet to trust in Jesus
20. A very entertaining story
21. God creating something out of nothing
22. An overwhelming response from God
23. A very powerful moment
24. God visiting a lady from out of nowhere
25. The joy of walking with the Lord
26. God treated me like a King twice in one week
27. A small blessing turning into a big one
28. A wonderful gift from God
29. Fear thou not, for I am with thee
30. Jesus is still alive and well
Conclusion

Special Thanks

I'm grateful in my heart for all the many people who contributed towards this project. So many prayed and offered help as I was putting this together. I am humbled by every act of kindness and every word of encouragement. I would like to give a special thank you to my friend and evangelist Todd Hicks and his wife for their donation without hesitation towards this effort for God. My friends, I believe God in heaven will reward you greatly for what you did. Also I would like to thank Miss Janine Burke and Kim White for their constant words of encouragement that refreshed my soul while writing. Thank you to my Godly parents who helped me every step of the way. Lastly I want to thank my lovely wife who helped me put this book together. Without her help this book would not be the same. I really appreciate everyone who helped make this happen.

With Love Bro Tony

Introduction

Welcome to volume two of Walking on the Water with Jesus. Once again we will unfold some unbelievable blessings sent from the Throne Room of Heaven. Every story within the pages of this book are fresh and new and they will magnify our great Lord once again. The power of God flows through each unique story you will read, and you will be touched in many different ways. We will cover a vast array of blessings that are moving and encouraging in every sense of the word. I'm very confident that these stories are some of the best that you may ever hear during your lifetime. May Gods Spirit minister to our hearts in the pages to come, and show us that He can still do the impossible even today.

As I was writing these stories down, the Power of God was very evident within my soul. Although I will be the first to admit that my strength is small, I am glad to report "that I can do all things through Christ which strengtheth me." This entire book was written in sixteen hours, and God's Spirit helped me every step of the way. Your heart will be blessed for sure, and your faith will be enlarged for His glory. May we all look to God for the help we so desperately need and not towards feeble man. Without God we can do nothing and we should always remember that.

My goal, as always, is to give God the glory for the great things He hath done. If this book does not bless your heart in various ways; I will be the first to ask your forgiveness. In the pages to come I will do my best to lift up God in ways that are different, exciting, and glorious for the cause of Christ. My prayer is that this book will bring hope to the hopeless and peace to the down of heart. May God use this book for His honor and praise in the years to come.

Phillipians 4:13 "I can do all things through Christ which strengtheneth me."

Chapter One
God's Golden Rule

The precious word of God speaks much about the subject we will cover in this chapter. God has a way of rewarding those who show kindness throughout their days on earth. God the Father gives all mankind a free will to exercise the right to show pity and grace towards others, however it is up to us whether we obey His leadership or not.

Often in my life I have decided to help others and the response from God has been wonderful. Hebrews 6:10 says, "For God is not unrighteous to forget your work and labour of love, which ye have shewed toward his name, in that ye have ministered to the saints, and do minister." Almost every single day of my life people ask me about sowing and reaping and does it really work. Constantly I will respond by giving them real stories from my life; which proves that sowing and reaping really does work. Perhaps the most well known scripture in the bible is found in Galatians 6:7. Here the bible tells us that, "Whatsoever a man soweth, that shall he also reap." The bible plainly expresses to us that if we sow bad seeds in life trouble will spring up later on, but if we sow good seeds blessings will come our way. We as humans refuse to plant good seeds on a daily basis and that decision often plagues us over and over again. The more I determine to help others, the more God in heaven seems to help me.

Just a short while ago, God proved himself to me and a friend of mine that He still gives good gifts unto his children. According to Micah 5:2 he is from everlasting to everlasting and he is still in control. Please let me prove it to you.

While at work one afternoon I was talking to a man about the mercy of Christ. This man proceeded to ask me about this subject and he craved the blessings that were daily coming my way. I told him that the good Lord has allowed me to sow hundreds of precious seeds in my life and they are starting to come back for me. This gentleman then asked me if I had ever heard of the Golden Rule; which is simply do unto others that which would be done unto you. I quickly replied sure I have and even though it will never take you to heaven, it is a great rule to live by. We then talked much about God's blessings and the joy of helping others. We both enjoyed the conversation and God met with us that afternoon.

As work concluded, and I made it to my car, the Lord burned this subject in my mind, and I was reminded of the importance of encouraging others. It was after arriving at my home, later that day that I would discover the realness of the conversation that just transpired a little earlier. I remember asking my wife if we received any mail that day and she said we sure did. She handed me a check that arrived at 3:30 that afternoon and it was from the Golden Rule Company. It came at a time when we desperately needed it, and it was for $399.24. God seemed to manifest himself to us that day and prove his love in an amazing way. The Golden Rule Company overcharged us nearly four hundred dollars and we happened to get the reimbursement check on that exact day. Earlier in the day, as I was talking to the man from my work it was exactly 3:30 in the afternoon, and that is when the check made it to my mail box as well.

God always seems to send help when we need it the most. Trust in the Lord at all times, and start to sow good seeds along your journey and God will show up in your life. After all the Golden Rule has stood the test of time and so has God's Holy book. Do what's right and the Lord promises to bless you every time.

Scriptures Chapter 1

Hebrews 6:10 "For God is not unrighteous to forget your work and labor of love, which ye have showed toward his name, in that ye have ministered to the saints, and do minister."

Galatians 6:7 "Be not deceived; God is not mocked: for whatsoever a man soweth, that shall he also reap."

Psalm 44:8 "In God we boast all the day long, and praise thy name forever. Selah."

Psalm 62:8 "Trust in him at all times; ye people, pour out your heart before him: God is a refuge for us. Selah."

Chapter 2
Holding Off the Rain

    We have a number of great stories contained within the covers of the Bible that blow our minds concerning our faith. According to Mark 4:39 we find that Jesus rebuked the wind and said peace be still and the wind ceased. Through Christ all things are possible and He proved it with the raging storm. It is through Christ that all things are possible, because He heard Joshua's prayer and made the sun stand still in heaven for a whole day. Joshua 10:14 declares that there was no day like that before or no day like it after that the Lord hearkened unto the voice of a man.

    Through Christ all things were possible in the life of Elijah, who was a man just like you and I according to James 5:17. He had the power to shut off the rain for three and a half years and to turn it back on through the power of God. We limit God far too much and it is high time we start believing that He can do anything like His word teaches. So many today explain away His miracles and fail to believe they can happen today. Hebrews 13:8 says, "Jesus is the same yesterday, today, and forever." I can still remember, not long ago, when a young man asked me if God can still stop the rain like He did back then. I responded by saying to him, "Sure he can because he did it for me one day and I have witnesses." Let me tell a story that will bless your heart and prove Gods power once again.

A few years back, I remember waking up to reports that there was a ninety percent chance of rain for the day, and so I prepared myself for it. My heart sank because nothing is worse than having to work in the rain. At this point in my life, the hand of the Lord could be seen on a daily basis to those around me, and I knew He could do the unthinkable.

At around eight that morning a young lady approached me with a prayer request that tested my faith. Her exact words were, "We know you have power with God so can you hold off the rain today." My response to her was I'll see what I can do and I'll try to hold off the rain till five thirty. Dark clouds seemed to dwell over our yard but there was no rain coming. As the day wore on and five thirty approached the sky grew darker, but still not a rain drop fell from the sky. It was five twenty nine when I made it safe and sound into the building and a man said to me, "Well, I guess your prayers worked because no rain hit us." I still remember looking at him and saying, "I held it off till five thirty but I'm not responsible after that." Just as the words left my mouth, five thirty struck and we were pelted with heavy rain that made the building shake. For around twenty five minutes it rained cats and dogs outside but not before five thirty.

The Lord is very capable of displaying His wonders no matter what age we live in. Depend on His word above anything else, and allow Him to work in an awesome way. Hebrews 11:6 says, "That without faith it is impossible to please him."

Scriptures Chapter 2

Mark 4:39 "And he arose, and rebuked the wind, and said unto the sea, Peace, be still. And the wind ceased, and there was a great calm."

Joshua 10:14 "And there was no day like that before it or after it, that the Lord hearkened unto the voice of a man: for the Lord fought for Israel."

James 5:17 "Elijah was a man subject to like passions as we are, and he prayed earnestly that it might not rain: and it rained not on the earth by the space of three years and six months."

Hebrews 13:8 "Jesus Christ the same yesterday, and to-day, and forever."

Hebrews 11:6 "But without Faith it is impossible to please him:"

Chapter 3
There is Rest in Christ

Sometimes, while on our journey through this life, we must take time to come apart and rest a while. God said in the Old Testament that on the seventh day He rested and He was refreshed. God knoweth the frame of man and He knows when enough is enough. Jesus told his disciples not to be overcharged with the cares of this life. The Lord also tells us to take all our burdens to the Lord and leave them there. According to the bible we must ordain certain times when we are to be wise about resting. Many of the great Christians that we read about and adore suffered premature health problems that could have been avoided if they would have rested more. When you are in the ministry and you love God it is hard to slow down and heed to the warning signals concerning your health. God has ordained rest for a reason, and He wants you to preserve your health so you can help more people for many more years.

According to statistics, the average preacher dies at around the age of forty five to fifty. The average life span of a person is seventy years of age and that is found in Psalm 90:10. There is sweet rest in Christ not just spiritually but also physically. Many good men and women die well before their time because they fail to get the proper rest they should. Statistics prove that a far greater percentage of people die due to stress rather than bad eating habits. The thing that is killing this country, in this generation, is uneasy spirits and stressed out people. I have had to train myself, over the years, to know when to say enough is enough, it is time to rest for a few days. In the remainder of this chapter I want to tell you a story that will show you the goodness of God. It is a story that refreshes me whenever I tell it. I pray it will refresh you as well.

    A few years back my batteries were very low and I was at the point of breaking down. My wife and I were raising our first child and I was working long hours, completing my first book, teaching, and many other little things. My wife and I sat down one day and discussed a possible vacation because it was long over do. Money was a definite issue at the time, but we had to do something. After talking it over I told my wife I would have to pray about the vacation and we would see what happens. The very next day we received a call from my sister-in-law with an answer to my prayer. They insisted that we go along with them to an indoor water park and they would pay our way. That week they paid for the room, food, Kabana, and many other things. It turned out to be a great week and the timing couldn't have been better. All in all they paid around one thousand two hundred dollars for us and refused to take any money. We will always remember there kindness till the day we die.

    Always keep in mind, child of God, that when you serve the Lord he always offers rest when you need it most. Just listen to God when He offers sweet rest and you will be glad you did. Rest is a sweet thing and we can only bear so much child of God.

Scriptures Chapter 3

Psalm 90:10 "The days of our years are threescore years and ten; and if by reason of strength they be fourscore years, yet is their strength labor and sorrow; for it is soon cut off, and we fly away."

1 Peter 5:7 "Casting all your care upon him; for he careth for you."

Chapter 4
Hearing a Sweet Voice on a Morning

One of my favorite songs growing up was the song Jesus is the Sweetest Name I Know. Its words seem to speak to me in a soft and moving way. This is also true concerning the voice of God. When He speaks, often it is in a sweet and lovely way that only His children can hear. Most of the time it is not loud and terrible, but rather tender and smooth as a morning dove. When His voice is heard, in our lives, it will grab our attention and it will give us peace in our hearts. There is nothing on earth like His gracious, eternal and life giving words that can stir the soul to no end.

When I think about His voice speaking to a heart, I think about the testimony of Gerald Crabb. By his own testimony, Mr. Crabb, who was a saved man, turned from the Lord and made a complete mess with his life. He let his family down, he lost his business and he failed the Lord through alcohol. He found himself working at a car wash and he only had the bottle to hold unto. One day as he was washing cars he said, from out of nowhere, he heard the sweetest voice he had ever heard and it was the Lord. Mr. Crabb said the Lord spoke to him and said I'm not done with you yet and if you will come back home I will forgive you of the mistakes you have made. Shortly after hearing God's voice, he began writing songs that are some of the best of this generation. God is a loving, patient, and forgiving God that treats us far better than we deserve. When His voice can be heard, sunrays of strength flood the soul and motivate us to do more for Him. For the rest of this chapter I will give you positive proof that He still speaks to hearts today.

On a Monday morning, as I was getting ready for work, I skipped breakfast as I was rushing out the door. I remember starting up the car and taking off to work. Before I left my housing complex, I realized I forgot my lunch. When I went to turn around that morning I suddenly heard the voice of God tell me to leave my lunch at home, because He would take care of me today. I followed the Lord's leadership and fully trusted that He would provide for me like He promised. I really didn't know how but I knew He would do something for me that day.

Later that day, at 11:20 a.m., a fellow co-worker approached me with some great news. He told me that Jimmie John Subs had provided us with around seventy five free subs to enjoy for that day. A sweet peace came over my soul because I knew that Christ provided for me like He said. What is even more incredible is the fact that all those subs were placed exactly in the area where I sit next to my bible. This story reminds me of young Samuel when he said, "Speak Lord for thy servant heareth." Praise the Lord.

Scriptures Chapter 4

1 Samuel 3:10 "And the Lord came, and stood, and called as at other times, Samuel, Samuel. Then Samuel answered, Speak; for thy servant heareth."

1 Kings 19:12 "And after the earthquake a fire; but the Lord was not in the fire: and after the fire a still small voice."

CHAPTER 5
A SERVICE
I WILL NEVER FORGET

There is a service that took place in a tent meeting, in Detroit Michigan, that still stands out in my mind. As I arrived there was excitement in the air, but before I left silence filled the church as God's judgment sweep through my soul.

Both preachers that night had wonderful reputations and are two of the very best men in this country. Both men preach in two completely different styles but both are powerful in their own unique way. One of these men preached like an Educated Isaiah and the other like a Fiery John the Baptist. One man has the biggest church in Michigan, and the other is possibly the greatest Evangelist in America. In other words, they are both anointed of God and are protected and sheltered by the Savior. Please permit me to give you a fatal story that should cause us to think twice before interrupting a service in a rude way when the Spirit of God is present.

As I arrived at the meeting that night joy rushed through my inner being, because of all the precious memories I had there through the years. Some of my fondest moments have taken place under that old tent, and the power of God is especially strong during those meetings. Some of the greatest preachers in the land mounted the pulpit that week and I was eager to hear from God. The good Lord has allowed me to pour much money into those meetings and it holds a special place in my heart.

When the service began that night everything seemed to flow well, and the singing seemed to be straight from Glory. After the song service concluded the first preacher was announced and he began his sermon. It seemed like the longer he preached the better it was. People's hearts seemed to be tuned into his message and we were receiving the Word with gladness. When the preacher arrived at the climax of his message something happened that swiftly changed the atmosphere of the night in a bad way.

From out of nowhere, as the preacher was speaking, the roaring of thunder rolled into the parking lot. The sound was so loud that it totally over took everything that the Man of God was saying. The sound had come from sixty tough, rugged bikers who wanted to make a grand entrance into Gods house. In my mind it was probably the rudest thing I had ever witnessed in my life.

It was exactly at that moment that I happened to make eye contact with the second preacher, who would speak that night, and we were both thinking the same thing. Proverbs 13:13 says "That whoso despiseth the word shall be destroyed." It seemed like God's spirit sweep over my soul and I knew God was going to judge that crowd for what they did. Sure enough as the second preacher mounted the pulpit, God's presence rested upon him for the next thirty minutes.

Near the end of his sermon, the preacher looked at me and said, "Bro Tony, someone is in trouble tonight and this will be their last chance to run to Christ." As it turned out no one accepted Christ that night as death was hovering over that tent. It was the very next day when we got a report that one of those bikers, who rudely distracted the gospel, was killed in a tragic way.

God has magnified His Word more than His own name; and when you laugh at it you will pay the ultimate price. A famous preacher has a message entitled Pay Day Someday. Be very careful how you treat the Lord, because no matter how tough you think you are, you are no match for Him. Always remember this verse "There is a way that seemeth right unto a man but the end thereof are the ways of death."

Scriptures Chapter 5

Proverbs 13:13 "Whoso despiseth the word shall be destroyed: but he that feareth the commandment shall be rewarded."

Proverbs 14:12 "There is a way that seemeth right unto a man; but the end thereof are the ways of death."

Psalm 138:2 "I will worship towards thy holy temple, and praise thy name for thy loving-kindness and for thy truth: for thou hast magnified thy word above all thy name."

Isaiah 64:1 "Oh that thou wouldest rend the heavens, that thou wouldest come down, that the mountains might flow down at thy presence."

Chapter 6
My Grace is Sufficient for Thee

The apostle Paul said in II Corinthians 12:9, "God's grace is sufficient for thee: for my strength is made perfect in weakness." Paul dealt with pressures that we will never be able to comprehend, but he still was effective for Christ. Paul never seemed to walk in his own power, but always in the power of God. Life can get overwhelming at times but God's grace is a beautiful thing. Many of the greatest people of all time went through pain, lose of land, deaths, hardships, and trails, but God always helped them through it. God has never promised to remove storms from our life however he has promised to give us the grace to go through it. Often in the midst of our afflictions when we think it can't get any worse God arrives on the scene to offer relief. You will often find Gods grace with the death of a loved one. Jesus had compassion on Mary and Martha when there brother died and he does the same for you and me. The Lord will issue certain times in our life when he will send grace in many different forms and fashions. The word grace basically means unmerited favor, or Gods riches at

Christ's expense. There have been many times in my life when the Lord has blessed me and sent things my way that I didn't have to work for. The story that I will now give proves Gods grace in my life and helps me to go another mile for Christ. The Lord is gracious and you will see it through this story.

One day as I was working in Detroit I noticed an unusual amount of churches with crosses on top of them. Nothing in this world means more to me then the cross of Jesus Christ. The great apostle Paul said it best in Galatians 6:14 when he wrote, "God forbid that I glory save in the cross of Jesus Christ." At my home I have a cd about the cross that I have listened to around 80 times. There is divine power in the cross and it has changed this world like nothing else ever has. I would venture to say that while working in Detroit that day I seen around 60 crosses in 3 hours. As we were driving home that day I remember getting very low on energy and very thirsty. As we came closer to the shop that day I bowed my head and said a simple prayer asking the Lord for a candy bar and a Pepsi. When we made it back to the shop I immediately headed towards the break room to see if my prayer was answered. Sure enough as I entered the break room someone had put four little Hersey bars on my bible. What's even more amazing is the fact that whoever did this took the time to make it in the form of a cross. Instantly God seemed to invade my heart in a new way and I had to take a seat and ponder what just happened. Around 10 seconds later a Mexican man touched my shoulder and asked me if I wanted a Pepsi for free. God answered my prayer in a stunning way and this story helps me every time I tell it.

Let me close this chapter by saying whenever we hear stories like this it should really cause us to thank God for the grace that he sends our way. Without the grace of God our life would be empty and void. The old song writer had it right when he said nothing in my hand I bring but simply to the cross I cling.

Scriptures Chapter 6

2 Corinthians 12:9 "And he said unto me, My grace is sufficient for thee: for my strength is made perfect in weakness. Most gladly therefore will I rather glory in my infirmities, that the power of Christ may rest upon me."

Galatians 6:14 "But God forbid that I should glory, save in the cross of our Lord Jesus Christ, by whom the world is crucified unto me, and I unto the world."

Chapter 7
A Sudden Change in the Air

No miracle that Jesus ever performed was quite like the day He calmed the Sea of Galilee. The storm was violent, the waves were crashing, and the disciples fear was very high. The whole area was on pins and needles and an uneasy feeling filled the air. The disciples on board truly felt like it was the end and they begged Jesus to do the impossible. What happened next shocked the world and proved the almighty power of God.

The Bible records that the Lord looked at the worst circumstance, known to man, and simply said, "Peace be still" and immediately there was a great calm. The birds started singing; the waves looked like a sheet of glass, and all stood in total amazement of what just transpired. This moment in time not only affected those on the ship, but also those on land.

According to Mark 5 we find that a man, who had six thousand demons, ran to Jesus and finally found peace in his soul when the Lord returned to shore. This man must have said to himself that if Christ can calm the raging sea, surely he can calm the storm in me. This calming of the sea prompted those disciples to make this statement "What manner of man is this that even the wind and the sea obey him?"

Throughout my time on earth I have often wondered if this was possible today. Can the Lord still do wonders in this day and age like he did back then? Praise God I'm glad to report, with this following story, that I have seen it with my own eyes. God is the God of the impossible and I'm thankful, in my soul, for this next story. Prepare to be amazed like we were that day and allow the Lord to minister to your heart with this story.

One Friday morning some of my coworkers and I got the call to pick up barrels on Woodward Ave. The sky looked pitch black, the atmosphere was gloomy and rain was most certainly coming our way. I was trying my best to keep our spirits up, but no one likes working in the rain and nothing seemed to help. What happened next still marvels me to this day.

As I was picking up barrels; the driver said to me that he hated working in weather like this and my response to him was swift and full of faith. I looked straight at him and said, "I will pray that God clears up the weather for us." To my amazement within thirty seconds every single dark cloud vanished from view and the sun was shining brightly upon us. Everyone's jaw dropped that morning and we had a wonderful day to work. The whole atmosphere changed and it felt like God was shining His light around us. The following Sunday I told this story at church and people's hearts were blessed.

We serve a supernatural God that can bring light to any situation, no matter how dark it may look. First John 1:7 says "but if we walk in the light, as he is in the light, we have fellowship one with another, and the blood of Jesus Christ his Son cleanseth us from all sin." What a joy to know that the Lord is always near and He is able to calm every storm that comes our way.

Scriptures Chapter 7

Mark 5:6 "But when he saw Jesus afar off, he ran and worshipped him."

Mark 4:41 "And they feared exceedingly, and said one to another, What manner of man is this, that even the wind and the sea obey him?"

1 John 1:7 "But if we walk in the light, as he is in the light, we have fellowship one with another, and the blood of Jesus Christ his Son cleanseth us from all sin."

Matthew 21:22 "And all things, whatsoever ye shall ask in prayer, believing, ye shall receive."

Chapter 8
O Taste and See That the Lord is Good

People who have never encountered the grace of God can never fully understand just how wonderful Jesus really is. When you are an outsider looking in the cross seems bloody, sad, and cruel and you will never understand it. However when you are washed in the blood everything becomes bright, transparent, and new. The love of God has a way of changing mankind's outlook concerning heaven and hell and spiritual matters.

One of my favorite songs ever is the song "The Longer I serve him the sweeter he grows." One of my favorite verses in the bible is psalm 34:8. That verse in the Bible says, "O taste and see that the Lord is good: blessed is the man that trusteth in him." Revelation 22:17 says, "Come let him take of the water of life freely." When a man or women partakes of the water of life and the bread of heaven there soul will be instantly satisfied. Jesus is everything you and I need, and when we accept him he will give us all the guidance and vision that one could ever desire. Jesus is sweet to the taste, easy on the eyes, and satisfying to the soul. When people begin to walk with Jesus they will find everything they need wrapped into one. He is altogether wonderful in every single way. Jesus came that we might have life, and have it more abundantly. The Lord is constantly blessing his own in new and exciting forms and fashions. This story I will now give is a prime example of his goodness towards his children. It may seem small but it touched this old sinner's heart. Allow me to show you how good the Lord is.

One night while I was playing with my baby girl, my wife told me she had to run and get some groceries. Before she left that night she asked me twice if I needed anything. At that point in time nothing came to my mind so I said no thanks. Around fifteen minutes after she left I started to crave a hot chocolate from Tim Horton's. As I went to pick up the phone to call her the Holy Spirit told me not to call but rather pray for it. Immediately I dropped my head and prayed that God would lay it on her to stop and get me one. After I prayed a sudden peace came over me and I knew it would come true. Around an hour later my wife walked in our house carrying two Tim Horton hot chocolates and some donuts. My first response was thank you Erin, and secondly I said God is good.

Let me just say that many will look at that story and say that is just by luck that things turned out like that. My response to that would be if it were only once or twice I could see it, but if it is on a daily basis then it must be God doing it. O taste and see that the Lord is good while you still have breath in your body. He will satisfy your every desire in a glorious new way.

Scriptures Chapter 8

Psalm 34:8 "O taste and see that the Lord is good: Blessed is the man that trusteth in him."

Revelation 22:17 "And the Spirit and the bride say, come. And let him that heareth say, come. And let him that is athirst come. And whosoever will, let him take the water of life freely."

John 10:10 "The thief cometh not, but to steal, and to kill, and to destroy: I am come that they might have life, and that they might have it more abundantly."

Chapter 9
Divine Protection Sent From Above

The Book of all books is filled with examples of God sending divine protection for His children. One might remember Daniel in the lion's den or Joseph in the pit. Maybe you could recall David when he was running from Saul or when he fought Goliath. In Psalms 18:2 it says, "The Lord is my Rock, and my fortress, and my deliver; my God, my strength, in whom I trust; my buckler, and the horn of my salvation, and my high tower." Isaiah 43:2 also tells us that, "When we pass through the waters, I will be with thee, and when we walk through the fire we shall not be burned." In Psalms 23:4 it says, "Yea though I walk through the valley of the shadow of death I will fear no evil, for thou art with me." A little further along in Psalms 27:1 it reads, "The Lord is my light and my salvation; whom shall I fear? The Lord is the strength of my life; of whom shall I be afraid." We also see in II Timothy 1:7 it states, "That God hath not given us the spirit of fear; but of Power, and of love, and of a sound mind."

We have the victory, and God enjoys making that known in the life of His children. When Satan wanted to attack Job, he accused God of setting up a hedge around him. Jesus Christ will defend us, protect us, and watch over us if we belong to him. He is a wonderful father and He has a way of keeping trouble at bay, more often than not.

In the line of work that I do, I am surrounded by danger on a daily basis. As I work on the road, I often find myself dodging traffic and avoiding accidents. I have had many close calls over the years and only, by the grace of God, am I still alive. Let me give you a little story that will be a blessing to you.

One Wednesday night, as the prayer requests were being taken, I remember asking the church for divine protection for the rest of the work week. Every time I look over the pages of my life, I realize that prayer has always been my saving grace.

This particular night I had to drive a separate car home then my family. On the way home I wanted to take the scenic route and enjoy the beauty of nature. I recall listening to gospel music and it was getting hard to see. All of the sudden I happened to look to my right and a deer was standing on the side of the road. The deer looked me in my eye and stood still like a statue. It was almost like God commanded that deer to stand still until I drove by.

Shortly after I drove by I saw the deer seemly unfreeze and gently walk across the road behind me. My mind went back to that prayer request taken at church forty minutes earlier and how I had asked for protection. James said that, "The effectual fervent prayer of a righteous man availeth much." I challenge you to turn back a few pages of your life and recall how many times God has sheltered you through life. Most Christians I know have stared death in the face often, but something always keeps them safe. Let me just say John had it right when he said "No man is able to pluck them out of my Fathers hand."

Scriptures Chapter 9

Psalm 18:2 "The Lord is my Rock, and my fortress, and my deliverer; my God, my strength, in whom I will trust; my buckler, and the horn of my salvation, and my high tower."

Psalm 23:4 "Yea, though I walk through the valley of the shadow of death, I will fear no evil: for thou art with me: thy rod and thy staff they comfort me."

Psalm 23:6 "Surely goodness and mercy shall follow me all the days of my life: and I will dwell in the house of the Lord forever."

Isaiah 43:2 "When thou passeth through the waters, I will be with thee: and through the rivers, they shall not overflow thee: when thou walkest through the fire, thou shalt not be burned; neither shall the flame kindle upon thee."

Psalm 27:1 "The Lord is my light and my salvation; whom shall I fear? The Lord is the strength of my life; of whom shall I be afraid?"

2 Timothy 1:7 "For God hath not given us the spirit of fear; but of power, and of love, and of a sound mind."

Job 1:10 "Hast not thou made a hedge about him, and about his house, and about all that he hath on every side? Thou hast blessed the work of his hands, and his substance is increased in the land."

James 5:16 "Confess your faults one to another, and pray one for another, that ye may be healed. The effectual fervent prayer of a righteous man availeth much."

John 10:28 "And I give unto them eternal life; and they shall never perish, neither shall any man pluck them out of my Father's hand."

Chapter 10
The Almighty Judgment of God

People all over this country have a warped concept of who God really is. Many hold to the theory that God needs us and that He would be hurting without our presence on planet earth. May I say to those who believe like this, you have been misguided by someone's false teaching somewhere along life's road. Calvary proves, beyond a shadow of a doubt, the love of God, but always remember that God is a God of anger as well. Psalm 90:7 says, "For we are consumed by thine anger, and by thy wrath are we troubled." Preachers are always quick to point out the love of God and they should, but there are just as many verses on His anger and fury throughout the Bible to balance it out. The average person I speak with cringes when I mention the judgment of God, but that does not change the reality of the truth.

It is sad to say that good men will argue with me, until they are blue in the face, about the thought of God's patience running out in a person's life. Mankind wants to jump over verses of this caliber because they are so worried about offending people. I have learned that no matter how gracious or sweet your words are someone, somewhere, will always find fault anyways. We cannot please everyone so just tell the truth whether they agree with you or not. God is angry with the wicked every day. Sometimes His patience runs out and His hammer drops after all other avenues of mercy are exhausted. Please allow me to express what I mean with the rest of this chapter.

    Not long ago, at my parent's house, a conversation took place that made the hair on my neck stand up. A man that I am close with asked me if God really kills people once they cross spiritual lines. When he asked this question I responded by giving him a number of verses and examples that were earth-shaking. After around a solid hour of examples about God slaying folks you could absolutely feel the presence of God in a remarkable way. The man I was talking with was shaking and looked very sick. Once I noticed how it was affecting him, I quickly ended the conversation out of respect for the man.

    Shortly after this conversation was complete I spoke with my father and he said, "Tony I want to show you something." My dad took me to a nearby table, sat me down, and handed me a Bible from the year 1856. He told me to flip through its pages and tell me what you think. As I took that old Bible I opened it up and it opened straight to I Samuel 2:6 and this is how it read, "The Lord KILLETH and he maketh alive: he bringeth down to the grave, and bringeth up." My eyes fell upon that verse and the power of God fell on me.

    In my private studies that week the Lord allowed me to read that verse around twenty times prior to opening my Dad's old Bible. I Samuel 2:33-34 teaches that God was so angry at Eli and his two sons that he promised to kill them in the flower of their age. Be very careful not to grieve God's Spirit too often throughout the days of your life because it can do you much harm. Always remember this verse as you conduct your life,

Psalm 7:13b "He hath also prepared for him the instruments of death; He ordaineth his arrows against the persecutors." God is indeed a God of Love but He is also very much a God of judgment.

Scriptures Chapter 10

Psalm 7:11 "God judgeth the righteous, and God is angry with the wicked every day."

Ephesians 4:30 "And grieve not the holy Spirit of God, whereby ye are sealed unto the day of redemption."

Psalm 90:7 "For we are consumed by thine anger, and by thy wrath are we troubled."
1 Samuel 2:6 "The Lord killeth, and maketh alive: he bringeth down to the grave, and he bringeth up."

Psalm 7:13 "He hath also prepared for him the instruments of death; he ordaineth his arrows against the persecutors."

Chapter 11
The Overshadowing of the Holy Ghost

There is nothing more powerful in this world then the overshadowing of the Holy Ghost. When God's spirit is present and moving, fear strikes the heart of man. In the Old Testament when the ark would go before the people, they would shake and quake with fear. In the New Testament, when Paul was preaching to Felix, the word of God says he trembled. Daniel 5 records that when the Holy Ghost showed up that Belshazzar's knees smote together. When the great Jonathon Edwards would preach during the great awakening, history says that people would have a fear of dropping off into hell before the morning light. The bible teaches in Luke that Mary was overshadowed by the Holy Ghost as she was carrying the Son of God. Hebrews 10:31 says "It is a fearful thing to fall into the hands of a living God."

When God's spirit is present in a service; it becomes hard to breathe, sinners grip the pews, palms get sweaty, and hearts skip a beat. When God's Holy Ghost overshadows a service you will never forget it till the day you die. God's spirit comes when it wants to and it leaves when it wants to. God's Spirit does not ask permission and it is always felt by those around him. It is breathtaking and scary when His presence can be felt. Many lose sleep, pace around, and hide in fear when the Spirit of God is doing His' work. The story you are about to read is powerful, and it will cause you to search your inner being. Till this day it remains one of the most amazing heart pounding stories that I could ever tell. God seemed to visit us that day and I do not know if I have ever felt a presence so strong.

A few years back, God opened up a door to witness to a young man named Shane, and it was beyond enlightening. From the time I got in the truck till the time I left the truck great power filled the air. Shane had been at the company for weeks, yet I had never had a chance to speak to him before. Shane was very nice and very interested in God. He would ask a question and I would answer with a number of verses and real stories. With each passing moment the feeling of conviction got stronger and stronger as I presented the gospel to him. Around twenty five minutes into our ride; it was so powerful we could hardly even shallow. It felt like God himself was sitting between us that night. Shane was shaking and I was as well. He looked at me with a look of fear and asked, "So you really think God is real?" My reply to him was sure I do and that is why as I pointed at the street sign in front of us.

Out of all the names that the street could have been it happened to be Jerusalem Street. We had been driving in the sticks when this took place and I was just about to tell him a story from Jerusalem to prove God was real. The timing was impeccable and the feeling was unmatched. As I concluded telling him this story we continued to drive and as we looked up, the next street was called Church Street. At this point God's anointed power was everywhere and silence filled the whole area. As we turned the corner we happened to arrive at our destination in Saline Michigan. When we stepped out of the truck to see if someone would show us where to place our signs something incredible happened. A drunken man staggered up to me and said one curse word and stopped immediately. He looked me straight in my eyes and said, "I can't do this you're a good man." God's power hit that man like a ton of bricks and he staggered away in shame. God's divine presence filled that entire area in a Holy way. Personally I have never seen anything like it before.

After this stunning incident took place we received word of where to place the signs. The person in charge led us around the back of a bar and asked us if we could lay the signs in a certain spot. To our surprise in the spot where we were told to lay our signs a church was painted on the back of the bar. In my thirty two years of living I have never seen a church painted on the back of a bar, but we did that night. Five seconds later I saw Shane bow his head and I asked him if he was alright. Shane then looked at me and said, "Just listen." He then turned up the radio and out of all the songs that could have come on it was a song called "Jesus Take the Wheel." We both shook our heads and unloaded our signs. Time almost seemed to stand still and we were speechless.

After our work was complete we had one final place to go and God's Spirit grew stronger and stronger. On the way to Chelsea there was a parade going on and the Gideon's were right in the middle of that crowd passing out bibles. When Shane had seen this, for some reason he made a sharp right turn and there was a huge cross staring us in the face. The power of God seemed like a shadow all around us and we will never forget that feeling. Shane actually called his mother that night and wanted to get things right with her. He told me that he needed to tell her that he loved her because he wasn't sure if he would make out of the truck alive. He didn't accept Christ but the Power was so real.

After we went home that night I was still shaking over what happened in that truck. It almost felt like walking through a page of the Bible that night. May we all have moments when God pays us a special visit from above. The Bible says in Psalm 8:4, "What is man, that thou art mindful of him? And the son of man that thou visitest him." There is nothing that can compare to a visit from the Holy One. Shane and I will never forget it throughout all of eternity.

This chapter would not be complete without this little side note. Around a month after this incident took place I was at a local barbershop and a precious Mexican lady was cutting my hair. This lady was very sweet and very friendly to all. As I went to tell her the above mentioned story she stopped me and said, "Tony do you know where I was born?" To be honest I had no earthy idea. Her answer totally shocked me when she said ,"Tony I was born in downtime Jerusalem." Out of all the places in the world that may have been the last place I would have guessed. Immediately my mind went back to that night with Shane. What a powerful moment in time. God is real my friends.

Scriptures Chapter 11

Daniel 5:6 "Then the King's countenance was changed, and his thoughts troubled him, so that the joints of his loins were loosed, and his knees smote one against another."

Hebrews 10:31 "It is a fearful thing to fall into the hands of a living God."

Psalm 8:4 "What is man, that thou art mindful of him? And the son of man, that thou visitest him?"

Chapter 12
Behold the Messiah

When John the Baptist came on the scene, with divine power on his life, he tried his absolute best to point the crowds to the Messiah. All of John's statements seemed to come from heaven, and every word he spoke got people's attention. The power of God flowed through his body and multitudes were coming from everywhere. One day according to the book of John 1:29 as people were in total awe of his message; he stopped and pointed toward the Messiah. As the people turned to see who he was pointing at, John said these words, "Behold the lamb of God that taketh away the sin of the world."

All the attention John had been receiving went directly to Jesus in a split second of time. John was showing the world that his sole purpose for living was to point others to the Messiah. When the Lord is lifted up great things will begin to happen. Lives will be touched, hearts will be mended, and souls will be redeemed. There are not many different roads to heaven but there is only one road to heaven and that is through Jesus Christ.

We as Christians need to get out of the way and allow Jesus to be magnified to a lost and dying world. Christ doesn't need us, but we sure do need him. He is the reason for the season, and we should lift him up every chance we get. John 12:32 says, "If I be lifted up from the earth, will draw all men unto me." The great old song says it best when it says, "Look and live my brother live, look to Jesus now and live."

I have always been taught that Israel is the center of the earth, and Calvary is the center of the universe. Jesus Christ is the pinnacle of everything that really matters, and his blood will never lose its power. May this powerful story point you to the Messiah in a glorious way, and touch your heart for His glory.

Every Christmas season, the most powerful musical in the world, takes center stage around this country. The musical is Handel's Messiah and it has impacted thousands for Christ. Every year it is performed, and every time it moves the soul. Fredrick Handel wrote the entire piece in just a few days, and it stirs the soul like nothing else can. Through the power of music, God's word is quoted in a magical way.

The first time I heard it I could do nothing but weep over its beauty. During the last song of this musical, the whole building rises to their feet, to give God the glory. Nothing on earth can compare to the feeling you have on the inside when the Hallelujah Chorus is being sung. Personally I believe every Christian living, owes it to their self, to see Handel's Messiah at least once in their lifetime. Powerful is the only word I could use to describe it. Allow me to tell you what happened not long ago in my life.

As I was working, in Detroit picking up cones, we stopped by an old church and seen a sign advertizing that Handel's Messiah was coming in December. While I was looking at the sign, a young man came to my mind that had never seen Handel's Messiah before. I then bowed my head and asked that God would use someone to buy that man tickets to Handel's

Messiah. My prayer was simply this, "Lord please give someone a burning desire to buy those tickets for that young man."

Around a week later, after church, I received a text message from that same young man that I prayed for. He revealed to me that my father came to him that night and said from out of nowhere the Lord told him to buy them both Handel's Messiah tickets. This man also said my dad promised to take him out to eat after the concert was over. My heart was overwhelmed by the convicting power of God, and I humbly give him the honor He deserves.

Sinner friend, it only takes one look at the Messiah and your life can take a drastic turn for the better. My heart will be forever thankful for Isaiah 9:6. The bible says in this verse, "For unto us a child is born, unto us a Son is given: and the government shall be upon his shoulder: and his name shall be called Wonderful, Counselor, The mighty God, The everlasting Father, the Prince of Peace."

Scriptures Chapter 12

John 1:29 "The next day John seeth Jesus coming unto him, and saith, Behold the Lamb of God, which taketh away the sin of the world."

John 12:32 "And I, if I be lifted up from the earth, will draw all men unto me."

Isaiah 9:6 "For unto us a child is born, unto us a son is given: and the government shall be upon his shoulder: and his name shall be called Wonderful, Counselor, The mighty God, the everlasting Father, The Prince of Peace."

Chapter 13
A Man's Best Friend

There is a special bond found throughout the pages of time between animals and mankind. It was Adam's job to name the animals, which God had created, and our connection with animals is undeniable. In the book of Genesis the bible teaches that before God ever sent a universal flood Noah called all the animals into the ark. Proverbs 12:10 teaches that a righteous man regardeth the life of his beast. God created animals for many different reasons, but one of the greatest reasons was to be a companion with man. God used Balaam's ass to rebuke his own master. God sent the raven's to minister to Elijah in his time of need.

Often times God uses animals to convey a message. In the book of Jonah God used a whale to get his man's attention. In the gospels he used a cock crowing thrice to signify Peter's denial of the Savior. All throughout the bible animals play an important role. After all Christ is the lion of the tribe of Judah, Satan is as a roaring lion, and we will all ride on white horses one day if we are saved. Jesus is the great Shepherd and we are his sheep.

There is a definite connection between humans and animals that has stood the test of time. According to many animal lovers perhaps the greatest connection between Man and Beast is the connection of dogs and there owners. It is commonly referred to as man's best friend. When you have a good faithful dog, they almost become like a family member. We had a dog name Max growing up and we were blessed to have him for many years. As time went on he became very special to us and we loved him dearly. There is an unexplainable relationship between man and dog that we can't put our finger on. For the rest of this chapter I will give you a story that will strengthen your faith in Christ. This is a feel good story and I pray you will gain hope through reading it.

    One day, shortly after I arrived home from work, our phone rang and it was my wife's mother. As my wife picked up the phone there was weeping on the other line because her dog Marley had come up missing. Marley is one of the sweetest dogs I've ever known and she is important to the entire family. We wondered how we could help so my wife made up fliers with Marley's picture on it. Hours and hours passed but there was still no sign of Marley anywhere. My wife's mother was worried as two hours turned into five hours without little Marley returning home. At around 10:00 p.m. that night my daughter Hope and I said a quick prayer for Marley to return back home. At 11:01 p.m., as I was lying in bed with my wife, a peace came over me and I told her Marley was home safe and sound. It was at 11:05 p.m. that our phone rang and I told my wife it was her mother telling us that Marley was with them again. Sure enough it was my mother -in- law telling us, with excitement, that her baby had returned home.

    When I think about this story it reminds me that God has everything under control and we need not fear when he is near. A dog may be man's best friend physically, but God is man's best friend spiritually. What a friend we have in Jesus.

The old song says He whispers sweet peace to me and He sure did that night.

Scriptures Chapter 13

Proverbs 12:10 "A righteous man regardeth the life of his beast:but the tender mercies of the wicked are cruel."

1 Kings 17:4 "And it shall be, that thou shalt drink of the brook; and I have commanded the ravens to feed thee there."

Proverbs 18:24 "A man that hath friends must show himself friendly; and there is a friend that sticketh closer than a brother."

Matthew 12:40 "For as Jonah was three days and three nights in the whale's belly; so shall the Son of man be three days and three nights in the heart of the earth."

Chapter 14
Where is the Lord God of Elijah?

When you start to list men throughout history, who had a touch of God on their life, you will not get very far until the name of Elijah is mentioned. Elijah's power with God was something to behold and it's something we should strive after. The bible tells us that Elijah brought down fire, brought a young boy back to life, and was caught up into heaven with a chariot of fire. As we examine his power, we must ask ourselves where is this power today?

James declared unto us, in the word of God, that Elijah was no different than us. Today we can still have this power if we hunger and thirst after it. In this chapter I will prove to you that God desires to give you the power of Elijah; if you will follow him with all your heart, soul, and mind. This chapter is also clear proof that God's power is present and with us today.

One day, as I was reading the bible at work, I found myself in 1 Kings, Chapter 18. This is the chapter where Elijah brought down the fire from heaven. As I was reading this great chapter my coworker and I heard a report on the news. The news reporter explained how our President and his workers of darkness were once again trying to steal religious liberties from Christians. When I heard this news I looked at my coworker and said, "I'm sick of this government trying to rob us of what God has given us." My coworker looked at me and said, "You better watch what you say Tony, they are probably listening." When he made that statement a power from above fell on me and I gave him a direct response he would never forget. I said, "Sir, I will gladly meet him on top of Mount Carmel right now and we can have a showdown on the mountain." Once those words left my lips a power from the glory world filled my soul and it lasted the rest of that day. Shortly after I made that statement amazing things started taking place.

First my boss notified me that I would be working a double shift, which I was not prepared for. My thoughts quickly went to 1 Kings 17, where God fed Elijah for three and a half years with a raven. I recall looking up into heaven and asking God to sustain me like Elijah. Immediately after making this request I looked down and staring back at me was a one dollar bill. I quickly picked it up and God spoke to me and said there is your drink. Directly after this happened I took a few more steps and I found another dollar and God said there is your snack. Shortly after finding that second dollar I happened to look around again and there was one last dollar and immediately my eyes fastened onto the words In God We Trust.

After all this took place I hurried back to the shop to tell my coworker what had just happened. When I returned to the shop I saw a note with a ten dollar bill that said, "Tony get gas with this money." At this point the power of Elijah filled my soul as strong as it ever had before and his glory was all around me. Right after this took place I looked up at the clock and noticed that it was time for my second shift to begin.

I arrived at the school and a voice whispered inside my

soul to go get a drink with the dollar God gave me. I quickly hurried to the break room and placed that dollar in the pop machine and God told me to get a Coke. At this particular time the Coke - Cola company had been placing share a coke with someone on their bottles and then it gave a name. As I pushed the button I received my coke and stood in amazement as I read the words Share a coke with Elijah. When I read that phrase it overwhelmed me. Out of all the names that could have been on the bottle that day, God made sure it was the name Elijah. I believe by God telling me to buy that coke and it being Elijah he was putting his stamp of approval on the statement I made earlier that day. The divine power I felt at that moment was priceless and I still have the bottle to this day as a reminder of what God did.

When my days are over and people form different views about my life, I want them to remember this story. It does not matter what people say about us it only matters what God knows about us. Thank God for his power and his Amazing Grace. Two weeks after that story had happened a dear woman took my book, Walking on the Water with Jesus, all around Israel and took many photos. She told me that when she went up on top of Mount Carmel with my book a power hit her like never before. She said, "Tony the power I felt that day is impossible to put into words." Many still ask the question, Where is the Lord God of Elijah? I hope after reading this chapter it cleared up that question for you.

Scriptures Chapter 14

2 Kings 2:14 "And he took the mantle of Elijah that fell from him, and smote the waters, and said, Where is the Lord

God of Elijah? And when he also had smitten the waters, they parted hither and thither: and Elisha went over."

Matthew 5:6 "Blessed are they which hunger and thirst after righteousness: for they shall be filled."

Chapter 15
What a Great God We Serve

For me to try to put into words just how great our God is seems impossible. His power is infinite, His grace is overwhelming, and His mercy is to all generations. The love of God is never failing, and His salvation is never ending. No words can describe this great God we serve. There is a song I learned as a child that says this "Wonderful grace of Jesus greater then all my sin, how shall my tongue describe it, where shall my praise begin." Thousands throughout the ages of time have tried to comprehend this God supreme, but we all fail to grasp the whole picture.

Psalm 48:1 says, "Great is the Lord, and greatly to be praised, in the city of our God, in the mountain of his holiness." Revelation 5:13 says ,"Every creature which is in heaven, and on the earth, and under the earth, and such are in the sea, and all that are in them, heard I saying, blessing, and honour, and glory, and power, be unto him that sitteth upon the throne, and unto the Lamb for ever and ever." Titus 2:13 says it like this, "Looking for that blessed hope, and glorious appearing of the great God and our Savior Jesus Christ." We, as His children, are longing for that wondrous day when we shall behold the Lord once and for all.

The Lord has given us hope, joy, peace, assurance, and everything we need as we wait for that glad day. The Lord has also given us divine light, His instruction manual, and His eternal promises as we labour here below. Our God is known as the Great Shepherd, the living bread, the Lamb of God, and the door to heaven. One of my favorite verses in the bible is Romans 8:32 which reveal's His greatness in a marvelous way. Romans 8:32 says, " He that spared not his own Son, but delivered him up for us all, how shall he not with him also freely give us all things?" Please permit me to give you a story that displays God's greatness in a very loving way. This story is an awesome picture of how God has pity on His children.

Something took place not long ago that is almost impossible to believe, but I have two witnesses that this indeed came to pass. Only our great God could make this possible and I praise his holy name for it. Let me declare exactly what God hath done for my soul.

Through the years, a host of different people have asked me if I had anything I would like one day as a gift. My answer has always been no, just a dipping dot ice cream machine. When I made this statement everyone would laugh, but I was always serious about what I said. Psalm 115:3 says, "But our God is in the heavens: he hath done whatsoever he hath pleased." The bible teaches us never to limit God, and I believe He can do the unthinkable for me.

One day I told my wife that I believed God was going to put it on someone's heart to give me a dipping dot machine, because he loved me. My wife did not give me much of a reaction, but if God be for us who can be against us. Around ten months later, my boss called me in his office with some amazing news. He said, "Tony, you won't believe this but they are giving away a free dipping dot machine and it is yours if you want it." My heart overflowed with joy as he told me the news. Although I've always wanted a dipping dot machine, I had to turn it down because I had limited space at home.

Isn't it amazing how God will bless us with things that are near and dear to our hearts? The bible asks this question "is anything to hard for God?" The answer to that question is no and I hope this story proves that to you. Over the years God has manifested His kindness towards me in many different ways. This story in particular proves His interest in me personally. What a great God we serve.

Scriptures Chapter 15

Romans 8:31 "What shall we then say to these things? If God be for us, who can be against us?"

Psalm 115:3 "But our God is in the heavens: he hath done whatsoever he hath pleased."

Titus 2:13 "Looking for that blessed hope, and the glorious appearing of the great God and our Savior Jesus Christ:"

Romans 8:32 "He that spared not his own Son, but delivered him up for us all, how shall he not with him also freely give us all things?"

Chapter 16
A Super Blessing

    This story is almost beyond description but I will try my best to put it into words. Anyone who knows me personally knows that I'm a big sports fan. When I was a child I dreamed of being like Magic Johnson or Barry Sanders. I would play or watch sports for hours a day, but today I would much rather be like Peter or Paul. With that said one fact still remains, I still enjoy a good game as well.

    Psalms 37:4 says "Delight thyself in the Lord; and he shall give thee the desires of thy heart." If you're a sports fan, a Christian or just someone who likes good stories, this one is for you. To this day it still thrills my soul and blesses me over and over again. It happened while I was at work one day; and God performed a miracle for me that I would have never dreamed could or would have happened. Let me tell you what took place.

    It was around two in the afternoon, when I started a conversation with a man. He mentioned that at his other job they would give him the rare opportunity to work at the Super Bowl hanging up different banners. As we were talking the Lord told me to get ready for a major blessing that would be coming my way. At the time I had no idea what that blessing would be, but I prepared my mind for something great.

Around two hours later I was talking to another man about work, and in the middle of his sentence he switched gears and asked if I liked sports. I then replied that I did. He then said, "I don't know why but something just told me to give you an item that was given to me." I then said to him "what would that be?" and his answer shocked me. He said I want to give you a Super Bowl football from the Super Bowl that was played in Detroit. I stood speechless because rarely do people give stuff like that away. He insisted and I couldn't change his mind.

To be honest I was prepared for a big blessing but not a Super Bowl football. God sure does love to bless His own. What makes this even more amazing is the fact that early that same morning something set the stage for all this to take place. At 9:04 a.m. I sent my wife a text that said have a SUPER day. Never, before that day, have I ever said that phrase but for some reason I said it that day. Little did I know that morning God was going to bless me with a SUPER day as well. The football was beautiful and this story still helps me to this very day. Psalms 21:2 says "Thou hast given him his heart's desire and hast not with-holden the requests of his lips." Selah.

Scriptures Chapter 16

Psalm 37:4 "Delight thyself also in the Lord: and he shall give thee the desires of thine heart."

Psalm 21:2 "Thou hast given him his heart's desire, and hast not withholden the request of his lips. Selah."

Chapter 17
My Help Cometh from the Lord

    Every single day of my life people ask me this question how can you trust God the way that you do? My response to that question is clear I am not trusting in my own weak abilities, but rather in the abilities of an infinite powerful God that has never failed. When we realize that He has been everywhere and has seen everything, we will also understand that He watches over His own as well. God has promised to hide us under the shadow of the almighty. He is our sword and shield and we are kept by the power of God. If we serve the Lord and trust in His abilities He will move heaven and earth on our behalf. Remember He is the Alpha and Omega and with Him all things are possible. He is a faithful and just God, and He is touched with the feelings of our infirmities. He guides, protects, provides, and overshadows those who walk with Him. When we look at life with that view we will have no problem trusting Him for our every need. Our God is in the heavens, and there is nothing to hard for Him. With the remainder of this chapter I will give you a story that will show the goodness of God once again.

As I was working, a short while back, I experienced a very trying day. Besides being very sick, I also had a bad headache and backache at the same time. About midway through the day, I recall having a desire to call my mom to ask her to pray for me. Calling off work was out of the question because we were hurting for money at the time. My sweet mother was kind enough to offer to pay for a day off in which I declined. My mother asked if I was sure and I told her that I have a God in heaven that will take care of me at church tonight. When those words left my lips I was absolutely sure that God would take care of me that night. Peace flooded my soul and I just knew a miracle would take place. Sure enough that night at church God performed a miracle in a wonderful way. That evening I set my bible down on the pew and headed for the back to use the restroom. When I made it back to my pew I found that there was a twenty dollar bill sitting on my Bible that wasn't there before. When my eyes laid hold upon this miracle my mind thought about my great God who sitteth upon his throne.

When we limit God we are only hurting ourselves. May I submit unto you that God has never failed one time, and it is impossible for Him to lie? God is always able to help us but only if we get out the way and allow him too. We have a God that knows the beginning from the end and he will always supply our every need.

Scriptures Chapter 17

Psalm 121:2 "My help cometh from the Lord, which made heaven and earth."

Luke 1:37 "For with God nothing shall be impossible."

Psalm 91:4 "He shall cover thee with his feathers, and under his wings shalt thou trust: his truth shall be thy shield and buckler."

Revelation 1:8 "I am Alpha and Omega, the beginning and the ending, saith the Lord, which is, and which was, and which is to come, the Almighty."

Psalm 37:25 "I have been young, and now am old; yet have I not seen the righteous forsaken, nor his seed begging bread."

Chapter 18
God is Always Pleased with Compassion

Nothing in this world pleases the heart of the Lord anymore then when people exercise compassion towards one another. Jude said that you will make an eternal difference in the kingdom of God if you will add this to your everyday life. Love is a power all its own and with it all the world can be at your disposal. Psalms 145:8 states that, "The Lord is full of compassion and great in mercy." Without love in our life, according to I Corinthians 13:2, we are nothing. God wants us to think on the cares of others throughout our existence on earth. When we live a life of compassion, God in return will allow people to return the favor someday. Every day of my life I look for ways to help others; because of that fact God uses others to help me. Although I could give you many stories to prove my point, I will give you one that should speak to your heart pretty clearly. Please allow God's spirit to open your heart to the need of helping others through this story.

My two favorite times of the year would have to be Thanksgiving and the Christmas seasons. During these few months, people actually display some good deeds and live like

Christ would want them to live. Excitement fills the air and a good spirit can be felt. May we all remember that twenty two percent of the world lives in poverty and God has been very good to us.

Around this time of year I'm always trying to find new ways to help the less fortunate. It was five years ago that I had an idea to give my annual company turkey to a sweet lady who was struggling badly. Immediately after I received my turkey that year I drove to the trailer park, where she lived, and surprised her with a thirteen pound turkey for Thanksgiving. When I gave her the gift she began to cry, gave me a big hug and thanked me very deeply. As I left her porch I had a warm feeling inside and I felt like God was pleased with me.

Two years later, I was trying to raise funds for some needy kids and God remembered my kindness. Within one glorious hour three different people came up to me with turkeys for the children. My heart was blessed that day. Two of the men, who had given me their turkeys, told me they don't know why but something told them to give them to me. I believe that God in heaven smote their hearts and caused them to help me in a special way. Besides the turkeys that year, God allowed me to raise around one thousand six hundred dollars for poor needy kids. In turn the kids had a wonderful holiday season that year.

When you help the needy God will always send something your way. I am very glad, to this day, that I showed compassion on the needy because God rewarded me abundantly. The good Lord said in Acts 20:35, "It is better to give then to receive."

Scriptures Chapter 18

Jude 22 "And of some have compassion, making a difference."

Psalm 145:8 "The Lord is gracious, and full of compassion; slow to anger, and of great mercy."

I Corinthians 13:2 "And though I have the gift of prophecy, and understand all mysteries, and all knowledge; and though I have all faith, so that I could remove mountains, and have not charity, I am nothing."

Acts 20:35 "It is more blessed to give than to receive."

Chapter 19
Tis so Sweet to Trust in Jesus

Without question, one of the greatest gospel songs to have ever been penned is the song Tis so Sweet to Trust in Jesus. Its peaceful words and Godly truths have a way of claiming a troubled soul. The lady that wrote this song was Miss Louisa Stead and she was a missionary for many years. Her life was filled with letdowns, setbacks, and heartbreaks. Although life at times was very rough, Miss Stead had a heart for God and she trusted Jesus for her every need.

Sometimes trusting the Lord through hardships in life is difficult but Miss Stead shows us the formula in this song. The fourth verse in her song reads like this, "I'm so glad I learned to trust thee, precious Jesus, Savior friend, and I know that thou art with me, wilt be with me till the end." Miss Stead was showing us that though we may not have all the answers, we serve a God who does. May we all live in faith trusting Christ every step of the way.

The bible teaches that He is a friend at all times, and He will never leave thee or forsake thee. Sometimes things come our way that totally take us off guard and bring us to our knees.

During these times in our life, we must understand that the trail of our faith is more precious than gold. God has a reason for everything done in our life and we must trust him at all times. It will be a special day in our lives when we learn to walk by faith not by sight. The bible says, "Draw nigh to God, and he will draw nigh unto you." When we trust the Lord with all our heart, good things will happen. Let me give you a marvelous story that will glorify the God we serve.

One day at work, during the month of December, God answered a prayer very rapidly for me. The Christmas season was upon us, and it was very busy at my company. My boss asked me to empty the trash in the office and I said, "No problem sir." While I was in the process of emptying the trash, I came to the office break room where God was about to prove himself to me. On the break room table sat a large display of candy, cheese, and a huge white chocolate pretzel, which caught my attention. I remember feeling funny about asking for the pretzel so instead I bowed my head right there and then and asked God to move on someone's heart to give it to me. Immediately after the prayer I went to leave the office and one of my bosses came towards me very quickly. It was almost like God himself told him to move my way. This man looked at me and said, "Tony come with me." As I followed him that day, he took me right back to the place where that pretzel was and said to take the whole display including the white chocolate pretzel. In less than fifteen seconds, after I prayed, the Lord allowed me to take that basket home with me.

When you trust the Lord with a heart of faith the impossible becomes possible. When you really think about it the Lord has never failed one time. If we can't trust him who can we trust?

Scriptures Chapter 19

Hebrews 13:5 "For he hath said, I will never leave thee, nor forsake thee."

Proverbs 3:5 "Trust in the Lord with all thine heart; and lean not unto thine own understanding."

Proverbs 17:17 "A friend loveth at all times, and a brother is born for adversity."

James 4:8 "Draw nigh unto God, and he will draw nigh unto you. Cleanse your hands, ye sinners; and purify your hearts, ye double minded"

Chapter 20
A Very Entertaining Story

  Christians are thought of by a lost world, to be boring and out of date. We are laughed at, scorned, rejected and despised. We are considered weak, brainwashed, and push over's. Whenever I hear these things I say to myself that is the furthest thing from the truth. Jesus is not weak, frail or the man upstairs. On the contrary He is powerful, alive and a miracle performer. God is known by the judgment which he executes. Jesus is very capable of handling any situation and He is just as amazing today as He was thousands of years ago.

  To be honest, my life is not boring in any way. If you walked in my shoes for a day you would see this statement to be true. God allows me to walk in faith, power and victory through his guidance. Every day of my life, God seems to be working and some things I witness are anything but boring. People on average do not read there bible and therefore they have a false concept of a real Christian. Many tried to get rid of Moses but they didn't have a chance to run off God's man. Peter was ignorant and unlearned, but he was powerful and he walked on the water. Nabal tried to disrespect David, and ten days later his heart died within him.

    A Christian that walks in the power of God is an unstoppable force. God will protect, shield, and defend his children at all costs. Joshua was an untouchable man and he won many battles with God. If I took the time I could give you hundreds of very entertaining stories I have heard that would thrill your heart to no end. Time after time God's hand has moved through the years and astounded those around me. With the rest of this chapter I will give you an entertaining story in every sense of the word.

    A short time ago, something arose in my life that God knew all about. This circumstance required prayer and it was a need that was precious to me. One morning I called my mother and we prayed about this matter in private. Later on that day, as I was studying and recalling all God's blessings on my life, my phone rang. As I picked up the phone the voice I heard was from a man I hadn't heard from in months. He proceeded to tell me that they were moving to Florida and he had something he wanted to give me. After a few minutes of talking he revealed to me that he wanted to give me a free oak entertainment center with; a thirty six inch TV, a five disc DVD player, surround sound and other neat items. This gift was absolutely amazing. God saw fit to answer my prayer and it was a blessing from heaven.

    Walking with God is the greatest honor that a man or women can receive, and there is nothing boring about it. When you are close to the Lord, blessings like this happen every day. The Bible teaches that if you walk with God his soul will delight in you. God will constantly bless those who do right in there life and bring honor to His holy name.

Scriptures Chapter 20

Psalm 9:16 "The Lord is known by the judgment which he executeth:"

1 Samuel 25:38 "And it came to pass about ten days after, that the Lord smote Nabel, and he died."

Acts 4:13 "Now when they saw the boldness of Peter and John, and perceived that they were ignorant men, they marveled; and they took knowledge of them, that they had been."

Chapter 21
God Creating Something Out of Nothing

The Lord Jesus Christ has an amazing ability to create something out of nothing. In the book of Genesis he breathed into mans nostrils and Adam became a living soul. The Bible records that God said let there be light and there was light. In sixth days everything we see before us was created by a Holy God.

According to the Bible, everything is in a perfect balance and heaven is His throne and the earth is His footstool. God has the sun, moon, stars, galaxies, and planet earth in perfect harmony. The Bible declares that the earth hangs on nothing, and that he sitteh upon the circle of the earth. The heavens declare His handiwork, and the clouds are nothing more than the dust of his feet.

No human can properly explain the order of the universe or what makes man's heart tick. We must conclude that without God we can do nothing, and his ways are not are ways. Some things can never be explained with are feeble explanations, so we must realize that God is in the heavens and He has everything under control.

Often in the Bible, we find God turning nothing into something. God caused dead bones too live again, blinded eyes to see, and the dead to return to life. The Lord caused the deaf to hear, the red sea to part, and the broken to be made whole. God remains the only one with the ability to create hope in a hopeless situation.

One of my favorite stories, in the Bible, would have to be when the Lord told Peter to catch a fish, open up its belly, and take out money so that he and Peter could pay their taxes. God proved the wonder of His promise when the money was exactly what they needed to the penny. I have always stood amazed of that miracle ever since I was a child. The story that I will share now is very similar to that story.

One day, while driving with a man from my work, I could not help but notice that he was down in the dumps. I quickly tried to help him in any way I could, but nothing seemed to work. After I tried a few different things I bowed my head and asked the Lord to do something special for this man. Around ten minutes later, as we were picking up cones, the man lifted up a cone and found a fresh ten dollar bill. It was no doubt from the Lord and it was the cleanest ten dollar bill I had ever seen. The first thing I thought about was Peter and the fish story.

After work that day I called my mom with this amazing story. My mother was shocked and the first thing she said was, "Tony that reminds me of the story of Peter and the fish." I then replied mom that is what I thought too. The Lord answered my prayer that day and proved again that He can do whatever He wants to, whenever he wants to. Psalms 40:13 says this, "Be pleased, O Lord, to deliver me: O Lord, make haste to help me."

Scriptures Chapter 21

Genesis 2:7 "And the Lord God formed man of the dust of the ground, and breathed into his nostrils the breath of life; and man became a living soul."

John 1:10 "He was in the world, and the world was made by him, and the world knew him not."

Isaiah 66:1 "Thus saith the Lord, The heaven is my throne, and the earth is my footstool: where is the house that ye build unto? And where is the place of my rest?"

Isaiah 40:17 "When the poor and needy seek water, and there is none, and there tongue faileth for thirst, I the Lord will hear them, I God of Israel will not forsake them."

Isaiah 40:22 "Let them bring them forth, and show us what shall happen: let them show the former things, what they shall be, that we may consider them, and know the latter end of them; or declare us things for to come."

Psalm 19:1 "The heavens declare the glory of God; and the firmament showeth his handiwork."

John 1:1 "In the beginning was the Word, and the Word was with God, and the Word was God."

John 15:5 "I am the vine, ye are the branches: He that abideth in me, and I in him, the same bringeth forth much fruit: for without me ye can do nothing."

Matthew 16:27 "For the Son of man shall come in the glory of his Father with his angels; and then he shall reward every man according to his works."

Nahum 1:3 "The Lord is slow to anger, and Great in power, and will not at all acquit the wicked: the Lord hath his why in the whirlwind and in the storm, and the clouds are the dust of his feet."

Chapter 22
An Overwhelming Response from God

Whenever you determine to help one of God's anointed, you will find that the rewards will be endless. Often times, God will tip over His eternal blessing bucket and pour you out blessings that you will not be able to bear. Everything I am can be traced back to the many times I've helped God's men. Through my giving, God in return has opened up a treasure box of gifts that are hard to put into words.

The book of Romans says it like this "How beautiful are the feet of them that preach the gospel of peace." True men of God are rare, but they are precious in the sight of God. Whenever I am around a man of God, I try my best to support them in any way I can. Nothing on earth is more glorious than a man of God preaching with divine power from on high. God expects us to help his men any chance we get. They are indeed worthy of double honor, and you will only benefit the cause of Christ when you hold up the preacher's hands.

God's men get tired, weary, and stressed out; it is our job to assist them often. The great Dr. John Hamblin told me one day, and I quote, "Bro Tony, you are special in the eyes of

God because you help His men." Just think, if we all had that testimony, what a difference we could make. God promises to reward us in a special fashion if we reach out by faith and encourage others. If this chapter does not prove to you that there are benefits to helping God's men, nothing will.

Last year the Lord gave me a great desire to help one of His very best servants in many different ways. Seemly all year I scrabbled, prayed, and went crazy to find ways to encourage this awesome man of God. Money was very tight, but wherever there's a will there is a way. After much struggle and determination, God allowed me to help him in a powerful fashion. God gave me peace about my labors and he rewarded me in a way that is hard to understand.

Within two weeks of time, the Lord used fifteen different people to give me eighteen items. Please let me say that again, fifteen people gave me eighteen items. The following is a list of things that people either gave me or offered me:

My mother gave sixty dollars for gas, a man gave forty dollars to help my family, a lady gave fifty dollars and told me the Lord wanted her to do it, a lady from my church gave me two huge tub's of gummy bears and said enjoy, a man from my work made me a sign I was praying about for free, my father in law offered to buy us a dog for two hundred and fifty dollars but we had to turn it down, another man bought me two pops and refused to let me pay for them, a man of God gave me a priceless item and said I was a blessing, another lady bought me a frosty and told me God wanted her to, a sweet lady brought me in my own set of cookies that God told her to bake, a lady bought me a sweet tea that I gave to someone else, a man from my work gave me money and told me to get whatever I wanted, and finally a precious couple took my family to a nice place for dinner and paid for it.

Almost every one of those people assured me that God directed them to help me. Other little gifts were also given to me and my heart was very warmed in those two weeks.

Over the years the Lord has pampered me, and blessed me in many ways. My goal in writing this chapter is to point you to the one in whom all blessings flow. Jesus promises to reward those who help His servants. This chapter alone should silence all those who doubt the blessings that come from helping God's men. May we all be compelled to dig a little deeper and allow God to use us in this way. If we will do this, God promises to send a bundle of blessings our way, and the results will be staggering.

Scriptures Chapter 22

Romans 10:15 "And how shall they preach, except they be sent? As it is written, how beautiful are the feet of them that preach the gospel of peace, and bring glad tidings of good things."

1 Timothy 5:17 "Let the elders that rule well be counted worthy of double honor, especially they who labor in the word and doctrine."

Malachi 3:10 "Bring ye all the tithes into the storehouse, that there may be meat in mine house, and prove me now herewith, saith the Lord of hosts, if I will not open up the windows of heaven, and pour you out a blessing, that there shall not be room enough to receive it."

Chapter 23
A Very Powerful Moment

When the pages of my life unfold and my race on earth is complete; this story will stand as one of the best in my life. The presence of God could be strongly felt throughout the whole course of this day. I will never forget it till the day I die. When you read this story, I pray that it dawns on us just how much God really does love each and every one of us.

Psalms 40:17 records that even though we are poor and needy, the Lord thinketh upon us. This story contains a series of little blessings that cheered my heart in a beautiful way. The fact is every blessing whether great or small is amazing if it comes from God. This story proves that Christ loves us and he answers our prayers according to his will.

While my family and I were on vacation in Alpena Michigan, last summer, God showed up early one Sunday morning in a breath taking fashion. As we were checking out of the hotel that morning, to travel back to our home church, God had a series of blessings prepared that could only come from Him.

Over and over that weekend we had passed a candy machine and I never seemed to have change. My precious little girl looked at me with innocent eyes and asked if we could get some candy. I responded to her by saying, "Hope, Daddy doesn't have money but God does. Let's pray for a quarter." Hope said ok Dad and right there and then we prayed for just one quarter.

After we prayed we headed back to our room to gather our things. On the way there Hope saw the pop machines and had to hit the buttons. She then looked inside the machine and there was a new quarter sitting there just for us. When I saw that quarter I knew God had answered our prayer. We went directly back to that candy machine and got Hope her candy, and we were both on cloud nine.

When we made it back to the room I immediately called my mom and told her this amazing story. After talking to my mom for a few minutes I hang up the phone and, immediately after doing so, Hope came up to me with another quarter in her hand. Someone had given her another quarter. After witnessing this again I was praising the Lord for His goodness towards my family. The next thing I recall doing is calling my mom again with some more good news.

I hung up the phone for the second time and Hope came straight up to me and asked for another quarter. I told her not to get greedy and that God had already given her two quarters. I reminded her that prayer is the answer for everything and that we could pray for one last quarter. We then said a quick prayer and around ten seconds later we got a knock on the door. It was my sister in-law, and she was standing there with one more quarter for Hope. It seemed like God was present in the room with us that day. After all this took place I fell to my knees and thanked the Lord for what he had done.

Once we had loaded up the car, it was time for our long ride home. On the way home we saw a sight to behold that sticks out in my mind. What we saw was a seventy five foot statue of Christ holding the World in his hands. It was a reminder to me that God has this whole world in the palms of His hands. I'm thankful for the thought that we serve a God that knows the path we take and wipes away every tear we cry. When I had seen that statue I thought of the verse that says "Be still and know that I am God."

Scriptures Chapter 23

Psalm 40:17 "But I am poor and needy; yet the Lord thinketh upon me: thou art my help and my deliverer; make no tarrying, O my God."

Psalm 46:10 "Be still, and know that I am God: I will be exalted among the heathen, I will be exalted in the earth."

Chapter 24
God Visiting a Lady From Out of Nowhere

In the book of John, chapter four, we find a story that reveals how God deals with mankind. We read in the chapter about a woman, who lived a life of pleasure and sin, all the days of her life. She had already been married five times and the man she was involved with was not her husband. This woman was so vile that the other women in the city did not want anything to do with her, because of her ungodly life style. As far as we can tell she was perfectly content with her sin and she was determined to die in that condition. However, thank God we that know this story know that Jesus could see a different future in this ladies life. He showed up when she was least expecting him too. It just took one visitation from God to completely change this women's destination and gave her something worth living for.

When we study God's word, we quickly realize that the Holy Spirit appears to us when we are not even thinking about Him. There have been wicked drunkards, through the years, that have received a visit from God while walking down the street. There have been drug addicts that have fallen under heavy conviction through a praying mother, often over the centuries of time. Church kids have been known to have screamed out for mercy through a preacher who was thundering the word of God from his sacred desk. The Bible teaches that God does whatever He desire's, at any given time, to grab mankind's attention throughout life. There are hundreds of stories I could reveal that prove this is true, but I will give you one that happened recently that blessed my soul.

One day, at my work, the Lord directed me to call my mother and tell her what was on my heart. I felt like, in my heart, God was going to place it on someone's mind to buy me some Reese candies; so I could give them to a precious man of God. To most people this may seem strange but I wanted to be a blessing to a preacher and I believed it by faith. This conversation happened in private and only my mother and I knew about it.

Shortly after our conversation, on a Monday morning, a lady approached me and said I have a gift for you. She then gave me a bag and said, "I hope you enjoy Tony." To my amazement inside the bag there were Reese trees for me to enjoy. After she gave them to me she said there was a story she wanted to share with me. She told me as she was shopping the other day from out of nowhere my name came to her mind and she had a strong desire to buy me some Reese trees. She said she didn't know why but she couldn't leave that store until she bought those for me. Once she told me this story, I asked her what day and what time this took place. She told me at 3:45 p.m. on Thursday this took place. What was amazing about this was that on Thursday at 3:35 p.m. I told my mother this would happen.

God has a way of showing up at just the right time and in just the right fashion. The Bible tells us that when Saul was persecuting the church; that is when a holy God decided to appear in a way that totally shocked him. We as humans do not know how and we don't know why, but He will tell us all about it in the bye and bye. God is past finding out and I have learned, over the years, that He comes when he wants to, and He leaves when He wants to.

We must determine to respond to God when He shows up and speaks to our hearts. The pages of time are full of stories like this one you just examined and in God's own unique way, He will show up whenever He wishes to. The Bible says, "That I am God and there is none else." This is how God has always dealt with mankind. Ask yourself why God would deal with that lady about something like that. To be honest, I can't explain how God moves and deals with us, I just know He does. God's Spirit can move people in a way that nothing else can. The moving of God is a powerful force that is unexplainable with the human tongue, but it can be felt in the soul of man. That is the wonder and beauty of a thrice holy God.

Scriptures Chapter 24

Isaiah 45:22 "Look unto me, and be ye saved, all the ends of the earth: for I am God, and there is none else."

John 4:29 "Come, see a man, which told me all things that I ever did: is not this the Christ?"

Chapter 25
The Joy of Walking With the Lord

The word of God teaches us in 3rd John verse 4 that a parent's greatest joy, this side of eternity, is that there children walk in truth. We, as children of God, are commanded to walk the straight and narrow path if we want the fullness of His power. God will give us all the tools possible to achieve this goal, but it is up to us to use them for His honor and glory. The biggest struggle that we face on a daily basis is the person that stares back at us in the mirror every morning. Often times we wander away from the Lord by our own free will. The Bible says in Psalm 4:3 that, "The Lord hath set apart the Godly for himself."

There have been rare men and women who have experienced great blessings of God through the years, and they would not change it for all the earth's riches. Enoch walked with God and he could feel the realness of the almighty in his life. Noah walked with God and he found grace in the eyes of the Lord. Charles Haddon Spurgeon walked with God and he became the most famous preacher in the World at the tender age of twenty. God has special things prepared for those who have paid the price and we can have them as well if we love God with all our hearts. If walking with the Lord was easy everyone would be doing it.

Last year alone, I'm thrilled to report, God allowed one hundred and eighty different people to give me three hundred and fifty six gifts in a single year. One family took us out to eat over fifty times. Please permit me to give you a typical day in the life of one who walks with God. This story is an example of how God blesses His own.

One day as my wife was walking into the bank and stranger asked her how old my daughter was. My wife responded by telling her that she was three years old. The women then told her to please wait there for a minute. The lady then went to her car to get something for my daughter. After a minute or so the stranger returned with a wrapped present in her hand and gave it to my daughter and drove away. When my little girl opened the present she found it was a Minnie Mouse puzzle. This gift was given to her by a perfect stranger. Later in the day, as my wife was driving in slippery conditions, she went to make a turn and she felt like God was keeping her car from turning. In a moment of time a car was going the wrong way on a one way street directly at her. God's hand of protection keep her from being in a head on collision and we give him the glory.

The day I just described to you is an example of an average day in a spirit filled Christian's life. Time would not allow me to explain to you the amazing wonders I behold on a daily basis and each day is a miracle in the making. Allow God to control your walk and talk of life and you too can know the joy of walking with the Savior. The old preacher had it right when he said, "God is good all the time."

Many of Gods children live far beneath their potential

and they refuse to walk in Power. Sad to say they live a life of defeat instead of a life of victory. James 4:17 still says, "He that knoweth to do good and doeth it not to him it is sin." God has a great life planed for us if we will follow his leadership and yield to his Spirit.

Scriptures Chapter 25

3 John 4 "I have no greater joy than to hear that my children walk in truth."

Psalm 4:3 "But know that the Lord hath set apart him that is Godly for himself: The Lord will hear when I call unto him."

Hebrews 11:5 "By Faith Enoch was translated that he should not see death; and was not found, because God had translated Him: for before his translation he had this testimony, that he pleased God."

Genesis 6:8 "But Noah found grace in the eyes of the Lord."

Ephesians 5:18 "And be not drunk with wine wherein is excess; but be ye filled with the Spirit;"

James 4:17 "Therefore to him that knoweth to do good, and doeth it not, to him it is sin."

Chapter 26
God Treated Me like a King Twice in One Week

One of the greatest mysteries known to man is why the King of kings treats His own with such respect and honor. We find in the Bible that Jesus, the King, humbled himself and washed his disciple's feet. The Bible also teaches that this King led the children of Israel around for forty years, and made sure that every need they ever had was taken care of. Throughout the word of God, this King calls us his friends. We also find throughout the scriptures that Christ loves us deeply and cares for us always. Psalm 68:19 teaches that daily this King of Glory loads us up with benefits. Earlier in Psalm 18:19 it teaches that He has brought us into a large place, and that He delights in us.

Romans 8:17 tells us that we are joint heirs with Jesus Christ. God's word also declares that all things are created for our good pleasure. In Ephesians 1:3 it states, "That He has blessed us with all spiritual blessings in heavenly places in Christ." While in I Peter 1:4 it tells us, "We have an inheritance incorruptible and undefiled that fadeth not away, reserved in heaven for you."

The song writer had it right when he wrote, "Who am I that a King would bleed and die for?" Another great song puts it like this, "I'm a child of the King, and he loves me I know." Revelation 1:6 declares that He hath made us Priests and Kings through His blood. Although we can never understand such love, we must admit Christ treats us like royalty, if we are His children. The following are two short stories proving His love once again. May God use these stories to convince your heart, of His love, in a special way.

One morning, before we started work, my driver stopped at Burger King to grab some breakfast. As we went to order our food, my heart was set on a sausage and egg sandwich and a small drink. When I made it up to the register I discovered that we just missed breakfast, so instead I ordered a cheeseburger and a drink. To be honest with you, I was disappointed because, I was really looking forward to having that sausage and egg sandwich.

While I was waiting for my meal, I noticed the door opened, in the back behind the counter, and a lady was coming directly towards me with a sandwich in her hand. She looked right at me and said, "Sir would you like a sausage and egg sandwich? I would like to give it to you for free." My reply was, "Sure I would and thank you very much." It was four days later when my driver and I went back to that Burger King and witnessed another blessing from God.

Earlier that morning my wife and I agreed to be a little more careful on how we spent our money. We always seem to be scrapping by but we never go without. I remembered, just before I walked into Burger King that morning, I decided not to get a meal that day but only a soda. As I walked up to the register a lady was standing there like a solider of God. The lady looked at me and said, "What would you like today?" and

I said I only wanted a large coke. The lady handed me a large cup and said that it was on the house today. It was almost like God himself told her to be ready to assist, because one of His servant's was coming through.

God's hand of mercy is very present in all our lives and it is up to us to notice when He is moving on our behalf. The precious old hymn says it like this "Why would he love me a sinner undone, why tell me why does he care." Let me close out this chapter with this verse. Psalm 24:7, "Lift up your heads, o ye gates; and be ye lift up, ye everlasting doors; and the King of Glory shall come in." When you open up your heart in submission to this King, He in return, will bring you into His royal family. To me that is a pretty good deal.

Scriptures Chapter 26

1 Timothy 1:17 "Now unto the King eternal, immortal, invisible, the only wise God, be honor and glory forever and ever. Amen."

Psalm 68:19 "Blessed be the Lord, who daily loadeth us with benefits, even the God of our salvation. Selah."

Psalm 18:19 "He brought me forth also into a large place; he delivered me, because he delighted in me".

Romans 8:17 "And if children, then heirs; heirs of God, and joint-heirs with Christ; if so be that we suffer with him, that we may be also glorified together."

Ephesians 1:3 "Blessed be the God and Father of our Lord Jesus Christ, who hath blessed us with all spiritual blessings in heavenly places in Christ:"

1 Peter 1:4 "To an inheritance incorruptible, and undefiled, and that fadeth not away, reserved in heaven for you,"

Revelation 1:6 "And hath made us kings and priests unto God and his Father; to him be glory and dominion forever and ever. Amen."

Revelation 19:16 "And he hath on his vesture and on his thigh a name written, KING OF KINGS, AND LORD OF LORDS."

Psalm 24:7 "Lift up your heads, O ye gates; and be ye lifted up, ye everlasting doors; and the King of glory shall come in."

Psalm 24:10 "Who is the King of Glory? The Lord of hosts, he is the King of glory. Selah."

Chapter 27
A Small Blessing Turning into a Big One

There is a story found in the book of John chapter 6 that shows the importance of giving the Lord what little we have and watching him multiply it beyond human comprehension. In John 6:9 we see a lad which only had five loaves and two small fishes. As the story unfolds we discover that the boy gave what he had and in verse 11 Jesus took it, blessed it, and five thousand were fed. Sometimes God expects us to give whatever we have to those around us so that He can show His power in a heavenly way.

One of my favorite songs of all time is a song entitled "Little is Much, When God Is in It." We serve an all seeing and all knowing God; that is a very present help in our time of need. The bible teaches that if we give the Lord our substance, He in return will fill our barns with blessings. Ecclesiastes 11:1 tells us to cast our bread upon the waters and God will give it back to us in His time. His ways are not our ways, neither are His thoughts our thoughts. Our job is to listen to Christ and His job is to honor His promise. I would venture to say nearly fifty times, in my life, God has led me to give what little I had and I have watched him bless those decisions four fold. Allow me to tell you a story that is simple yet profound.

One Wednesday night, as I was getting ready for church, God clearly brought a lady to my mind and told me to give her my last five dollars. That money was intended to go into my gas tank, but I was positive God wanted me to do this. The Lord seemed to whisper to my soul and said if you will do this I will bless you richly.

When we arrived at the house of God, that dear lady was on my heart. She had recently been saved and she was extremely faithful to the Lord. I remember shaking her hand and giving her my last five dollars. She developed a tear in her eye and I knew the Lord was in it.

After this brief exchange I took my seat and opened up the hymn book. As I was studying the song Great is Thy Faithfulness, a man slipped in behind me and took his seat. This man then suddenly grabbed me by the shoulder and dropped a hundred dollars in my lap. When this took place almost immediately the Lord spoke to my heart and said I'm a debtor to no man. It was just by giving that lady five dollars that the Lord gave me nineteen times more then I gave out.

Please allow the Lord to take your little lunch and fed many others around you. It's a wonder why more people don't trust Christ with their little lunch, because the fact remains, He will surely reward you from His storehouse of love.

Scriptures Chapter 27

John 6: 9 "There is a lad here, which hath five barley loaves, and two small fishes: but what are they among so many?"

Ecclesiastes 11:1 "Cast thy bread upon the waters: for thou shalt find after many days."

Isaiah 55:8 "For my thoughts are not your thoughts, neither are your ways my ways, saith the Lord."

Chapter 28
A Wonderful Gift from God

Every human; young, old, rich, poor, bond or free, love to receive gifts throughout the days of their life. Romans 6:23 teaches "That the gift of God is eternal life through Jesus Christ our Lord." Often times a thoughtful gift can lift your spirit and brighten your day. James 1:17 says "That every good gift and every perfect gift cometh from above." We must give credit where credit is due when it comes to gifts that we receive.

Thankfulness is a major thing with the Lord, and we must be careful not to become cold and greedy in our life. Most people I know are so very blessed. These people have a roof over their heads, shoes on their feet, a number of cars, and toys galore. Our Great Savior has showered us with gifts untold and it is time we thank Him for what he has done.

Once in awhile things happen that humble us to the lowest degree. The Lord will move in such a gracious way, at different times, and it will literally bring us to tears. This next story is one of those types of stories. Its rarity makes it neat, and it will cheer you up and cause you to reflect on God's goodness towards us.

While I was at work one afternoon, I was asked to go on the road and pick up some signs that we had put out weeks earlier. On the way to the jobsite, I began talking to a good man and he mentioned that he had a slightly used Harley Davidson leather coat. When he mentioned that coat I knew instantly that I wanted to buy it from him for a friend of mine. Harley Davidson items are very rare and very expensive, but I was determined to buy that coat for my friend.

We started talking details and right away it was apparent to me that he didn't want to sell it. I offered him two hundred and fifty dollars, but I could tell it was special to him. After our conversation was complete that day he told me he would think it over. I then told him that I wanted to buy it for a man of God, but if he was uncomfortable please don't sell it. A few days went by and still no word on the coat.

I can remember praying that God would change his heart and allow me to buy it from him. After a few days went by, this same man approached me on a Monday morning with the coat in his hand. We talked for a minute and he said, "I don't want to sell this coat to you I would rather give it to you." He went on to say that God told him to give me the coat and he was sure of it. I asked if he was positive and he said, "Give it to that preacher friend of yours." My heart melted and I could not believe his kindness towards me. I find that hardly a day goes by without me praising the Lord for gifts like that. I believed God answered my prayer and it in turn blessed my heart.

If we took the time to reflect back on all the wonderful gifts God has sent our way, it would no doubt bless us over and over again. May we never be guilty of being unthankful for all the gifts He sends our way. He deserves all the praise for what He has done.

Scriptures Chapter 28

Romans 6:23 "For the wages of sin is death; but the gift of God is eternal life through Jesus Christ our Lord."

James 1:17 "Every good gift and every perfect gift is from above, and cometh down from the Father of lights, with whom is no variableness neither shadow of turning."

Chapter 29
Fear Thou Not:
For I am With Thee

    The benefits and blessings of being a child of God are impossible to explain. Peter had it right when he said that it is joy unspeakable and full of glory. There are thousands of promises found throughout the Bible and we will deal with a great one in this chapter.

    The word of God often teaches that, the born again child of God, receives special protection from the obstacles that this world throws their way. The three Hebrew children found a fourth man in the fire. Jonah found deliverance from the belly of the whale. David said this in Psalm 18:29, "For by thee I have run through a troop; and by my God have I leaped over a wall." Isaiah declares that, "no weapon formed against thee shall prosper." The Bible teaches that God is a very present help in trouble. The Lord always promises to deliver his own when problems are looming in our life.

    Isaiah 41:10 has been a favorite verse for many wonderful saints throughout the years. It reads like this, "Fear thou not; for I am with thee: be not dismayed; for I am thy God: I will strengthen thee; yea, I will help thee; yea, I will hold thee with my right hand of my righteousness." Many Giants of the Faith have rested in peace having this verse burned into their heart and mind. No matter what comes our way, this verse gives us confidence that God will be there every step of the way.

Often times in my life, sudden events have come my way that has threatened my future but God has sheltered me from all danger. Psalm 91:4 says, "He shall cover thee with his feathers and under his wings shalt thou trust: his truth shall be thy shield and buckler." More times than I could ever explain the Lord has overshadowed me with love and compassion. We find in Luke 15 the wonderful account of Christ leaving the ninety and nine and going after the one sheep in danger. The following story reminds me of that very account in the Bible.

Not long ago as I was on my way to work, the weather turned horrible and extremely slick. Living in Michigan, I found myself driving in some of the worst conditions I have ever seen. That day there were many accidents all around me; cars were in ditches, trucks were sliding into other trucks, and people had no control of their vehicles. My own personal car handles very well in the snow, but on this day I had no traction on the icy roads. My goal that morning was just to make it to work in one piece and I found even that to be a tough task.

My speed that morning never exceeded twenty miles per hour and I was nervous even being on the road. As I neared my destination, I was stopped by a red light and had major problems even stopping. When the light turned green, I recall, looking to my right and seeing a young man coming directly towards me going at around forty five miles per hour. It was to my amazement that the young man slammed on his brakes and somehow stopped his car on a dime. There was no way on earth he could have stopped in those conditions without help from God. To say it was impossible in those conditions would have been an understatement. We were both in total awe at what happened that day.

After that change of events, I arrived at work that morning and had a wonderful day. Psalm 33:8 says, "Let all the earth fear the Lord: let all the inhabitants of the world stand in awe of him." Moses said it best when he said, "Stand still and see the salvation of the Lord." When the Savior is driving the car you will have no need for an airbag. The Lord is all the protection we need.

Scriptures Chapter 29

1 Peter 1:8 "Whom having not seen, ye love; in whom, though now ye see him not, yet believing, ye rejoice with joy unspeakable and full of glory."

Psalm 34:7 "The angel of the Lord encampeth round about them that fear him, and delivereth them."

Daniel 3:25 "He answered and said, Lo, I see four men loose, walking in the midst of the fire, and they have no hurt; and the form of the fourth is like the Son of God."

Chapter 30
Jesus is Still Alive and Well

What sets us apart, as Christians, from every other religion on earth is the fact that our God got up on resurrection morning; while other leaders lie silent in the grave. If Christ would have stayed in the tomb we would be of all men most miserable. Jesus is alive and well and his power to redeem fallen men will never change. We have complete confidence as children of God that we can boldly enter into the throne room of grace, all thanks to the blood of this risen lamb. Hebrews 13:8 declares that Jesus is the same yesterday, today and forever. The following story will highlight the fact that Jesus is still alive and well, and He is willing and able to hear your feeble cry.

Not long ago, I received glorious news that a friend of mine, Charlene Parker, wanted to take pictures with my book as she travelled through the Holy Land. When I heard this news I was speechless and humbled. All throughout the next several weeks she would send me photos she took from Israel. The pictures that she took were absolutely outstanding. Charlene had pictures from; on top of Mount Carmel, alongside the Sea of Galilee, in Bethlehem, by Mount Calvary, and of course inside the empty tomb of Jesus.

When the final day arrived for Charlene to finish her tour of Israel, she happened to be inside the empty tomb. All throughout that week we were praying for seventy two degree weather with sunshine as she took those pictures. God wonderfully granted our prayers as the weather was a perfect seventy two degrees and sunny. The pictures could not have been more beautiful, but what took place that day after I saw the pictures was even more marvelous.

Immediately after I seen the pictures I asked God to direct me to the exact verses He wanted me to read for the day. I flipped open my Bible to Luke Chapter 24:6 where it says, "He is not here but is risen." Once I read the first six verses of that chapter, a peace came over me that I could never describe and I knew God directed me to those verses. Hours later as I was arriving home, I looked and my neighbor Dan was standing in my yard just like a statue. I opened the door and Dan said to me, with much joy, "Tony guess what I read today?" I responded by saying, "What did you read," and he said, "Tony I read Luke 24 under the inspiration of the Holy Ghost." He then told me at around eleven thirty that morning God told him to read that chapter and it opened his eyes like never before. When Dan told me this news tears began to flow down my face because earlier that same morning at the same exact time God also told me to read those exact same verses. Folks only God can do something like that.

The odds of the above story happening on the same day as Charlene was in the empty tomb is nearly impossible. Thank God for Matthew 19:26 which says, "With men this is impossible but with God all things are possible." Jesus is still alive and well everyone and He is doing just fine.

Scriptures Chapter 30

Luke 24:6 "He is not here, but is risen: remember how he spake unto you when he was yet in Galilee."

Matthew 19:26 "But Jesus beheld them, and said unto them, with men this is impossible; but with God all things are possible."

Conclusion

As we conclude this project, I would personally like to thank you for taking the time to read this book. I pray that your heart was blessed and your soul was stirred with each story. As I travel through this life, I cannot help but notice just how many people live a life of defeat on a daily basis. God had never intended for us to dwell in a state of depression. John 10:10 declares, that "Christ came that we may have life, and that we might have it more abundantly." The bible has every answer to any problem life throws our way. The greatest challenge we have in life is to remain positive and happy on a constant basis no matter how bad life gets.

My reason for writing these stories is to get folks to understand that God loves them very much and He wants the best for them. The vast majority of people I will ever meet make the mistake of blaming God for the problems they face, instead of Satan. The Bible declares that the devil is a master deceiver and he is out to destroy our lives. Satan wants nothing more than for us to dwell in a state of depression all the days of our life. We must train ourselves to know that we have the victory through Christ, and we have already won the war.

One day Satan will be thrown into a lake of fire and we will dance on a street of Gold for all eternity. God shed his blood for the sins of the world, so that we could escape the flames of hell. An old song says it like this "The love of God is greater far then tongue or pen could ever tell, it goes beyond the highest star and reaches to the lowest hell." Through God's word we find that He has offered us eternal life through Jesus Christ our Lord. Hebrews 2:9 proclaims, "That he tasted death for every man." We all know John 3:16 "For God so loved the world, that he gave his only begotten Son, that whosoever believeth in him should not perish but have everlasting life." Salvation of the soul is available to all mankind, but it is up to us to receive His free gift.

John 1:12 says, "But as many as received him to them gave he power to become the sons of God, even to them that believe on his name." There will be times in all of our lives when we will feel a tug from another world. During those rare and unusual times, God will invite you to come for the saving of your soul. Although God can lead you to the Water of Life, He cannot make you drink. It is up to you to receive or reject this free gift of salvation that is offered during your lifetime.

My goal in giving you these stories is to cause you to hunger for Christ like you never have before. Romans 10:13 says, "For whosoever shall call upon the name of the Lord shall be saved." If you will seek God when He is calling you, he has promised to hear your cry for help. Like the thief on the cross, you must admit your lost condition and trust in what Christ did on the cross for the redemption of your soul. You must believe that Christ died for you, that he was buried for you, and that he rose again the third day for you according to the scriptures. The only way to gain access into heaven is to come through Christ and through Christ alone. Millions have believed the gospel through the years, and millions have found a home in glory upon death.

When you come through Christ and Christ alone you will find acceptance from a Holy God. The bible says, "When I see the blood I will pass over you." Ephesians 1:7 says, "In whom we have redemption through his blood, the forgiveness of sins." Salvation was never meant to be hard, but rather very simple." Run to Christ while you feel His spirit pleading with you and you will find peace. Please do not wait too long you may never have tomorrow. Hebrews 9:27 declares, "And as it is appointed unto men once to die and after this the judgment." Do not face God with the knowledge you have; accept His free gift today while you have a chance. May God bless you all.

Scriptures Chapter ~ Conclusion

John 10:10 "I am come that they might have life, and that they might have it more abundantly."
Hebrews 2:9 "That he by the grace of God should taste death for every man."

John 3:16 "For God so loved the world, that he gave his only begotton Son, that whosoever believeth in him should not perish, but have everlasting life."

John 1:12 "But as many as received him, to them gave he power to become the sons of God, even to them that believe on his name."

Romans 10:13 "For whosoever shall call upon the name of the Lord shall be saved."

Ephesians 1:7 "In whom we have redemption through

his blood, the forgiveness of sins, according to the riches of his grace."

Hebrews 9:27 "And as it is appointed unto a man once to die, but after this the judgment."

Isaiah 55:6 "Seek ye the Lord while he may be found, call ye upon him while is near."

ANTHONY RITTHALER

Published By Parables

OUR MISSION

The primary mission of Published By Parables, a Christian publisher, is to publish Contemporary and Classic Christian books from an evangelical perspective that honors Christ and promotes the values and virtues of His Kingdom.

Are You An Aspiring Christian Author?

We fulfill our mission best by providing Christian authors and writers publishing options that are uniquely Christian, quick, affordable and easy to understand -- in an effort to please Christ who has called us to a writing ministry. We know the challenges of getting published, especially if you're a first-time author. God, who called you to write your book, will provide the grace sufficient to the task of getting it published.

We understand the value of a dollar; know the importance of producing a quality product; and publish what we publish for the glory of God.

Surf and Explore our site --
then use our easy-to-use "Tell Us" button
to tell us about yourself and about your book.

We're a one-stop, full-service Christian publisher.
We know our limits. We know our capabilities.
You won't be disappointed.

www.PublishedByParables.com

ANTHONY RITTHALER

PUBLISHED *by* PARABLE
Earthly Stories with a Heavenly Meaning

PUBLISHED by
PARABLES
Earthly Stories with a Heavenly Meaning

Anthony Ritthaler

Soaring With Eagles

A Book Of Freedom, Strength and Power

PUBLISHED by PARABLES
Earthly Stories with a Heavenly Meaning

ANTHONY RITTHALER

Pathways To The Past

Each volume stands alone as an Individual Book
Each volume stands together with others
to enhance the value of your collection

Build your Personal, Pastoral or Church Library
Pathways To The Past contains an ever-expanding list of
Christendom's most influencial authors

Augustine of Hippo
Athanasius
E. M. Bounds
John Bunyan
Brother Lawrence
Jessie Penn-Lewis
Bernard of Clairvaux
Andrew Murray
Watchman Nee
Arthur W. Pink
Hannah Whitall Smith
R. A. Torrey
A. W. Tozer
Jean-Pierre de Caussade
Thomas Watson
And many, many more.

Title: Soaring with Eagles
Anthony Ritthaler
Rights: All Rights Reserved
ISBN 978-1-945698-12-5
Doctrinal theology, Inspiration
Salvation, Meditation
Other books by this author include: Walking On The Water With Jesus (Volume 1 and 2) and A Devil From The Beginning.

Anthony Ritthaler

Soaring With Eagles

A Book Of Freedom, Strength and Power

PUBLISHED by PARABLES
Earthly Stories with a Heavenly Meaning

ANTHONY RITTHALER

Tony's Words Of Freedom, Strength and Power

"The Devil is a liar,
but an Eagle just flies higher."

"When danger is all around
the Eagle takes off to higher ground."

"We have a choice as Christians:
we can hang with the crows, or soar with the pros."

"Your finest hour will always be
when you soar with God's Power."

"Fly with the Lord in Power, Strength, and Glory
and never allow Satan to write your life's story."

"When others around you complain and cry,
be mature take off and fly."

"Whenever you soar with God
this world will think your odd."

"When you are fighting the World, the flesh, and the Devil allow the Holy Spirit to move you to a higher level."

"The greatest person in life is not he who obtains the most, but it is he who is controlled by the blessed Holy Ghost."

"If you desire to be rare, that's when God can take you anywhere."

"Those who have the touch from on High will always give Satan a black eye."

"An Eagle often flies alone, but his journey leads to Gods Throne."

"When you're facing all the Demons of Hell, just fly to God and sing it is well."

"When like the Eagle you soar to the mountain, God will allow you to drink from His fountain."

"When an Eagle takes flight he never looks back, but that won't stop the Pharisees from taking smack."

Table of Contents

Tony's Words Of Freedom, Strength and Power
Special Thanks
Introduction
1. God's Power on Full Display
2. Angels Among Us
3. Good Things Come to Those Who Wait
4. Prayer is Always the Answer
5. Peace be Still
6. The Highway to Hell
7. Jesus is Always Right on Time
8. Sheltered in the Arms of Jesus
9. Soaring with Eagles

10. I Put off the Old Coat and Put on the New
11. A Blissful Moment in Time
12. Hiding under the Shadows of the Almighty
13. All Things are Possible with God
14. Red and Yellow, Black and White, Their All Precious in His Sight
15. The Importance of Waiting on God
16. Jesus Knows Exactly What He is Doing
17. Surely Goodness and Mercy Shall follow Me All the Days of My Life
18. Love Conquers All
Conclusion

Special Thanks

There are five preachers in particular that I want to thank for their influence upon this book. Without their help through the years there is no way on earth this book would be possible. A big thank you goes out to Dr. Lawrence Mendez for his impact on my life. Without your preaching sir I would not be where I am today. Thank you Dr. Kidd for teaching me how to walk with the Lord; your impact on my life has been humbling. Thanks Evangelist Larry Bell for teaching me integrity through the life you live. Brother you are a rock sir and I love you so much in the Lord.

A very special thank you goes out to Evangelist Todd Hicks for always being there for me. My friend you have been a great encouragement and I'm honored to know you. Last but not least I want to thank my dear Pastor Timothy Ammon for his dedication over the years. Pastor I've learned a great deal through your ministry and it's a joy to serve at Hope Baptist Church.

Thanks to everyone else that also helped me along this road. I love you all so very much.

With Love
Bro Tony

Introduction

Welcome to my brand new project called, "Soaring with Eagles" I'm honored you would take time to read this book. I'm confident that you will not be disappointed. Each inspirational story has been coated with prayer with the conviction that this book will lift you to greater heights with God. This book will be a blessing and an encouragement to anyone searching for a deeper walk with the Master.

There are a variety of powerful, unique stories that will bless folks from all walks of life. As you read this project I'm confident that the Spirit of Almighty God will challenge you, bless you and cause you to hunger for power with God. Every story in this book has one ultimate purpose: to bring glory to the risen Lamb. Soaring with Eagles will encourage pastors, equip saints, and convict the sinner.

May Gods blessed Holy Spirit do a work in each and every life that takes time to dive into this book. Soaring with Eagles is meant for all Christians not just a select few. God wants us all to soar to heights not yet discovered and this book will give you the tools to make that happen.

My prayer is that thousands who live in fear and dismay will raise up out of there depressed state and will soar to God with complete confidence that Christ loves them and longs to use them like never before.

Enjoy the book everyone and soar for His honor and for His Glory all the days of your life.

Phillipians 4:13 "I can do all things through Christ which strengtheneth me."

Chapter One

God's Power on Full Display

Throughout history there have been countless warriors of the faith who have seen and done wonders through a spirit filled life. Men and women, who have ignored the skeptics and have accomplished marvelous things through the power of a higher source. Men like Charles Finney: he once saw 50,000 people saved in one week; or women like Fanny Crosby who was used by God to touch millions of lives through her beautiful hymns.

In days of old many Christians could move mountains through the strength of their prayer lives. Today, unfortunately, these stories are rare: and it's all due to how people live.

Hebrews 13:8 says," Jesus Christ is the same yesterday, today, and forever." The Bible clearly tells us that God never changes, and He never will. Sadly it's us who have changed and we have no one to blame but ourselves for the lack of miracles we see on a daily basis. Please allow the following story to minister to you and fire you back up for God again.

A few years ago, God in heaven opened up a door for my family and allowed us to move from a condo in Canton, Michigan to a house in Romulus, Michigan. To watch God work throughout the moving process was humbling in every way. Quickly, after we moved in, we discovered that a new roof was needed. We had about 6,000 dollars left over from the move so I contacted a man I knew about putting a new roof on for us. The man's name was Miguel and he, along with his whole family, agreed to do our roof for just over 5,000 dollars. The labor took around 5 days and we were amazed by the work he and his family did. Miguel notified me that he ran out of daylight to put on the sealer that would prevent water from getting under our roof but Monday after work He would complete it for us.

Monday came and as we were working we received horrible news and it came suddenly. The news report said rain is coming and it's coming fast so be ready. When we heard the news Miguel immediately left to go put the sealer on but on his way to my house rain pounded the area. Once I personally heard the news I quickly begged the Lord to keep my roof safe and God heard my feeble cry.

My dear mother happened to be over that day and she had a front row seat to one of the greatest miracles she ever witnessed. She told me over the phone that it was raining everywhere around her except in our yard. My mom said rain was pounding every house around her but God refused to allow the rain to come inside our fence. For over 40 minutes this took place and she said it looked like a hand was holding it back. God proved His power that day and through His grace our roof was spared.

We serve a God of wonders and a God who wants to display His power like in days gone by. What we saw that day left many speechless and we will remember this story forever. Folks, nothing is too hard for God and the clouds are nothing more than the dust of His feet.

Chapter 2

Angels Among Us

Whether people choose to believe it or not I'm telling you by the authenticity of the Word of God angels are among us. The Bible is loaded with accounts from the Old Testament and the New Testament of angels appearing suddenly with a message from the Lord.

Personally I know of five times in my life where God sent an angel along my pathway and so many could give the same testimony. If God would open our spiritual eyes we would stand in amazement by how many angels were standing nearby. The Bible says in II Kings 6:17 that Elisha prayed for God to open a young man's eyes and when He did the mountain was full of horses and chariots of fire. Angels are among us folks and that's why it's so important to live right. You see, most people who see angels walk with God. The following story was a blessing to me and I pray it will be a blessing to you.

One Saturday night as I was preparing my Sunday morning lesson verses started dancing through my mind about the subject of angels. Within thirty minutes I had over 100 verses written down about angels and around ten stories of folks that met them from people I know. Power filled my house and peace filled my heart as I wrote down the title of my message, "Angels among us." The very next morning as we were traveling to the church the Spirit of God was present and I could not wait to teach this little lesson. I remember walking into the building and being approached by one of my teens and her glow was amazing. Before anyone else arrived that morning she began to tell me all about her week and the angel she meet. The story she gave me was incredible and it was very detailed. After hearing her story I had no doubt in my mind that God had sent an angel her way to simply encourage her. After she gave me this story the bus arrived and a few more teens joined us for the message. A young women came that morning. I had never seen her before, and, imagine this -- out of all the names she could of had it was the name, Angelica. She told me after class that day that something told her to come to church that morning so she came. Angelica was never there before and she has never come back but she came that day. The Power of God was with us that morning and all the teens were weeping after they heard this message.

My friends, angels are very much among us and I venture to say you have come across a few in your day, Psalms 34:7 says this, "The angel of the Lord encampeth round about them that fear Him, and delivereth them."

Keep your eyes open my friends for you never know when one is nearby.

Chapter 3

Good Things Come to Those Who Wait

The Word of God is full of stories that express the great benefits of waiting on God. Psalms 15:4 says, "For whatsoever things were written aforetime were written for our learning, that we through patience and comfort of the scriptures might have hope." God led men to pen down these stories so that generations to come could learn how to conduct their lives properly. Perhaps the greatest story about waiting on God and enjoying its benefits is the story about Abraham and Isaac. We all understand that Abraham was a man of great faith; who trusted God every step of the way. Time after time throughout his life God tested his faith by bringing trials into his life. Each test was passed with flying colors and each trial brought him closer to the Lord.

One day God appeared to Abraham and told him that even though he was to old to produce offspring Abraham would! He was destined by God to become a father again and his elderly wife Sarah would bring forth the promised seed. Although Abraham did not understand how this could happen he trusted God for 25 years and never gave up. At 90 years of age Sarah gave birth and Abraham became the father of Isaac. God called Abraham a friend of God, a term He never gave anyone else and it's all due to Abraham's faith in God. How many of us would have doubted God and thrown in the towel before 25 years had passed?

Many people lose out on God's blessings because they grow weary of waiting on God. The Bible still teaches that "all things work together for good to them that love God, to them who are called according to his purpose." Sometimes God will bring instant answers to prayer; but not always. We pray and our prayers are answered according to His timing. Everything will work out according to His will. We must learn how to lean on Him for every need rather than ourselves. God has a plan and purpose for everything that happens. If you're going through a trial please understand that God has a reason for it. The more you trust God the greater your life will turn out. This next story will prove that good things come to those who wait and who pray.

The Word of God tells us in Psalms 37:4 to "delight thyself also in the Lord; and He shall give thee desires of thine heart." Personally I cling to this promise daily along with many other promises from God's Word. We serve a gracious and loving God who desires to bless us through the course of our lives. I believe that when we love God and serve others God will be sure to reward us with desires we have as well. My dear wife is a music teacher and she does not ask for much at all. One day she came to me with two requests to pray over. She said, "I've always wanted a piano so I can practice at home and teach my children music. I also would like a curio cabinet to store my different little items in." My response to my dear wife was that we will make this a matter of prayer and trust God for as long as it takes. Around one year later we received a call from Erin's mother that was a blessing beyond measure. Through this phone call it was made known to us that a dear lady in Hillsdale, Michigan felt led to give us a piano. She told my wife that she wanted to give her the piano to be a blessing to our family. Shortly after this conversation ended our telephone rang again and this time it was my wife's best friend Megan on the other line. Megan said, "Erin, do you have any room for a curio cabinet I want to give it to you. Folks, after waiting a whole year for God's direction He saw fit to bless us with both gifts within the same hour.

Chapter 4

Prayer Is Always The Answer

What ever happened to people who could get a hold of God without much struggle? Let me ask another question. Whatever happened to people who lived with clean hands, clean minds, and clean hearts?

In these last days finding this combination in people is like finding a needle in a haystack. Christians today have filthy, darkened hearts, and dirty minds. Psalms 66:18 clearly states, "If I regard iniquity in my heart the Lord will not hear me." Christians all over this country spend most of their time trying to impress people and they don't even care about pleasing God. Christians in this day and age fill their lives with busy schedules and they forget all about God. Men of God who mounted the pulpits 200 years ago lived clean lives and prayed for hours every day and it' brought revival. Today preachers are too busy to pray and it shows through their preaching. Revival seems to be a thing of the past and that's because members and pastors have become lazy in the work of God. The Bible teaches over and over again that Gods power is available to those who hunger and thirst after righteousness. We need a whole army of people with passion again who care more about pleasing God than they do pleasing themselves.

The following story demonstrates the importance of having a clean life before God. People depend on us to pray for them and if we are away from God they will walk away empty. Allow this story to help you live a holy life.

A dear man from my work came to me broke and crying one day and I could tell he needed help. This man did not attend church but he was always a blessing to me so I wanted to be a blessing to him. This man quickly asked for money and I quickly said I'm broke but God is not. We bowed our heads right there and I said a quick prayer. My exact words were, "Lord this man has been a blessing to me, please help him in Jesus name amen." I'm glad to report that night after work a woman knocked on this man's door with a check for 2,500 dollars. God will not work through an unclean vessel and it's essential to others that we are effective prayer warriors. Ask yourself right now: when is the last time I know that God heard and answered my prayer? If it's been a while come clean with the Lord today? Souls of men and women hang in the balance.

CHAPTER 5

PEACE BE STILL

It's amazing to me that the worst storm the disciples ever encountered was calmed by just three words, "PEACE BE STILL". When Jesus is close by fear melts away by the sweet sound of His voice. Millions of people all around this universe run to doctors, shrinks, and educated people when trouble arises and those same people leave empty and void of help. Jesus is willing and waiting to help us but most will make Him their last option. There is great power in the name of Jesus Christ and if we have any sense about us we will run to His loving arms when tragedy strikes. The Word of God says in Psalms 34:19,"Many are the afflictions of the righteous but the Lord delivereth out of them all". No matter what storm we find ourselves in we can find deliverance through just three words from the Master "PEACE BE STILL" Allow God to speak to your heart through this next story.

One afternoon, while waiting for my food at McDonalds, I struck up a conversation with a dear woman and her young daughter. The conversation was going well and God's

Spirit was convicting their hearts. As we were speaking I remember looking over to my right and seeing that young daughter start shaking and foaming at the mouth. I quickly turned to the mother and asked what was going on and she said a seizure and this is a big one. People began to rush to her aid to help but I knew we serve the greatest doctor of all. I quickly stepped back and uttered three words, "peace be still". When I said those words that young girl stopped shaking and her body calmed completely down instantly. Her dear mother sat her down so that she could recover. As I went to leave that young girl looked my way and smiled.

Why do we have so much fear when Jesus is near? Stop going to earthly counselors when troubles come! Go to the only one who can calm you spirit - the Lord Jesus Christ. Amen and Amen.

Chapter 6

The Highway to Hell

The greatest tool the devil uses in destroying people is wicked, ungodly music. The devil uses his music to influence and pollute the minds of untold millions. God's music will always bring joy, peace and contentment. The devil's music will preach pain, rebellion and misery. Many of the famous rock and roll singers willingly admit that they worship Satan. Nothing will cause people to slide towards hell's flames faster than wicked music. Every time I hear rock and roll in public it grieves my spirit and it makes me very uneasy.

There have been thousands of murders, suicides and fatal decisions caused by people who were under the influence of rock and roll music. Every teen I've ever known who has listened to this music over the years has paid a high price. Once this music enters someone's brain, the chains of bondage will enter into their souls and the devil will enter into their life. The devil will use his music to steal every ounce of joy and power from that person's life. Don't fall prey to the devil. If you listen to this junk get rid of it as fast as you can.

The following story was such a blessing to me because it shut the devil up for a little while. May God bless you through this simple story.

Around four years ago I was at work having one of those stressful, tiresome days and I could not wait to go home. My head was hurting and my body was worn out. I can remember looking at the clock and noticing we only had about an hour left. Moments later a man came in and started blasting a song on the radio called, "Highway to Hell." The absolute last thing I needed at that time was to hear that song so I prayed that God would turn that nonsense off for me. Seconds later the bay door of the shop opened and the wind that rushed in messed with the signal and static filled the air. Three people tried to fix the radio but they could not do it. Finally a man got frustrated and unplugged the radio for good. The rest of the day was peaceful and I'm thankful God answered that prayer.

Why would anyone allow the devil to flood their mind with that trash? If I were you I would leave the devil where he is standing and I would run to Jesus and never look back. Thank God for the victory we have in Christ Jesus.

Please throw the devils music in the trash and replace it with songs that honor God.

If you do, I promise you can leave the highway to hell and you can travel on the highway to heaven.

Chapter 7

Jesus is Always Right on Time

The account of Jesus raising Lazarus from the dead has blessed me my entire life. When others were wondering why Jesus was taking so long, Jesus knew what He was doing and the timing was absolutely perfect. Jesus should never be doubted by fallen man and if He made a promise from His Word it will come to pass. Jesus promised to never leave us nor forsake us and to supply our every need. We, as Christians, doubt God's Word so often and it really affect's our lives. We must understand through life we will have many ups and downs but we will never be alone in this journey. We must trust God at all times and believe that He is working on our behalf. Jesus knows the beginning from the end and if we can't trust Him then who can we trust? Jesus is working behind the scenes of your life and just because you can't see Him it does not mean He is not there. Let me share a story that will help us realize the beauty of God's perfect timing.

Not long ago we fell on hard times and we were concerned

about finances. We had no idea how God would provide. We just knew that He would. During challenging times the devil works overtime to discourage us and cause us to doubt God. My wife asked me how will we get the money to pay our bills. I had no answer. I just knew God would take care of it. Minutes later I received a check in the mail for $554.10. The timing was perfect and we gave God the glory. Shortly after this happened more money came in and it was for $94.79. After the second check came in I looked at my wife and said, "Honey, God has everything under control and His timing is always perfect."

All around the world, on a daily basis, God in heaven does things of this nature for His children. We serve a great God who loves and cares for us. It's high time we stop doubting the Lord and start trusting His every move in our lives. God will never fail us one time.

Chapter 8

Sheltered in the Arms of Jesus

The Word of God teaches in Matthew 18:10 that every child has a guardian angel watching over them. So many people around this world could stand up and tell stories of how their children were heading into danger and something kept them safe. There is an unseen hand of love that hovers around children all around this earth. Personally I've seen this with my daughter numerous times and my wife and I have stood in amazement by all the times God has shown mercy on her. There has always been a special relationship between Jesus and children and that relationship will never change. Jesus loves to reach down and hold children in His arms and He sends His angels to shelter them from many dangerous situations. There are a lot of stories I can give on this subject that would bless your heart but I will just give you one to prove Matthew 18:10 is true.

A few months ago my family and I took a trip to Hillsdale, Michigan to spend time with friends and family. The weather was awesome that week and the fellowship was a blessing as well. My daughter fell in love with the four-wheeler that week and we had a blast driving that thing around. On the last day of our stay in Hillsdale my daughter Hope wanted to ride the four-wheeler one last time so we jumped on and took one final ride. We drove to many different places, up and down hills, around the property and eventually we ended up in a corn field. My daughter said, "Daddy go faster, go faster, so I said, "Hold on tight and we will." We started going very fast and I underestimated how much land we had left and I was running out of room to stop safely. My only option was to slam on the brakes and when I did my precious daughter went flying off the four-wheeler. When she landed on the ground it was like she landed on a pillow and there was no doubt an angel was close by. I quickly parked the four-wheeler and asked Hope if she was O.K. She looked at me and said, "I'm O.K. daddy; let's ride again." Anything could have happened that day especially at the speed we were going but God showed mercy on us that day.

Isn't it wonderful how Jesus shelters children? No man or woman can explain moments like this but we just know it happens. Thank God for a merciful and loving God.

Chapter 9

Soaring With Eagles

    The chapter that you are about to read will make the hairs on the back of your neck stand up. I'm confident that this chapter will stand out in your mind as one of the most powerful stories you have ever read. For three solid weeks the Lord over shadowed me and the details of this story will amaze you. Even when I look back at this story now, I still stand in awe by what God did throughout the course of these three weeks. There is no possible way with human tongue I could properly explain every single event that took place but with the help of God I will do my best. Please give me your undivided attention as we travel through a three week period that was totally ordained by God. May God's power fall upon you while you read this story.

    One day as my three year old daughter and I were walking through Cracker Barrel I saw something that caught my eye. The moment I laid my eyes upon it I knew, without a shadow of a doubt, I wanted to get it for a preacher friend of mine. What my daughter and I saw that day was amazing to behold and very unique. The item was a four foot statue of an eagle sitting on top of the Liberty Bell and it was a limited edition. Once I decided to get this statue I pulled my daughter close to me and we both prayed for it right there in the store with everyone looking at us. Our prayer to the Lord was full of faith and we asked Him to send the money quickly. Two days later while driving up the road at 2:45 PM God gave me peace that our prayer had been heard. When I arrived home that day I looked in the mail box and there were two checks waiting there for me. One check was for 873 dollars and the other check was for 94 dollars. After receiving these checks we went to the bank and cashed them and went straight back to the Cracked Barrel and bought that eagle statue. We took the statue to my parent's house and stored it there for the night and they loved it as well. On my drive home that night I remember God dealing with me stronger than He ever had before about teaching a lesson called, "Soaring with Eagles". All that night the Lord dealt with me about it and when the morning light hit I had total peace about teaching it the following Sunday morning. The moment I publicly announced I was teaching on the subject, "Soaring with Eagles" God's power struck me like never before – it was awesome! Immediately after this happened I sent a text to a woman and told her what I was teaching and I said, "never in my life had I felt God so strongly." As these words left my mouth a horn beeped from the distance and a truck pulled up for me to unload at work. When it got closer I noticed the company name and out of all the names it could have been it was the Allied Eagle Company. We unloaded 837 items from the truck and every item had an eagle on it. Moments later I received a call from a man I hadn't heard from in a while and he had amazing news. The man on the other line said, "Tony, I'm working at a new golf course right now and I want you to know that anytime you want to golf for the rest of your life you can for free." I responded by saying wow sir, what coarse is this? He responded back and said, "EAGLE CREST," Tony. Out of all the golf courses it could have been it was the one with the word Eagle in it.

All throughout the remainder of that week leading up to Sunday there were eagles at literally every place I went. We knocked on eleven doors that Saturday and every single house had something with eagles on it. In one week we had seen over 1,500 items with eagles on them. Every move we made and every step we took that week was directed by God Almighty.

Sunday finally arrived and I was fired up to preach. We brought that big eagle statue into the services and recorded the message that morning. God moved in a mighty way and four teens were born again. To describe the power we all felt that day is impossible and so many lives were changed. After the service concluded God started dealing with my heart to preach a volume two of this message, because more needed to be helped. I'll never forget after the service a man took us to I-Hops and God was still dealing with me. At I-Hops they give you a name of someone famous from the past and when it's your time to eat they call you by that name to your table. Out of all the names we could have received that Sunday we received Mr. Glen Frey , the lead singer of the musical group called - The Eagles. On the way to Hillsdale, Michigan the following day I asked the Lord to make it clear if He wanted me to teach a volume two of this message. At the moment I had this thought I looked and I saw a seventy-five foot eagle balloon starting back at me and I surrendered to God's will right then and there.

All through out that next week as well eagles were everywhere and so was God's presence. When Sunday arrived we preached, "Soaring with Eagles - Volume two" and a wind from another world swept through that place. A young man from our church was kind enough to record both messages so I asked him to turn it into a video for me. The young man agreed and what happened next is staggering. The very next morning this young man was walking with his boss with my messages in his hand and from out of nowhere a real live eagle landed at his feet. This young man said the eagle was older and it stared at him for what seemed like an eternity before it flew off. He also said his boss was shaking and he stood in amazement that day. The following Saturday, the preacher I wanted to give that statue too was in town, so I went to see him and brought the eagle statue with me. The preacher loved the statue and we took a picture together. After this took place a guest preacher stood up and this is what he said," Folks I do not know why but tonight God changed my message and I want to preach a message called "Soaring with Eagles." I'm telling you God moved across that church and we saw five saved that night.

    At the end of these three powerful weeks, on the final day of these amazing events, God did one last thing that put a stamp of approval on it all. As I was driving home on a Monday morning from work it felt like God grabbed my steering wheel and led me in a different direction. I felt like the Lord was driving the car and he led me to a gas station. When I got out of the car I could not believe my eyes. At the Arab owned gas station there was a four foot tall eagle statue on top of the Liberty Bell with an American flag sticking out of it. When I saw that eagle statue I thanked God for the powerful three weeks He allowed me to experience.

    So many other things happened in those three weeks that I did not include in this chapter but I assure you they were all from God. All in all, we had seen over 2,000 items with eagles on them in three weeks. Never in my life have I sensed such power as I did for that time period and I will never forget it till the day I die.

In closing this chapter I want to quote Isaiah 40:31. "But they that wait upon the Lord shall renew their strength; they shall mount up with wings as eagles; they shall run, and not be weary; and they shall walk, and not faint."

Chapter 10

I Put Off the Old Coat and Put on the New

Whenever a person makes their way towards Jesus Christ and accepts His free gift of salvation, automatically he goes from rags to riches spiritually. When we are born we inherit a sinful nature, but when we are born again we receive a brand new nature. In the book of II Corinthians 5:17 Jesus tells us that if any man be in Christ he is a new creature, old things are passed away; behold all things are become new. Although we cannot see it with the natural eye salvation brings instant change from God. At the moment of conversion God takes off are old, filthy, stinky rags and puts on a new, clean and fresh garment of righteousness. Isaiah 64:6 says, "all our righteousness' are as filthy rags." But Psalms 103:12 declares that our sins are "forever removed and forgotten" when we are washed in the blood. It is a spiritual cleansing that sticks with you forever. Salvation brings a sudden change and a new standing with God. We are no longer vile and wretched in the sight of God but instead we are justified and pure through the sacrifice of Christ. Salvation is the greatest thing that can ever happen to you and if you have it you ought to tell others about it. An old black preacher once said, "When I got born the first time momma told me about it, but when I got born the second time I told momma about it." When you match the dingy, old, dirty coat up against God's new amazing coat there is no comparison. Thank God for His love, mercy and compassion. We are so unworthy. For the rest of this chapter I will share with you a story from my past that fits this chapter perfectly. People enjoy this story and it is a good picture of His mercy on us. Allow God to bless your heart with this story.

Many years ago as we were serving God in the city of Detroit God granted me a special blessing one night. My mother had been telling me that it was time to get a new suit because all of my suits were either dated, worn out or old. At that time I was sending all my money to help the church in Detroit; and, I felt guilty about the idea of buying myself a suit. I told my mom that if God wanted me to have a suit He would lead someone else to buy one for me. The Bible says in Matthew 6:28 "take no thought for raiment for He would provide it in due season if I trusted in Him." Around a week after our conversation took place a godly man asked if he could speak to me after the service. He took me to his van and pulled out a beautiful blue suit and said I hope it fits. He went on to say that the Lord smote his heart and told him to buy it for me. That suit was very nice and I wore it for ten years. Matthews 6:33 says it like this, "Seek ye first the kingdom of God and his righteousness and all these other things will be added unto you." It was a great feeling that night to take off my old used worn out coat and slip on that beautiful new one. Philippians 4:19 says "But my God shall supply all your need according to His riches in glory by Christ Jesus." Blessings from God never get old, but only newer and newer the more you tell them. Thank God for salvation, and how He cleans us up through the blood of His precious Son.

Chapter 11

A Blissful Moment in Time

Nothing in this world thrills and excites me more than reading about great men and women who changed the landscape of their generation through faith. When I read history I marvel at the dedication and effort that people made to make this world a better place.

Billy Sunday preached daily and fought the Devil constantly and saw around one million saved. Charles Spurgeon read 6 books a week, preached 10 times a week wrote 140 books, preached to 10 million, and personally answered around 500 letters a week. Fanny Crosby wrote around 500 songs a year for about 40 straight years. History is filled with such people who were instrumental in changing the world for the kingdom of God.

In the following story I will tell you about a miracle that happened as I was studying about a great man named Phillip Bliss. As I express to you this story think of how rare this story really is and let's give glory to the matchless name of Jesus. I sure hope you enjoy this story.

One night around 5 years ago I was sitting in my chair reading about a songwriter named Phillip Bliss. As I was reading the Holy Spirit was turning me inside out and tears were streaming down my face. Phillip Bliss was responsible for penning some of the greatest hymns ever written and he was totally surrendered to Christ. D.L. Moody once said. "Mr. Bliss was the most talented man he ever met but yet the most humble as well. Another man said, "He never seen Mr. Bliss in public without a smile and a glow." I remember reading for hours that night and feeling weak from weeping.

The very next night we had Wednesday evening service and my dear pastor Timothy Ammon wanted to speak to me after services. After the preaching concluded we went into his office and talked for a minute. Pastor Ammon then gave me a package and said, "This is a book just for you. Tony for many years, people have tried to get this book from me but I didn't have peace about giving it away but now I do, please enjoy it." Pastor closed by saying, "Open it in your car." I said, "Sure."

When I opened my car I sat down and began to unwrap it. As I read the title I could not believe my eyes. The book was entitled, "The life and times of Phillip Bliss" and it was from the 1800's. As I gazed on that book God's power fell on me for around 30 minutes. Folks that is beyond rare; AMEN. Two years later I felt a need to reach out to a young man who was hungry for God. My mindset that day was to feed him as much hymn history as possible and some how I got around to sharing with him the history of Phillip Bliss. The very next day something outstanding took place. While working in Detroit I received a long text from the same young man I talked with the day before. He said, "Tony, are you sitting down?" I responded, "Yes Sir." He proceeded to tell a story that was hard to believe. He said, "Tony, as I was working at Wal-Mart this morning I heard a voice over the loud speaker that said Phillip Bliss report to the front." He said, "I ran up to the front to see if I could catch him but no one was there."

The day before we talked about Phillip Bliss who lived in the 1800's and the next day that exact name blasted over the loud speaker so everyone could hear that wonderful name.

I'm grateful for God's amazing kindness. He is such a great Savior

Chapter 12

Hiding Under the Shadows of the Almighty

As I grow older in the Lord I find myself somewhere in the book of Psalms every day. The book of Psalms covers every aspect of life and its pages refresh me daily. Many great Christian's today run to the book of Psalms whenever danger is near and I must admit I do too. Nearly every verse in this wonderful book will motivate you to serve God at a higher level than you did the day before.

With the rest of this chapter I want to highlight what God can do for those who hide under the shadow of the Almighty. I pray this chapter magnifies the name of our Great God.

A few years ago as I was on the internet listening to music I heard that the Talley's were going to be in my area singing for God's glory. I've always liked the Talley's songs and their family has a rich history of honoring the Lord so I quickly bought two tickets for my dad and me. All throughout the day of the concert God directed me to Psalms 91 and He would not give me peace about reading anything else that day. As we arrived at the church to hear the singing God swept over my soul that night. My main desire, that night, was to hear the singing, meet the Talley's and give them a signed book. When the concert was over people flooded their table so I stayed behind and read Psalms 91:4 over and over again. A great peace filled my heart as I read that great verse for the final time. Once the reading was over I walked up to the Talley's CD table and we talked for a minute. Mrs. Debra Talley stopped in mid sentence and said I have something for you to have sir; wait a second. Mrs. Talley then came back with a book and said I am going to sign my favorite verse in here for you. She grabbed the writer's pen and wrote down Psalms 91:4 and smiled at me. Folks it is not by accident she signed that verse for that is the exact verse God directed me to all day.

When we abide under his wings we will always be better for it. Trust God, do what He says, for His power is great and His understanding is infinite. Life is very simple get out of the way and let Jesus lead the why. Abide under the shadows of the Almighty and God will help you all your days.

CHAPTER 13

ALL THINGS ARE POSSIBLE WITH GOD

Never allow negative hurtful people to rob you of your dreams. There are folks all over the world that will cast doubt and gloom on our visions and dreams and the best thing we can do is eliminate those people from our lives. The older I'm getting the more I'm surrounding myself with folks that truly share in my visions and will support me instead of drain me. Always remember as long as Joseph was around his jealous family his life never took off for God's glory. When he got away from these bad influences he soared with God and became second in command in the land of Egypt.

All the great business people of this world warn against listening to bad advice and as Christians we need to heed the same advice. I don't care how long someone has been going to church if they offer no support and bad advice I'm junking it because it will harm me later down the road. The Bible says that we ought to obey God rather than man. Believe in yourself and trust that God can do anything whether others think so or not. With God anything is possible and these events that follow will prove just that.

I woke up one Saturday morning and I could not get a gospel singing group from Tennessee out of my mind. The group that was on my mind was a famous group called Legacy Five. The Lord laid it heavy on my heart that morning to get them my book, "Walking on the water with Jesus" as soon as possible. My first thought was to send a book to their address but God quickly changed my mind and I dropped to my knees in prayer. My prayer to God was simply this, "Lord please allow this book to make it to the Legacy Five safe and sound. Thank you Lord, amen." After my prayer had ended I noticed that I had received a picture and it was from my dear wife. My wife was stopped by a red light and she looked over and right next to her was the Legacy Five tour bus and she took a picture. When she sent the picture it happened to be just minutes from where we lived. Legacy Five was performing just miles up the road so I went to take them my book. Before I got out of the car I asked the Lord to make it easy and God answered my prayer. I opened my car door and just a matter of steps away, was Scott Fowler, lead singer of Legacy Five and I handed him the book.

Months later God laid it on my heart to get a book to Mr. Jason Crabb which was not an easy feat. I found out that my dear friend Brad Ledbetter was singing at the National Quartet Convention and that Jason Crabb would be there as well. Mr. Crabb is one of the most famous singers in America and the odds of getting a book to him were nearly impossible but my friend agreed to try. At the National Quartet Convention there are thousands of people and hundreds of singers. For the next few days I prayed about this situation and after two days I received a message from my friend and it was amazing news. Brad Ledbetter said, "Tony, you won't believe this but they put Jason Crabb's booth right next to mine so I can get him your book." My response was, "oh I believe it brother because prayers work." We both gave God the glory for what he did that day.

Around 6 months later as I was teaching my teen class I made the statement that my next goal was to get my book to Mr. Bill Gaither. After making this statement a teen shouted out, "You will never get it to him. He is the most famous song writer in the world." I quickly told the young man never to make that statement and that God would answer this prayer through faith.

A few months later Gaither tickets became available to me and I told my mom this is ordained of God and I ordered two tickets to see Bill Gaither. All throughout the day of that concert I told my mother we are going for a reason; trust me God will make it easy. Normally the Gaithers pack out arenas easily but on this night they had a low turnout. My mother sat back in amazement as I walked directly up to all the Gaither members and gave them my book. Nothing is impossible with God and this last story will be a final stamp of authority on this subject.

Many experts will agree that the hardest challenge in the world today is for a common man to get an opportunity to speak to the president, or presidential candidates. Many people laughed when I told them that by the end of the year I would get my book to Mr. Ted Cruz. Folks, no one is laughing now. In three short months after making this statement God raised up three people who I never met to personally hand my book to Mr. Ted Cruz. The odds of this happening were off the charts and I still praise God for what He did in all these different events.

The moral of this story is simple. Don't allow others to

control your; life rather allow God's Spirit to. Soar with God, without the permission of others. All my life people have hurt me, tried to stop me, and cast doubt on what I'm doing but the less I listen to that noise the more I attain joy. Always remember people called Einstein and Edison stupid when they were young but history records they changed the world through their wisdom. The great book, "The Cat in the Hat," was rejected 27 times before a publisher accepted it. Before Mr. Seuss died millions upon millions were sold.

People will always rise up to stop you when you go to make a difference. My advice, kill them with kindness and go on for the glory of God. Jude 22 "And of some have compassion making a difference."

Chapter 14

Red and Yellow; Black and White; They're All Precious in His Sight

There was a song I learned as a little boy that spoke volumes to my soul concerning the mind of God. The song is titled, "Jesus loves the little children of the world." Within this little song was a phrase that opened up God's mind and God's heart to me at a very young age. The phrase reads like this, "Red and yellow; black and white; they're all precious in His sight." Jesus died for all the children of the world. Once I allowed this song to sink into my heart I realized that God is not a racist nor does He prejudge anyone. No! God is loving and caring. Jesus wants the best for each of us. Many do not see this. Most people that I've come across allow Satan to convince them that anytime something goes wrong it is God's fault. Always remember Jesus willingly died for the sins of the world and Satan is the great deceiver. If the Devil can get people to believe this he will take their hope, their strength, and eventually their life.

Statistics say that around 80% of what people say or do is negative in its nature. The Devil has folks confused and defeated before they even make it out of their bed each morning. There is a spiritual battle that rages daily and it takes place between our ears. God wants your mind according to Philippians 2:5 and Satan wants it as well according to II Corinthians 4:4 . How our lives turn out is totally dependent on who we allow to control our minds. We must train ourselves to think positive and Godly in this present evil world. If we don't we are no match for the Devil. No matter what your problems are, the answer is found in a great God who cares for you whether you believe it or not.

This next story proves to the world that through prayer anything is obtainable. Allow God to encourage you with this following story.

Every day of my life I rub shoulders with folks that willingly tell me about their many problems. It amazes me what some go through and it breaks my heart. People are giving up on life and depression is claiming thousands every year. All I can do as a man of God is offer hope through a man named Jesus Christ. Some will receive it and some will reject it but my job is to reach out with a loving heart. One day a man approached me and his list of problems were longer than anyone I've ever met. Every day he carried bitterness and unforgiveness around with him and I could see the pain on his face. This man has always been kind to me but if anyone brought up God he would curse and scream. One day he asked me if I wanted a pop and for some reason it touched my heart and I said, "Sure my friend and thank you." I remember looking at him and saying, "Sir I will pray that God shows compassion on you tonight for helping me just now. He looked at me and said ," Tony, all my life it has been a train wreak and I do not believe in God like you do." I turned to him and said," We will talk tomorrow, let me know what happens." The very next day he came to me with joy and told me a wonderful story that thrilled my soul.

He said," Tony, as I was walking up my driveway today towards my house I looked and there was $40 staring back at me." He said," Tony that was the first time in my life something good has happened to me." I said, "Randy, God did that for you to prove that He loves and cares for you," Randy walked away smiling while holding that $40 in his hands.

If we let go of our bitterness and look towards the Son things will always become brighter on our pathway. Let me close with this verse in Psalms 16:11 that says, " Thou wilt shew me the path of life: in thy presence is fulness of joy; at thy right hand there are pleasures for evermore."

Chapter 15

The Importance of Waiting on God

Every single day of my life I try to stress the importance of waiting on God in every decision we make. There are literally hundreds of verses about being patient and waiting for the guidance of a loving Savior. In my 35 years in church I've sadly watched teenager after teenager gather many scars and regrets through quick decisions made without God's help. Even sadder is the large number of adults I've known who have found themselves in a world of hurt because they tried to outrun God instead of listening to His Spirit.

Proverbs 14:12 teaches that, "There is a way which seemeth right unto a man, but the end there of are the ways of death."

Never trust your feelings, flesh and emotions over God's Word which never fails. Feelings and emotions change daily but for 6,000 years God's Word has never changed. Every decision we make needs to be ordered by the Lord. With God's leadership we will find peace and rest. Anything outside of this will result in ruin and it will be as sinking sand. Psalm

46:10 has helped me more often than any verse in God's holy Word when it comes to waiting on God. In nearly every Bible bookstore in this country you will find this phrase, "be still and know that I am God."

I hope and pray that this following story will stress the importance of waiting on God in our everyday life.

Not long ago my dear wife came to me and asked if we could look for a 42 inch flat screen TV. It had been a while since we got anything for ourselves so I said sure lets go take a look. We got in the car and traveled 20 minutes to a store and looked at all their TV's. As we were looking I began to feel a sense of peace. I told my wife that tonight is not the night, lets wait a few weeks. We went home that night obeying the voice of God and not our flesh and God was pleased. About 2 weeks later we received a call from a dear friend and the news was glorious. The women on the other line said to my wife, "Erin, do you need a 42 inch flat screen TV? I've only used it a few times." We quickly said "yes, we would." Not only did God reward us for waiting, He gave us exactly the same TV we were looking at a few weeks earlier at the store.

We will have a greater sense of joy and peace if we learn to wait on God. If we learn this simple principle of God life will be much more enjoyable. Thank God's for his sweet Holy Spirit in our lives. I do not want to ever be in a hurry while serving God however I want to be in a position where I can hear his still small voice at any time wherever I am. Many miss his voice because they attempt to out run the Lord. That is always a mistake in whatever decision we make. Waiting on God is so important and I hope many have learned this truth through reading this simple chapter.

Chapter 16

Jesus Knows Exactly What He's Doing

Sometimes things happen that shock us. Circumstances get out of our control. Jesus, according to His Word, is the King of Kings and Lord of Lords and He is exactly what we need when times get rough. We will never understand why friends and family die suddenly, but we must understand that there is a reason for everything that takes place. Sometimes things happen to grab our attention and cause us to think about eternity. Hebrews 9:27 still teaches that there is an appointment with death that we all must keep. Heaven and hell are very real and we must prepare to meet our God. Many times in order to get one's attention He causes hardships and tragedy to unfold so that we will look up and seek the salvation we so desperately need. Nothing happens by accident and everything happens by design. If life always went good we would never think about eternity and we would die suddenly and wake up in a darkened hell. With love divine He tries in every way to get you to think about your final state when you leave this life.

This story proves that God understands your situation and He will gladly be there if you will invite Him in. Allow me to help you with this story.

One day at work a man I'm very close to received word that his cousin sadly passed away in a tragic motorcycle accident at a very young age. My heart broke for this man and I wondered what I could do to help. As the day went on something within me told me to give him one verse in the Bible -- Matthew 11:28. This is a famous verse in the Bible which says, "Come unto me, all ye that labor and are heavy laden and I will give you rest," That night he went home and couldn't sleep and read this verse over and over again. Never before that day had he taken a liking to the Bible but God got a hold of his heart. The next morning he approached me and said you picked a good verse and I want you to know that I read it over and over again. I said I'm proud of you and I'm glad you read that verse. After our conversation I had to go on the road to Detroit to pick up equipment. All through the day I was praying for this man and Matthew 11:28 kept running through my mind. As we neared the close of the day and we threw the last sign on our truck I noticed a huge church to my right. Next to the church was a big sign with a verse attached to it. Out of all the verses in the Bible that it could have been it happened to be Matthew 11:28, "Come unto me all ye that labor and are heavy laden and I will give you rest."

You see, my friend God knows what He is doing. God sends so many warnings throughout our lives to cause us to look to His cross where He paid the price for us. We try our best to ignore Him, but we are only lying to ourselves. All you have to do is run to Christ and He will give you rest. One day life will end, and eternity will begin. Stop running away from the Lord, but rather look and live my brother live. Just think about it, without this tragedy in this man's life he may have never read that verse. God wants to rescue you today if you will only give Him a chance.

Chapter 17

Surely Goodness and Mercy Shall Follow Me All the Days of My Life

All young people at a very early age need to read Psalms 23:6. This verse without a doubt can change the course of a young person's life if it is understood and followed. Psalms 23:6 reads like this, "surely goodness and mercy shall follow me all the days of my life: and I will dwell in the house of the Lord forever.

Faithfulness according to God's Word is the greatest thing a person can have and without it blessings from God will disappear. If a person is inconsistent in the things of the Lord they will struggle all the days of their life.

As a very young man I had a desire to have the blessings of God in my life so I tithed on every check and was at church every service. I'm 35 years old now and I have never regretted that decision. Day after day God sends His goodness my way and it's all because I've been faithful toward the things of God.

God made a promise in Psalms 23:6 that will never fade away but it's up to us to obey His Word and reap the benefits. Let me give you this story to prove that this verse is true.

A few years back God told me to teach on the subject, "Surely goodness and mercy shall follow me all the days of my life." My goal in teaching that morning was to drive home the point that God has special blessings for those who serve Him. That morning alone we used around 75 verses and 10 stories proving this was true and God was really moving on their young hearts. At the close of the class I told the kids that every day something special happens for our family because we love God and want to be faithful to Him.

Hours later after this statement my mother said someone dropped off a gift with my name on it. I remember opening the package and inside was 96 Reese peanut butter cups. Instantly my mind went back to the message I taught that day and joy filled my soul.

Let me close this chapter by saying this, "many want blessings in their lives but when you mention faithfulness it stops them cold in their tracks." If you will be faithful to God then God will be faithful to you. Serve God all your days and you will never regret it. Give him every corner of your heart and the results will be overwhelming.

Chapter 18

Love Conquers All

All Christians around this country need to take the time, once a week, to read 1 Corinthians chapter 13. Paul, under the inspiration of the Holy Spirit, tells us over and over that if we live our lives without love we are really not living at all. Paul made this statement in 1 Corinthians 13:2, "And though I have all faith, so that I could remove mountains and have not charity, I am nothing.

Far too many Christians try to function without love and as a consequence they live as spiritually dead people, causing dead churches.

Pastors all around this country preach hard and pound on the pulpit and people go out of their services worse than they came in because love is not flowing through the services. Any man of God that makes a difference will have a balance of doctrine and love. To have one without the other is a false balance and proverbs 11:1 says that a false balance is an abomination unto the Lord. Without a steady dose of love a church will crumble.

If this is true in a church that is ordained by God it is

also true in a biblical marriage that is also ordained by God. Matthew 19:6 says, "Wherefore they are no more twain but one flesh. What God hath joined together, let no man put asunder." God has always intended for all marriages to thrive and last forever but sadly many fall apart because love vanishes from the marriage. Even God had to give His people a bill of divorce because they were backslidden and lost their love for Him and cheated on Him. When love is present in a marriage all things are possible. However if it leaves it will quickly become impossible.

A relationship is dictated by how much love dwells within a home. God has always intended for marriage to last forever and I hope this story proves the second part of Matthew 19:6, "What God hath joined together let no man put sunder.

Around a year ago my wedding ring came up missing and I had no earthly idea where it was. After a day of looking for it I told my wife that I had misplaced it. We were scheduled to go to Hillsdale, Michigan that week so we went and never looked back. I assured my wife that once we got back from Hillsdale I would find it and I didn't want her to worry. We spent three great days in Hillsdale and we arrived back home on a Sunday night. After we unpacked from our trip I made a point to look everywhere for that ring but I could not find it. The very next morning, before I left for work, I made one final attempt to find the ring but I could not find it. I worked a full shift that day and on my way home something amazing happened. Songs of love and assurance rapidly flowed through my mind and a peace flooded my soul. Somehow and someway I just knew my ring was safe and sound and the remainder of my drive was pleasant. I remember pulling in my yard and thanking God for keeping my ring safe. As I opened the door I looked on the grass and without taking a step I reached down and picked up my ring like nothing ever happened. Three months later after playing basketball my ring came up missing again. For over 4 months I could not find my ring. Never during that time did I worry or stress over it because I knew God would keep it safe. Sure enough, as I was listening to gospel music one day I looked down and in between the seats of my car my ring was looking back at me. What's amazing about this is that I found it on our 7th year anniversary. Romans 8:38-9 is so powerful when you read these verses in its entirety. Romans 8: 38-39 says, "For I am persuaded that neither death, nor life, nor angels, nor principalities, nor powers, nor things present, nor things to come, nor heights, nor depths, nor any other creature shall be able to separate us from the love of God, which is in Christ Jesus our Lord.

CONCLUSION

As we conclude this book I hope something within these pages motivated you to serve God better in these last days. We all understand that as the rapture approaches the fiery darts of the wicked will only increase. It's not good enough to be just a lukewarm Christian in these last days. We need people on fire for God. This generation of people is going to hell, at a record pace, and it is because we as Christians have lost our power with God. Soaring with Eagles is meant to infuse life back into those who have grown weary from the battle. Christians are dropping like flies, backsliding, and falling by the wayside in record numbers. Many who do come look like death warmed over. Oh how we need life and liberty back in our churches. We always heard the statement that says, "as goes our churches so goes the nation" As long as the power of God is missing from our churches, people as a whole, will grow darker in their hearts around this great nation. When the fire of God returns in people's hearts again we will see amazing results. However if it does not return then revival is hopeless. Life is too short and God is too good for us to live a half hearted Christian life.

Jesus deserves our very best and I pray God's Spirit has refreshed you as you read this book. I pray that we will take an examination of our lives and ask ourselves are we closer to

God right now than we were yesterday. If the answer is no then we need to ask God to renew us like the eagles for His honor and glory. My prayer is that this book will affect millions in the years to come and that revival fires will spread through this feeble effort. Thank God for his Power that is available to us. We must hunger and long after it.

    With Love
    Brother Tony
    Isaiah 40:31

BUILDING BLOCKS THAT WILL LEAD YOU TO GOD'S POWER

Before completely closing out this book I feel led by the Lord to give you some building blocks from God's Word that will lead you to God's power in your life. God's power is not for a chosen few like so many believe but it is for any child of God who wants it from the depths of their soul. If you wish to soar with God it will not be easy but I will give you the recipe for success from God's holy book. We will discuss 15 words from the Bible that will lift any Christian to new heights with God if they are followed and added to people's lives. The fifteen words are joy, strength, power, peace, giving, soul winning, prayer, wisdom, love, faithfulness, compassion, studying, patience, singing and faith. We will write out each word and give verses along with each word. If you add these verses to your life I promise you will be soaring with eagles soon. The verses I will give you have always helped me and I know they will help you as well. Read each verse carefully. Add these words to your life and you will be amazed at where you will be with God a year from now. I hope these verses help you see the importance of getting close to the lord and winning battles in your own personal life.

ADD COMPASSION TO YOUR LIFE

Jude 1:22 And of some have compassion, making a difference:

Matthew 15:32 Then Jesus called his disciples unto him, and said, I have compassion on the multitude, because they continue with me now three days, and have nothing to eat: and I will not send them away fasting, lest they faint in the way.

\Luke 15:20 And he arose, and came to his father. But when he was yet a great way off, his father saw him, and had compassion, and ran, and fell on his neck, and kissed him.

Matthew 9:36 But when he saw the multitudes, he was moved with compassion on them, because they fainted, and were scattered abroad, as sheep having no shepherd.

Mark 1:41 And Jesus, moved with compassion, put forth his hand, and touched him, and saith unto him, I will; be thou clean.

1Peter 3:8 Finally, be ye all of one mind, having compassion one of another, love as brethren, be pitiful, be courteous:

1John 3:17 But whoso hath this world's good, and seeth his brother have need, and shutteth up his bowels of compassion from him, how dwelleth the love of God in him?

Psalm 78:38 But he, being full of compassion, forgave their iniquity, and destroyed them not: yea, many a time turned he his anger away, and did not stir up all his wrath.

Psalm 86:15 But thou, O Lord, art a God full of compassion, and gracious, longsuffering, and plenteous in mercy and truth.

Psalm 145:8 The LORD is gracious, and full of compassion; slow to anger, and of great mercy.

ADD FAITH TO YOUR LIFE

Hebrews 11:1 Now faith is the substance of things hoped for, the evidence of things not seen.

Hebrews 11:6 But without faith it is impossible to please him: for he that cometh to God must believe that he is, and that he is a rewarder of them that diligently seek him.

Matthew 15:28 Then Jesus answered and said unto her, O woman, great is thy faith: be it unto thee even as thou wilt. And her daughter was made whole from that very hour.

Matthew 8:10 When Jesus heard it, he marvelled, and said to them that followed, Verily I say unto you, I have not found so great faith, no, not in Israel.

Matthew 17:20 And Jesus said unto them, Because of your unbelief: for verily I say unto you, If ye have faith as a grain of mustard seed, ye shall say unto this mountain, Remove hence to yonder place; and it shall remove; and nothing shall be impossible unto you.

Romans 10:17 So then faith cometh by hearing, and hearing by the Word of God.

James 1:6 But let him ask in faith, nothing wavering. For he that wavereth is like a wave of the sea driven with the wind and tossed.

2Peter 1:1 Simon Peter, a servant and an apostle of Jesus Christ, to them that have obtained like precious faith with us through the righteousness of God and our Saviour Jesus Christ:

1Peter 1:7 That the trial of your faith, being much more precious than of gold that perisheth, though it be tried with fire, might be found unto praise and honour and glory at the appearing of Jesus Christ:

James 2:5 Hearken, my beloved brethren, Hath not God chosen the poor of this world rich in faith, and heirs of the kingdom which he hath promised to them that love him?

ADD FAITHFULNESS TO YOUR LIFE

Hebrews 10:25 Not forsaking the assembling of ourselves together, as the manner of some is; but exhorting one another: and so much the more, as ye see the day approaching.

Psalm 84:10 For a day in thy courts is better than a thousand. I had rather be a doorkeeper in the house of my God, than to dwell in the tents of wickedness.

Psalm 27:4 One thing have I desired of the LORD, that will I seek after; that I may dwell in the house of the LORD all the days of my life, to behold the beauty of the LORD, and to enquire in his temple.

Psalm 23:6 Surely goodness and mercy shall follow me all the days of my life: and I will dwell in the house of the LORD for ever.

Psalm 100:4 Enter into his gates with thanksgiving, and into his courts with praise: be thankful unto him, and bless his name.

1Corinthians 4:2 Moreover it is required in stewards, that a man be found faithful.

Psalm 122:1 A Song of degrees of David. I was glad when they said unto me, Let us go into the house of the LORD.

Mark 12:30 And thou shalt love the Lord thy God with all thy heart, and with all thy soul, and with all thy mind, and with all thy strength: this is the first commandment.

Romans 12:1 I beseech you therefore, brethren, by the mercies of God, that ye present your bodies a living sacrifice, holy, acceptable unto God, which is your reasonable service.

Joshua 24:15 And if it seem evil unto you to serve the LORD, choose you this day whom ye will serve; whether the gods which your fathers served that were on the other side of the flood, or the gods of the Amorites, in whose land ye dwell: but as for me and my house, we will serve the LORD.

ADD GIVING TO YOUR LIFE

Luke 6:38 Give, and it shall be given unto you; good measure, pressed down, and shaken together, and running over, shall men give into your bosom. For with the same measure that ye mete withal it shall be measured to you again.

Acts 20:35 I have shewed you all things, how that so labouring ye ought to support the weak, and to remember the Words of the Lord Jesus, how he said, It is more blessed to give than to receive.

2Corinthians 9:7 Every man according as he purposeth in his heart, so let him give; not grudgingly, or of necessity: for God loveth a cheerful giver.

Matthew 5:42 Give to him that asketh thee, and from him that would borrow of thee turn not thou away.

Matthew 19:21 Jesus said unto him, If thou wilt be perfect, go and sell that thou hast, and give to the poor, and thou shalt have treasure in heaven: and come and follow me.

Acts 3:6 Then Peter said, Silver and gold have I none; but such as I have give I thee: In the name of Jesus Christ of Nazareth rise up and walk.

John 3:16 For God so loved the world, that he gave his only begotten Son, that whosoever believeth in him should not perish, but have everlasting life.

1John 3:16 Hereby perceive we the love of God, because he laid down his life for us: and we ought to lay down our lives for the brethren.

Romans 8:32 He that spared not his own Son, but delivered him up for us all, how shall he not with him also freely give us all things?

James 1:5 If any of you lack wisdom, let him ask of God, that giveth to all men liberally, and upbraideth not; and it shall be given him.

ADD JOY TO YOUR LIFE

Psalm 16:11 Thou wilt shew me the path of life: in thy presence is fulness of joy; at thy right hand there are pleasures for evermore.

Nehemiah 8:10 Then he said unto them, Go your way, eat the fat, and drink the sweet, and send portions unto them for whom nothing is prepared: for this day is holy unto our Lord: neither be ye sorry; for the joy of the LORD is your strength.

1Peter 1:8 Whom having not seen, ye love; in whom, though now ye see him not, yet believing, ye rejoice with joy unspeakable and full of glory:

Jude 1:24 Now unto him that is able to keep you from falling, and to present you faultless before the presence of his glory with exceeding joy,

1John 1:4 And these things write we unto you, that your joy may be full.

Hebrews 12:2 Looking unto Jesus the author and finisher of our faith; who for the joy that was set before him endured the cross, despising the shame, and is set down at the right hand of the throne of God.

Isaiah 35:10 And the ransomed of the LORD shall return, and come to Zion with songs and everlasting joy upon their heads: they shall obtain joy and gladness, and sorrow and sighing shall flee away.

Psalm 30:5 For his anger endureth but a moment; in his favour is life: weeping may endure for a night, but joy cometh in the morning.

Luke 15:10 Likewise, I say unto you, there is joy in the presence of the angels of God over one sinner that repenteth.

John 15:11 These things have I spoken unto you, that my joy might remain in you, and that your joy might be full.

ADD LOVE TO YOUR LIFE

Proverbs 10:12 Hatred stirreth up strifes: but love covereth all sins.

Jude 1:21 Keep yourselves in the love of God, looking for the mercy of our Lord Jesus Christ unto eternal life.

Romans 13:10 Love worketh no ill to his neighbour: therefore love is the fulfilling of the law.

2Corinthians 13:11 Finally, brethren, farewell. Be perfect, be of good comfort, be of one mind, live in peace; and the God of love and peace shall be with you.

John 15:13 Greater love hath no man than this, that a man lay down his life for his friends.

Ephesians 3:19 And to know the love of Christ, which passeth knowledge, that ye might be filled with all the fulness of God.

2Timothy 1:7 For God hath not given us the spirit of fear; but of power, and of love, and of a sound mind.

Revelation 1:5 And from Jesus Christ, who is the faithful witness, and the first begotten of the dead, and the prince of the kings of the earth. Unto him that loved us, and washed us from our sins in his own blood,

1John 4:8 He that loveth not knoweth not God; for God is love.

John 14:15 If ye love me, keep my commandments.

ADD PATIENCE TO YOUR LIFE

Romans 15:5 Now the God of patience and consolation grant you to be likeminded one toward another according to Christ Jesus:

Romans 5:3 And not only so, but we glory in tribulations also: knowing that tribulation worketh patience;

James 1:3 Knowing this, that the trying of your faith worketh patience.

James 5:11 Behold, we count them happy which endure. Ye have heard of the patience of Job, and have seen the end of the Lord; that the Lord is very pitiful, and of tender mercy.

Titus 2:2 That the aged men be sober, grave, temperate, sound in faith, in charity, in patience.

2Peter 1:6 And to knowledge temperance; and to temperance patience; and to patience godliness;

Hebrews 12:1 Wherefore seeing we also are compassed about with so great a cloud of witnesses, let us lay aside every weight, and the sin which doth so easily beset us, and let us run with patience the race that is set before us,

Revelation 3:10 Because thou hast kept the word of my patience, I also will keep thee from the hour of temptation, which shall come upon all the world, to try them that dwell upon the earth.

Luke 8:15 But that on the good ground are they, which in an honest and good heart, having heard the word, keep it, and bring forth fruit with patience.

2Corinthians 6:4 But in all things approving ourselves as the ministers of God, in much patience, in afflictions, in necessities, in distresses,

ADD PEACE TO YOUR LIFE

Isaiah 26:3 Thou wilt keep him in perfect peace, whose mind is stayed on thee: because he trusteth in thee.

Ephesians 2:14 For he is our peace, who hath made both one, and hath broken down the middle wall of partition between us;

Psalm 34:14 Depart from evil, and do good; seek peace, and pursue it.

Luke 2:14 Glory to God in the highest, and on earth peace, good will toward men.

Romans 1:7 To all that be in Rome, beloved of God, called to be saints: Grace to you and peace from God our Father, and the Lord Jesus Christ.

John 14:27 Peace I leave with you, my peace I give unto you: not as the world giveth, give I unto you. Let not your heart be troubled, neither let it be afraid.

John 16:33 These things I have spoken unto you, that in me ye might have peace. In the world ye shall have tribulation: but be of good cheer; I have overcome the world.

Isaiah 48:18 O that thou hadst hearkened to my commandments! then had thy peace been as a river, and thy righteousness as the waves of the sea:

Colossians 3:15 And let the peace of God rule in your hearts, to the which also ye are called in one body; and be ye thankful.

2Peter 1:2 Grace and peace be multiplied unto you through the knowledge of God, and of Jesus our Lord,

ADD POWER TO YOUR LIFE

Philippians 3:10 That I may know him, and the power of his resurrection, and the fellowship of his sufferings, being made conformable unto his death;

Luke 24:49 And, behold, I send the promise of my Father upon you: but tarry ye in the city of Jerusalem, until ye be endued with power from on high.

2Corinthians 12:9 And he said unto me, My grace is sufficient for thee: for my strength is made perfect in weakness. Most gladly therefore will I rather glory in my infirmities, that the power of Christ may rest upon me.

Ephesians 3:20 Now unto him that is able to do exceeding abundantly above all that we ask or think, according to the power that worketh in us,

Ephesians 1:19 And what is the exceeding greatness of his power to us-ward who believe, according to the working of his mighty power,

Romans 15:13 Now the God of hope fill you with all joy and peace in believing, that ye may abound in hope, through the power of the Holy Ghost.

Genesis 32:28 And he said, Thy name shall be called no more Jacob, but Israel: for as a prince hast thou power with God and with men, and hast prevailed.

Isaiah 40:29 He giveth power to the faint; and to them that have no might he increaseth strength.

Acts 1:8 But ye shall receive power, after that the Holy Ghost is come upon you: and ye shall be witnesses unto me both in Jerusalem, and in all Judaea, and in Samaria, and unto the uttermost part of the earth.

Luke 4:14 And Jesus returned in the power of the Spirit into Galilee: and there went out a fame of him through all the region round about.

ADD PRAYER TO YOUR LIFE

Acts 4:31 And when they had prayed, the place was shaken where they were assembled together; and they were all filled with the Holy Ghost, and they spake the Word of God with boldness.

Jude 1:20 But ye, beloved, building up yourselves on your most holy faith, praying in the Holy Ghost,

1 Thessalonians 5:17 Pray without ceasing.

Psalm 34:15 The eyes of the LORD are upon the righteous, and his ears are open unto their cry.

Jeremiah 33:3 Call unto me, and I will answer thee, and shew thee great and mighty things, which thou knowest not.

James 5:16 Confess your faults one to another, and pray one for another, that ye may be healed. The effectual fervent prayer of a righteous man availeth much.

Daniel 6:10 Now when Daniel knew that the writing was signed, he went into his house; and his windows being open in his chamber toward Jerusalem, he kneeled upon his knees three times a day, and prayed, and gave thanks before his God, as he did aforetime.

Psalm 55:17 Evening, and morning, and at noon, will I pray, and cry aloud: and he shall hear my voice.

Psalm 5:3 My voice shalt thou hear in the morning, O LORD; in the morning will I direct my prayer unto thee, and will look up.

Acts 9:40 But Peter put them all forth,and kneeled down, and prayed; and turning him to the body said, Tabitha, arise. And she opened her eyes; and when she saw Peter, she sat up.

ADD SINGING TO YOUR LIFE

Ephesians 5:19 Speaking to yourselves in psalms and hymns and spiritual songs, singing and making melody in your heart to the Lord;

Colossians 3:16 Let the word of Christ dwell in you richly in all wisdom; teaching and admonishing one another in psalms and hymns and spiritual songs, singing with grace in your hearts to the Lord.

Psalm 100:2 Serve the LORD with gladness: come before his presence with singing.

Psalm 126:2 Then was our mouth filled with laughter, and our tongue with singing: then said they among the heathen, The LORD hath done great things for them.

Revelation 5:9 And they sung a new song, saying, Thou art worthy to take the book, and to open the seals thereof: for thou wast slain, and hast redeemed us to God by thy blood out of every kindred, and tongue, and people, and nation;

Psalm 40:3 And he hath put a new song in my mouth, even praise unto our God: many shall see it, and fear, and shall trust in the LORD.

Psalm 18:49 Therefore will I give thanks unto thee, O LORD, among the heathen, and sing praises unto thy name.

Psalm 30:4 Sing unto the LORD, O ye saints of his, and give thanks at the remembrance of his holiness.

Psalm 138:5 Yea, they shall sing in the ways of the LORD: for great is the glory of the LORD.

Song of Solomon 2:12 The flowers appear on the earth; the time of the singing of birds is come, and the voice of the turtle is heard in our land;

ADD SOUL WINNING TO YOUR LIFE

Matthew 4:19 And he saith unto them, Follow me, and I will make you fishers of men.

Mark 16:15 And he said unto them, Go ye into all the world, and preach the gospel to every creature.

Luke 14:23 And the lord said unto the servant, Go out into the highways and hedges, and compel them to come in, that my house may be filled.

Psalm 126:6 He that goeth forth and weepeth, bearing precious seed, shall doubtless come again with rejoicing, bringing his sheaves with him.

Acts 20:26 Wherefore I take you to record this day, that I am pure from the blood of all men.

Matthew 6:20 But lay up for yourselves treasures in heaven, where neither moth nor rust doth corrupt, and where thieves do not break through nor steal:

Luke 19:10 For the Son of man is come to seek and to save that which was lost.

Matthew 28:19 Go ye therefore, and teach all nations, baptizing them in the name of the Father, and of the Son, and of the Holy Ghost:

Mark 5:20 And he departed, and began to publish in Decapolis how great things Jesus had done for him: and all men did marvel.

Romans 10:1 Brethren, my heart's desire and prayer for Israel is, that they might be saved.

ADD STRENGTH TO YOUR LIFE

Ephesians 6:10 Finally, my brethren, be strong in the Lord, and in the power of his might.

Philippians 4:13 I can do all things through Christ which strengtheneth me.

Psalm 18:32 It is God that girdeth me with strength, and maketh my way perfect.

Psalm 27:1 A Psalm of David. The LORD is my light and my salvation; whom shall I fear? the LORD is the strength of my life; of whom shall I be afraid?

Exodus 15:2 The LORD is my strength and song, and he is become my salvation: he is my God, and I will prepare him an habitation; my father's God, and I will exalt him.

2Samuel 22:33 God is my strength and power: and he maketh my way perfect.

Proverbs 10:29 The way of the LORD is strength to the upright: but destruction shall be to the workers of iniquity

Isaiah 12:2 Behold, God is my salvation; I will trust, and not be afraid: for the LORD JEHOVAH is my strength and my song; he also is become my salvation.

Psalm 29:11 The LORD will give strength unto his people; the LORD will bless his people with peace.

Psalm 46:1 To the chief Musician for the sons of Korah, A Song upon Alamoth. God is our refuge and strength, a very present help in trouble.

ADD STUDYING TO YOUR LIFE

1 Timothy 4:13 Till I come, give attendance to reading, to exhortation, to doctrine.

2 Timothy 2:15 Study to shew thyself approved unto God, a workman that needeth not to be ashamed, rightly dividing the word of truth.

Acts 17:11 These were more noble than those in Thessalonica, in that they received the word with all readiness of mind, and searched the scriptures daily, whether those things were so.

John 5:39 Search the scriptures; for in them ye think ye have eternal life: and they are they which testify of me.

Hebrews 4:12 For the word of God is quick, and powerful, and sharper than any twoedged sword, piercing even to the dividing asunder of soul and spirit, and of the joints and marrow, and is a discerner of the thoughts and intents of the heart.

Psalm 104:34 My meditation of him shall be sweet: I will be glad in the LORD.

Job 23:12 Neither have I gone back from the commandment of his lips; I have esteemed the words of his mouth more than my necessary food.

Psalm 119:105 NUN. Thy word is a lamp unto my feet, and a light unto my path.

Psalm 119:11 Thy word have I hid in mine heart, that I might not sin against thee.

Psalm 119:133 Order my steps in thy word: and let not any iniquity have dominion over me.

ADD WISDOM TO YOUR LIFE

Proverbs 1:7 The fear of the LORD is the beginning of knowledge: but fools despise wisdom and instruction.

Acts 6:10 And they were not able to resist the wisdom and the spirit by which he spake.

Luke 2:52 And Jesus increased in wisdom and stature, and in favour with God and man.

Proverbs 3:13 Happy is the man that findeth wisdom, and the man that getteth understanding.

Proverbs 4:7 Wisdom is the principal thing; therefore get wisdom: and with all thy getting get understanding.

Revelation 5:12 Saying with a loud voice, Worthy is the Lamb that was slain to receive power, and riches, and wisdom, and strength, and honour, and glory, and blessing.

Daniel 1:20 And in all matters of wisdom and understanding, that the king enquired of them, he found them ten times better than all the magicians and astrologers that were in all his realm.

Proverbs 16:16 How much better is it to get wisdom than gold! and to get understanding rather to be chosen than silver!

Proverbs 8:11 For wisdom is better than rubies; and all the things that may be desired are not to be compared to it.

Proverbs 9:10 The fear of the LORD is the beginning of wisdom: and the knowledge of the holy is understanding.

Published By Parables

OUR MISSION

The primary mission of Published By Parables, a Christian publisher, is to publish Contemporary and Classic Christian books from an evangelical perspective that honors Christ and promotes the values and virtues of His Kingdom.

Are You An Aspiring Christian Author?

We fulfill our mission best by providing Christian authors and writers publishing options that are uniquely Christian, quick, affordable and easy to understand -- in an effort to please Christ who has called us to a writing ministry. We know the challenges of getting published, especially if you're a first-time author. God, who called you to write your book, will provide the grace sufficient to the task of getting it published.

We understand the value of a dollar; know the importance of producing a quality product; and publish what we publish for the glory of God.

Surf and Explore our site --
then use our easy-to-use "Tell Us" button
to tell us about yourself and about your book.

We're a one-stop, full-service Christian publisher.
We know our limits. We know our capabilities.
You won't be disappointed.

www.PublishedByParables.com

PUBLISHED by PARABLES
Earthly Stories with a Heavenly Meaning

PUBLISHED by
PARABLES
Earthly Stories with a Heavenly Meaning

Anthony Ritthaler

Soaring With Eagles
Volume 2

A Book Of Freedom, Strength and Power

PUBLISHED by PARABLES
Earthly Stories with a Heavenly Meaning

ANTHONY RITTHALER

Pathways To The Past

Each volume stands alone as an Individual Book
Each volume stands together with others
to enhance the value of your collection

Build your Personal, Pastoral or Church Library
Pathways To The Past contains an ever-expanding list of
Christendom's most influencial authors

Augustine of Hippo
Athanasius
E. M. Bounds
John Bunyan
Brother Lawrence
Jessie Penn-Lewis
Bernard of Clairvaux
Andrew Murray
Watchman Nee
Arthur W. Pink
Hannah Whitall Smith
R. A. Torrey
A. W. Tozer
Jean-Pierre de Caussade
Thomas Watson
And many, many more.

Title: Soaring with Eagles Volume 2 A Book Of Freedom, Strength and Power
Anthony Ritthaler

Rights: All Rights Reserved
ISBN 978-1-945698-16-3
Doctrinal theology, Inspiration
Salvation, Meditation
Other books by this author include: Walking On The Water With Jesus (Volume 1 and 2), A Devil From The Beginning and Soaring With Eagles Volume 1

Anthony Ritthaler

Soaring With Eagles
Volume 2

A Book Of Freedom, Strength and Power

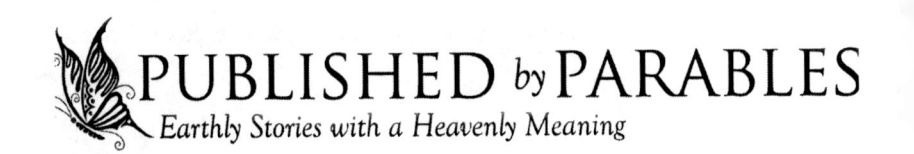

PUBLISHED by PARABLES
Earthly Stories with a Heavenly Meaning

ANTHONY RITTHALER

Tony's Words Of Freedom, Strength and Power

"The Devil is a liar,
but an Eagle just flies higher."

"When danger is all around
the Eagle takes off to higher ground."

"We have a choice as Christians:
we can hang with the crows, or soar with the pros."

"Your finest hour will always be
when you soar with God's Power."

"Fly with the Lord in Power, Strength, and Glory
and never allow Satan to write your life's story."

"When others around you complain and cry,
be mature take off and fly."

"Whenever you soar with God
this world will think your odd."

"When you are fighting the World, the flesh, and the Devil allow the Holy Spirit to move you to a higher level."

"The greatest person in life is not he who obtains the most, but it is he who is controlled by the blessed Holy Ghost."

"If you desire to be rare, that's when God can take you anywhere."

"Those who have the touch from on High will always give Satan a black eye."

"An Eagle often flies alone, but his journey leads to Gods Throne."

"When you're facing all the Demons of Hell, just fly to God and sing it is well."

"When like the Eagle you soar to the mountain, God will allow you to drink from His fountain."

"When an Eagle takes flight he never looks back, but that won't stop the Pharisees from taking smack."

Table of Contents

Tony's Words Of Freedom, Strength and Power
Table Of Contents
Special Thanks
Introduction

1. How Excellent is Thy Loving Kindness, Oh God!
2. How to Get Victory Over Depression
3. Three Things That Eagles Have That Christian's Need Desperately
4. The Power of a Good Testimony
5. Jesus Calmed My Storm on the Inside
6. Rejoice in the Lord Always, No Matter How Bad You Feel
7. A Friend Like No Other
8. The Stamp of Approval from Almighty God
9. If You Will Give God Your Little Lunch, He Can Multiply it for Years to Come
10. Feeling God's Angels All Around

11. Pay It Forward
12. Getting A Big Surprise While Driving Home One Night
13. Our God Knows What We Have Need Of
14. There's a Miracle in the Making
15. Jesus is Always There When We Need Him
16. The Lord Will Hear When I Call Upon Him
17. Call Unto Me and I Will Answer Thee
18. The Goodness of God Leadeth Thee to Repentance
19. But My God Shall Supply All Your Need
20. Amazing Grace, How Sweet the Sound
Conclusion

Special Thanks

I want to donate this special thanks portion to five special men that have been such an encouragement to me. Four of these men are radio hosts, and all five men practice what they preach. My respect and admiration for these men of God is hard to put into words and I hope through this section of the book you will seek to know them all yourself. Every one of these men are the real deal, and I'm honored that God has brought them my way and I thank Him every day for it. When I examine these men's lives, I see integrity, hard work, Godly charity, a vision for the lost, kindness, and faith. Let me list these five men and pay them the honor they so richly deserve.

The first man I would like to thank today is Bro Richard Frazier, host of The Richard Frazier Show on 760 Wurl Radio Moody Alabama. Bro Frazier has given his life to help other people's ministries and so many love this wonderful saint of God. You will be hard pressed to find a kinder Christian, and my respect for him is off the charts. Bro Frazier has had me on his show, he prays for me and my family, and he has been a true support to my ministry. Bro Frazier is one of these rare

Christians that walks with the fruit of the spirit and it shines through on a daily basis. Bro Frazier, thanks for being a friend, a support, a blessing, and a prayer warrior for me. May God continue to bless your ministry in many glorious way's.

The next man I would like to mention in my special thanks is Bro Bob Hill, host of Wbni Christian Radio. Bro Hill has truly humbled me by his financial support, his pure heart, and his support in passing my books to those in need. Nearly every day he blesses me with either a prayer, a word of advice, or a kind word from above. This world really needs more men like this and words on paper will never capture the blessing Bro Hill has been. Thank you my friend for your belief in my ministry and for being such an encouragement to me. Your friendship really touches my heart.

The third person I would like to praise for a moment is the great Nate Fortner, host of the Authors Minute and owner of Whosoever Press. Bro Fortner is a singer, an author, a business owner, a mentor, a friend, and a support to so many around this country. God sent Bro Fortner along my pathway at a time that was a blessing and my life has only become better through his influence upon my life. Folks, you need to look up Bro Fortner and get to know him on a personal level. Bro Nate Fortner is one of the most talented men in America and yet one of the most humble at the same time. Often, I find myself taking notes of how he conducts his life and I try to add these traits to mine as well. Bro Fortner, I want to thank you for all of your support through the years, and I pray great blessings on your life. You're a great man and I praise God for the example you set for a world that needs Jesus. Keep up the awesome work, I love you man of God.

The next man I want to thank is Bro Ken Mitchell, President of Missions Radio. When I think of character, faith, and dedication, Bro Mitchell comes to mind instantly. Every day of his life, Bro Mitchell goes out of his way to enrich someone else's life, and his heart is completely controlled by the Lord. The impact of his ministry is vast, and the rare gifts that he possesses are a blessing. Time and time again, Bro Mitchell has proven to be a friend, a servant, a giver, and a great testimony to those around him. Without men like Bro Mitchell, this world would be a far darker place. Bro Mitchell, I would not be where I am right now without your impact on my life. Thank you from the bottom of my heart for the blessing you have been over the last few years.

Last, but not least, I want to say a big thank you to my friend, Mr. John Jeffries, owner of Published By Parables Ministry. Bro Jeffries is my publisher, my friend, and one of my heroes in the faith. His constant help blesses me, and his old fashion character inspires me every day. Bro Jeffries has a heavy burden to reach the world and his outstanding heart helps him touch so many. Without Bro Jeffries help towards my ministry, we would not be where we are today. There is no way I could thank him enough for his support, his love, and his labor towards these books. Bro Jeffries, thanks for allowing my dreams to come true through your ministry, and thanks for being a man who I can look up to.

Folks, this world needs Christians like the five I just mentioned. Far too many use the Christian name for the wrong reasons, but these men make God smile. Thanks once again to all you men for being such a joy to know and an encouragement to this old sinner. God bless you all in a special way.

Introduction

Welcome to Volume Two of Soaring With Eagles; where once again the central theme will center around the great power of our Savior, Jesus Christ. Every story will bring honor to God above, and each story will motivate you to soar to higher ground. Churches around this country are filled with just average Christians who refuse to throw up the white flag of surrender and the cause of Christ suffers because of it. God wants us to be on fire for His glory; making a difference in a hopeless world. God expects His children to have a hunger to seek revival in their own personal life and I pray these stories will give you that desire.

As you read these stories, allow God to do a work in your heart. May the Holy Spirit of God speak to your heart as you read, and allow Him to change you from the inside out.

Sadly, when I go into churches in these last days, it's like I'm forced to watch an episode of the Walking Dead. People have no joy, they stagger around like zombies, spiritually speaking. They won't sing, they won't shout, they won't grow, they are half asleep, they have no direction, no drive, no purpose, and they make no impact for Christ. Folks, we need revival in our hearts again and a passion to reach the lost.

My prayer with this book is that these stories will charge you back up for God again, and cause you to thirst after His power. We serve a God that wants to show His power in all of our lives, but it will not happen unless we get serious again. Please enjoy the stories to come and allow God to transform you by His amazing grace.

Chapter One

How Excellent is Thy Loving Kindness, Oh God!

The God we serve is a God of tender compassion and loving kindness. If we have a desire to live for Him, he will honor us with things we desire and love. The Bible says in James 1:17, "Every good gift and every perfect gift is from above". Our Heavenly Father has a special place in His heart for those that put Him first in their life. The Bible says in Matthew 6:33 "Seek ye first the Kingdom of God, and His righteousness, and all these things shall be added unto you". When our children listen and obey us, we have a tendency to want to be a blessing in return because they make us proud. God in Heaven does the same thing for those that serve Him. The Bible says in Isaiah 1:19 "If ye be willing and obedient, ye shall eat the good of the land". We are serving a gracious and kind God who writes down all the good seeds we sow, and in His time he will reward us with things near and dear to our hearts. God knows our frame, he knows what we desire and he looks forward to blessing us in ways that are special to us. The Bible says in

Psalm 37:4 "Delight thyself also in the Lord; and he shall give thee the desires of thine heart". When our lives please God, we can expect great blessings to come our way because that is how God operates. The Bible says in Psalm 68:19 "Blessed be the Lord, who daily loadeth us with benefits". As we live life down here we should always be at peace knowing that God shelters us in the palm of his hand. The next story will show the world that God really cares for His own and will bless us if we put Him first.

One day, while working in Canton, Michigan, we passed a restaurant that I heard so much about but had never been to before. The restaurant was called IHOP, where they serve endless pancakes morning, noon, and night. The man I was working with couldn't believe I had never been there and he told me I needed to go as soon as possible. I remember looking at this man and saying, "Sir, if God wants me to go to IHOP he will reveal it unto me". Around two weeks later, a woman approached me at church with a gift for me and my wife, Erin. The woman looked at me and said "Tony, I thought you may like this, so enjoy". After we thanked this dear woman of God, we opened the gift and to our amazement it was a gift card for $250 to IHOP. God seen fit to make a way for us to enjoy this wonderful place and now Erin's Grandfather takes us every Sunday and refuses to let us pay. The Lord knows how to bless us in special ways and this was a blessing to me. We shall close out this chapter with Psalm 34:15 "The eyes of the Lord are upon the righteous, and His ears are open unto their cry".

Scriptures For This Chapter

Psalm 37:4 "Delight thyself also in the Lord; and He shall give thee the desires of thine heart."

Isaiah 1:19 "If ye be willing and obedient, ye shall eat the good of the land:"

Matthew 6:33 "But seek ye first the kingdom of God, and His righteousness: and all these things shall be added unto you."

Chapter 2

How to Get Victory Over Depression

In these last days of darkness, depression is sweeping through our land at an alarming rate. The Devil is having a field day with people's minds and millions are committing suicide because of it. In the Book of John, Ch. 10:10, the Bible declares "That the thief cometh not, but to steal, and to kill, and to destroy" and sadly this is happening all over this world. The Bible teaches us in I Peter 5:8 that the Devil, "As a roaring lion, walketh about, seeking whom he may devour". Folks, the Devil is on the warpath more now than he has ever been before because he knows his time is short. Satan is completely controlling people's minds in these last days and his ultimate goal is to keep us depressed and weak on a daily basis. Every single day of my life I talk to people in deep depression and it breaks my heart. The man in Mark Ch. 5 was possessed with around 6000 demons in one human body. Day in and day out this man remained in a hopeless state, crying and cutting himself with stones.

Satan sat back and laughed at this man's misery and he does the same with all mankind. If he can fill your heart and mind with his never ending lies, he will then keep you in his prison with no intentions of ever letting you out. The Bible says in II Timothy 2:26 that "The Devil takes people captive at his own will". In Luke 13 we read about a woman who was bound by Satan for 18 long, miserable years. Satan is the master deceiver and sadly he has a larger following than Jesus Christ. So many across this world make the mistake of allowing the devil to influence them and this decision results in total regret and misery. God has designed men to have peace, joy, love, and liberty but people would rather listen to lies more than truth and it bites them like an adder. Depression has risen at an incredible rate over the last 10 years and instead of running to the answer, people run to drugs, alcohol, parties, and doctors. People who run to these avenues of help usually come back far worse than they were before they went.

With the remainder of this chapter, I want to point you to the answer and it is the cure to all man's diseases and it has always been the formula for success so listen up. The key to victory always begins in one's head. The battle begins in the mind and Christ wants to capture your thoughts with glorious heavenly things. Satan, on the other hand, will flood our minds with doubt and questions that trouble our souls. Whenever you are overwhelmed with emotions and fear, leave Satan in the dust and run to Jesus as fast as you possibly can. The Bible says in I John 4:18 "That perfect love casteth out fear". The Word of God also tells us in Hebrews 2:14-15 that the lord came to "Deliver them who through fear of death were all their lifetime subject to bondage". The scriptures tell us in II Timothy 1:7 "That God hath not given us the spirit of fear; but of power, and of love, and of a sound mind". There is only one way to have joy unspeakable and full of glory and that is through the Lord, Jesus Christ. When the maniac lost all hope he made a great choice and ran to Jesus because he knew within his heart Christ was the only one who could break the chains of bondage in his life. The Bible records that after this choice was made, this crazy man was never the same again. The Bible clearly states in Mark Ch. 5:15 "And they come to Jesus, and see him that was possessed with the Devil, and had the legion sitting, and clothed, and in his right mind: and they were afraid".

There is good news my friends, no matter how low you feel, or how many mistakes you make, there is Hope through a forgiving God who longs to clean up our lives and minds through his blood. The Bible says in Isaiah 26:3 "Thou wilt keep him in perfect peace, whose mind is stayed on thee: because he trusteth in thee. The Bible also says in Philippians 4:7 "And the peace of God, which passeth all understanding, shall keep your hearts and minds through Christ Jesus". The Word of God tells us in I Peter 1:13 "To gird up the lions of your mind" and in Philippians 2:5 the Lord says "Let this mind be in you which was also in Christ Jesus". The Bible declares that Jesus is the God of peace found in Romans 16:20, and that he the prince of peace in Isaiah 9:6. You see Satan can offer you cheap thrills and fun but it is impossible for him to offer peace and that's what the world needs more than anything else. Jesus is the only person who can offer abiding peace and He promises if we will draw nigh to him he will draw nigh to us. If you feed your spirit more than you feed your flesh, you will quickly start to gain victories in your life. God has never designed us to live defeated, sad, depressed, and confused, but rather he designed us to have peace, joy, freedom, and liberty through Christ. Always remember God is not the author of confusion and we will always offer help, mercy, pardon, forgiveness, and victory when we need answers. The Bible says in Luke 4:18 "The spirit of the Lord is upon me, because he hath anointed me to preach the gospel to the poor; He hath sent me to hear the broken-hearted, to preach deliverance to the captives, and recovering of sight to the blind, to set at liberty them that are bruised".

My friends, Jesus is willing and able to give you rest, don't delay; get to Jesus today. Refuse to allow Satan to deceive you any longer, submit to God's calling and you can be delivered from depression. Surround your life with Godly music, Godly people, and Godly preaching and it will guard you from the valleys of depression. Saturate yourself with God's word and allow His peace to invade your heart. Jesus is the answer and he can still bring out those which are bound with chains. The Bible declares in John 8:32 "And ye shall know the truth, and the truth shall set you free". Realize today that your only hope for everlasting joy and victory resides in Jesus, God's son. The Bible says in I Corinthians 15:57 "But thanks be to God, which giveth us the victory through our Lord Jesus Christ". The Word of God says in I John 5:4 "For whatsoever is born of God overcometh the world: and this is the victory that overcometh the world, even our faith". There is no pain you feel that He cannot heal. There is no storm that He cannot calm. There is no burden that He cannot lift. And there is no sin He cannot forgive. The Bible says in I John 1:9 "If we confess our sins, He is faithful and just to forgive us our sins, and to cleanse us from all unrighteousness". If you feel like you're going to drown from the waves of depression, reach out to Jesus and he will deliver you. The Bible says in Psalm 40:2 "He brought me up also out of a horrible pit, out of the miry clay, and set my feet upon a rock, and established my goings". Jesus is the answer and if you need help, burdens are lifted at Calvary.

Scriptures For This Chapter

Psalm 40:2 "He brought me up also out of a horrible pit, out of a miry clay, and set my feet upon a rock, and established my goings."

Isaiah 9:6 "For unto us a child is born, unto us a son is given: and the government shall be upon His shoulder: and His name shall be called wonderful, counselor, the Mighty God, the everlasting Father, the Prince of Peace."

Isaiah 26:3 "Thou wilt keep him in perfect peace, whose mind is stayed on thee: because he trusteth in thee."

Mark 5:15 "And they come to Jesus, and see him that was possessed with the Devil, and had the legion, sitting, and clothed, and in his right mind: and they were afraid."

Luke 13:16 "And ought not this woman, being a daughter of Abraham, whom Satan hath bound, lo, these eighteen years, be loosed from this bond on the Sabbath Day?"

John 8:32 "And ye shall know the truth, and the truth shall make you free."

II Timothy 2:26 "And that they may recover themselves out of the snare of the devil, who are taken captive by him at his will."

James 4:7 "Submit yourselves therefore to God. Resist the Devil, and he will flee from you."

I Peter 1:8 "Whom having not seen, ye love; in whom, though now ye see Him not, yet believing, ye rejoice with joy unspeakable and full of glory."

I Peter 1:13 "Wherefore gird up the loins of your mind, be sober, and hope to the end for the grace that is to be brought unto you at the revelation of Jesus Christ."

I John 1:9 "If we confess our sins, He is faithful and just to forgive us our sins, and to cleanse us from all unrighteousness."

Chapter 3

Three Things That Eagles Have That Christian's Need Desperately

If you have never done a deep study about eagles and their many special gifts, you are really missing out. Everything about the eagle is remarkable and they have always represented liberty, freedom, power, and conquerors.

God designed them to be unique and rare and the Bible describes them as very special. We as Christians should all take notes of the many unique qualities of eagles and we should do our best to add them to our lives. There are not very many Christians that are soaring with God anymore, and it is killing revival in our churches. In days gone by so many saints of God excelled like the eagle in so many areas. But, my friends, it's not the same anymore. Christians are now content with being lukewarm in these last days and this wicked mindset literally makes God sick. With the remainder of this chapter I want to highlight three amazing traits that eagles possess and I pray to

God that we develop a desire to add them to our life. May we all have a great desire to soar like the eagle all the days of our life.

The first thing that I would like to point out that the eagle has that we desperately need is great vision. It is said that an eagle can see at least ten times farther than humans can. God has designed an eagle's eye to see things coming from miles away and this gift allows them to react quicker, hunt better, and accomplish far more because of keen awareness. Folks in church are content with being average and we have totally lost our vision for a lost world dying and going to Hell. The Bible says in Proverbs 29:18 "Where there is no vision the people perish". The eagle uses its eyesight as a great advantage and it allows them to gain an edge over his enemies.

The Bible describes the last day church as wretched, and miserable, and poor, and blind, and naked. The Eagle wins many battles and is a victor in nearly everything it does, while most saints I know just struggle to get out of bed each morning. Christians, we need to open our eyes to the reality that people need the Lord and the world needs us to have a vision like Jesus again.

The Devil has literally rocked the church to sleep and it's high time that we awake out of our dead condition. The eagle is always prepared through its great vision and that's why they are respected like no other bird that exists. Christians, we need to beg God for the vision to make a difference in a crooked and perverse generation.

Allow God to give you a supernatural vision like the

eagle to reach a dark world in need of Christ. If we seek after a great vision, our churches could see revival once again.

    The second thing the eagle has that Christians really need is great strength. An eagle has ten times the grip pressure humans do and they are feared by all. We as Christians are expected and commanded to be strong in the Lord. The Book of Ephesians 6:10 says this "Finally, my brethren, be strong in the Lord, and in the power of His might". We are commanded to walk in the fruit of the spirit while putting on the whole armor of God. The Bible says in Isaiah 40:31 that an eagle will constantly renew their strength year in and year out and they can soar to heights unknown. The Bible commands Christians to get stronger as time goes on and to grow in His grace. Most Christians are either going backwards or staying neutral and the Devil beats them up. We need more David's who have a power from another world and are not afraid to step up to their Goliath's. We need more Sampson's, Joshua's, and Gideon's who fear God, not man. So many Christians walk around defeated, weak, helpless, and powerless, as the Devil slaps them around. We as Christians are meant to experience victories, triumphs, and blessings as we grow stronger in the Lord every day. The Bible says in Romans 8:31 "What shall we then say to these things? If God be for us, who can be against us?" The Word of God also says this in II Corinthians 2:14 "Now thanks be unto God which always causeth us to triumph in Christ".

    There is nothing more amazing than an eagle in flight, and most Christians will only watch in wonder because of their refusal to be strong Christians. God wants us to get stronger day in and day out and without this quality in our lives we will never win battles over the enemy. Allow God to fill you with His power and strength and your life will begin to take off.

The last thing that an eagle has that Christians need is a spirit that is in submission to the wind. It is very clear throughout God's word that the wind is a type of the Holy Ghost and an eagle will allow the wind to carry him where he needs to go. For the majority of the eagle's life he will use the strength of the wind and not his own and this is why he is so successful. We as Christians need to really take note of this. Christians are dropping out of God's will at a record pace because they are doing things in their own strength without God's spirit. The Bible clearly declares in Philippians 4:13 that "I can do all things through Christ which strengtheneth me". When we rely on God's unending strength and ability rather than our own, the results are staggering. Far too often as we travel through this life we make the mistake of trusting in our own ability and we grow weary very quickly. Christians are falling over and over because they are not allowing God to control them and use them for His honor and glory. The Book of Galatians says "This I say then, walk in the spirit, and ye shall not fulfill the lusts of the flesh". An eagle remains fresh, strong, and victorious all because he yields to the wind for the longevity of his life. In the Book of John 15:5 Jesus said "For without me ye can do nothing". Without the power of the Holy Ghost controlling our lives on a regular basis, the end result will always be failure. The eagle is showing us by example that we can never soar to new heights without the influence of the wind from another world. Never operate in your own strength, learn how the eagle conducts itself and add these three qualities to your life. The eagle is the king of the air and if we want to fly with the Lord we must have a vision for the lost, great strength of the Lord, and a total submission to the wind from above.

Let's close this chapter with this power verse and I pray this verse will be the testimony of all our lives. II Samuel 1:23 "Saul and Jonathan were lovely and pleasant in their lives, and in their death they were not divided: they were swifter than eagles, they were stronger than lions".

Scriptures For This Chapter

II Samuel 1:23 "Saul and Jonathan were lovely and pleasant in their lives, and in their death they were not divided: they were swifter than eagles, they were stronger than lions."

Proverbs 29:18 "Where there is no vision, the people perish: but he that keepeth the law, happy is he."

Isaiah 40:31 "But they that wait upon the Lord shall renew their strength; they shall mount up with wings as eagles; they shall run, and not be weary; and they walk, and not faint."

John 15:5 "I am the vine, ye are the branches: he that abideth in me, and I in him, the same bringeth forth much fruit: for without me ye can do nothing."

Romans 8:31 "What shall we then say to these things? If God be for us, who can be against us?"

II Corinthians 2:14 "Now thanks be unto God, which always causeth us to triumph in Christ, and maketh manifest the savior of His knowledge by us in every place."

Galatians 5:16 "This I say then, walk in the spirit, and ye shall not fulfill the lusts of the flesh."

Ephesians 6:10 "Finally, my brethren, be strong in the Lord, and in the power of His might."

Philippians 4:13 "I can do all things through Christ which strengtheneth me."

Chapter 4

The Power of a Good Testimony

There is nothing in this world that carries more value with God like a good testimony does. The Bible says in Psalm Ch. 4:3 "But know that the Lord hath set apart him that is godly for himself". There is no denying the fact that Joseph, Joshua, Daniel, John the Baptist, Elijah, and others like them had an extra special influence and annoitting than the average Christian did in their day. God wants us to be holy as He is holy and in this day the way His children live breaks His heart. Christians seem to forget that the Lord of glory watches our lives and records our works in a book. This thought alone should cause His children to have a desire to walk the straight and narrow, but sadly, many don't even care.

My Dad did a wonderful job to instill in me as a young boy the fear of the Lord and the importance of a good testimony. Ever since I've been a little boy, I've been extremely careful of what I say, what I do, and where I go. The Bible says in Proverbs 1:7 "The fear of the Lord is the beginning of knowledge: but fools despise wisdom and instruction". As I live my life, I fully understand that I do not have the power to live other's lives for them, but I do have the power to walk in a way that pleases God. The Bible teaches in Colossians 1:10 "That we should walk worthy of the Lord unto all pleasing, being fruitful in every good work, and increasing in the knowledge of God. Paul begs Christians in Romans 12:1 "To present their bodies as a living sacrifice, holy, acceptable unto God, which is your responsible service". The Bible commands us to live in a way that is pleasing to God and as a result we will be a sweet fragrance in the nostrils of God. The Bible says in Philippians Ch. 2:15 "That we may be blameless and harmless, the sons of God, without rebuke, in the midst of a crooked and a perverse nation, among whom ye shine as lights in the world". Jesus commanded us in Matthew Ch. 5:16 "To let our light so shine before men, that they may see your good works, and glorify your father which is in Heaven". In my entire life I can only remember saying one curse word at the age of five. Never in my life have I drank a beer, been to a worldly party, smoked cigarettes, done drugs, or hung out with the evil crowd. Can you give that kind of testimony?

The Book of Psalm Ch. 1:1 says this "Blessed is the man that walketh not in the council of the ungodly, nor standeth in the ways of sinners, not sitteth in the seat of the scornful". But his delight is in the law of the Lord; and in his law doth he meditate day and night. God desires and expects us all to bring honor to His precious son and we cannot accomplish this if we buddy up with Satan most of the week. Jesus himself said this in Matthew 6:24 "No man can serve two masters". God wants us to serve him with every single fiber of our being. The

Bible says this in mark 12:30 "And thou shalt love the Lord thy God with all thy heart, with all thy soul, with all thy mind, and with all thy strength: this is the first commandment". Far too many Christians try to live in the world throughout the week and then play the part as Christian on Sundays. This kind of lifestyle literally makes God sick, and He clarifies this in Revelation Ch. 3:16 "Without living pure and clean before the Lord we will never reach our full potential". Every day as we get out of bed in the morning we should make a clear choice to die to self and serve the Savior. The Bible says this in Matthew 16:24 "Then said Jesus unto His disciples, if any man will come after me, let him deny himself, and take up his cross, and follow me". How important is your testimony to you? People are constantly watching our lives and they are just waiting for us to stumble. When Jesus ministered during His time on earth literally thousands of lost and religious people hung on every word not to learn but to only find fault. My greatest fear in life is to make a major mistake that will bring a reproach to the Lord Almighty. The pressure to walk on the water is heavy but it is not heavier than the cross our Lord carried. We all should do our part to be a light that shines forth to a dark world. The Bible tells us in Proverbs 4:18 "But the path of the just is as a shining light, that shineth more and more unto the perfect day". Let me ask you a question; are you shining more and more every day? Does the world see a difference in your life? We owe it to the Lord to be that light that He commands us to be. When people saw Elijah coming they stopped and took notice because they knew he had a testimony second to none. When you show up on the scene do people sense this about you? Every one of us should take our walk with the Lord seriously and I fear in these days it's not important like it should be. As long as people live half-hearted, people will remain hopeless and destitute of peace because we are dropping the ball. People depend on us to be an example that they can learn from. Are you comparable to a David, a Jeremiah, a Stephen, or a Moses? Sadly, most can be compared to a Lot or Judas. What kind of testimony do you possess?

As I close out this chapter I want to share a blessing with you that cheered my heart concerning my testimony. On Facebook they had a link posted where people could go on there and see who they're comparable to from the Bible. The comparison is computed due to ones way of life, and testimony as a whole. I submitted my profile and Facebook compared me to John the Baptist and the Angel Gabriel. Although I know I'm not even close, it blessed me beyond measure. I'm wondering as we close the page on this chapter who would you be compared to if you submitted your information? Live right everyone, God takes it very serious, I promise.

Scriptures For This Chapter

Psalm 4:3 "But know that they Lord hath set apart him that is Godly for himself: the Lord will hear when I call unto Him."

Psalm 1:1 "Blessed is the man that walketh not in the council of the ungodly, nor standeth in the way of sinners, nor sitteth in the seat of the scornful."

Proverbs 1:7 "The fear of the Lord is the beginning of knowledge: but fools despise wisdom and instruction."

Proverbs 4:18 "But the path of the just is as a shining light, that shineth more and more unto the perfect day."

Matthew 5:16 "Let your light so shine before men, that they may see your good works, and glorify your father which is in Heaven."

Matthew 7:13 "Enter ye in at the straight gate: for wide is the gate, and broad is the way, that leadeth to destruction, and many there be which go in thereat."

Matthew 6:24 "No man can serve two masters: for either he will hate the one, and love the other: or else he will hold to the one, and despise the other, ye cannot serve God and mammon."

Matthew 16:24 "Then said Jesus unto His disciples, if any man will come after me, let him deny himself, and take up his cross, and follow me."

Mark 12:30 "And thou shalt love the Lord thy God with all thy heart, and with all thy soul, and with all thy mind, and with all thy strength; this is the first commandment."

Romans 12:1 "I beseech you therefore, brethren, by the mercies of God, that ye present your bodies a living sacrifice, holy, acceptable unto God which is your reasonable service."

Philippians 2:15 "That ye may be blameless and harmless, the sons of God, without rebuke, in the midst of a crooked and perverse nation, among whom ye shine as lights in the world."

Colossians 1:10 "That ye might walk worthy of the Lord unto all pleasing, being fruitful in every good work, and increasing in the knowledge of God."

I Peter 1:16 "Because it is written, be ye holy; for I am holy."

Revelation 3:16 "So then because thou art lukewarm, and neither cold nor hot, I will spew thee out of my mouth."

CHAPTER 5

JESUS CALMED MY STORM ON THE INSIDE

Jesus has the ability to calm every storm that comes our way, but we must believe he can. So many Christians are sinking in the pit of doubt, but Jesus wants to set them on a solid rock by His marvelous grace. When is the last time you heard God's voice? If it's been a long time, may I suggest you lighten the load of noise surrounding your life and open your ears to that still small voice. Too many people in these last days are stressed to the max, and they are ready to explode at any second. Christians do not seem to have the ability to hear God's voice anymore and it's leading them astray. We as saints of God should all be in a position to hear His voice, and if we can't it's our fault, not God's. Whenever our spirit is troubled, we can go to the rock of ages and find relief. Sometimes our hearts and minds race and we find ourselves feeling overcharged with the cares of this life. The Devil wants us to rush, go fast, and worry about everything. God wants us to slow down, wait on Him, and be at peace. Sometimes in this fast moving society, we as Christians must learn to slow down, calm our emotions, and listen for His voice. The next story is a wonderful story that will bless your soul. Allow God to help you as you take in this blessed story.

One morning I woke up to reports that the weather was turning bad and there was a 100% chance of rain. The news also said that rain would start at around 7:30 A.M. and last until 3:00 P.M. When I heard this news, it troubled me because the homecoming football game was on this exact day and the lines for the field had to be perfect, so I began to worry. When I arrived at 7:00 A.M. that morning, the sky looked pitch black so I felt naturally rushed. When I went into the building I quickly grabbed the painter and the things I needed and hurried to the field to paint the football lines for the big game. The sky grew darker and darker and I was working at a high speed to beat the rain. My soul was troubled and my emotions were getting out of control and I had no clue how I would get the field done in time. Moments after these thoughts rushed through my mind I felt a peace from above saying "turn the machine down and take your time, it will not rain until you're finished with your work". After feeling this peace, I followed the Lord's voice and turned the machine to its slowest level and had total confidence that God spoke to me. I'll never forget the instant change of emotions that day and I had not one fear that it would rain until the job was complete. Instead of being stressed, I began to sing, and worship God right there on the field. When I finished the field it was 9:00 A.M. and the sky looked like something from a horror film but still no rain. On my way back to park the painter in the shed I kept the painter on slow and stopped to talk to a man named John for around 10 minutes. Once this was over, I did another job that lasted around 15 minutes and then I started to head towards the shop. On my way back I saw a woman rushing to throw trash away so I stopped to give her a hand. The woman looked at me and said "rain is coming, find shelter". When she said this I told her "once I park this painter in the shed the rain will come, but not until then". Around 3 minutes later I arrived in the shed and rain pounded the building. God held off the rain that day and Huron High won their game.

The Lord wants us to trust His word, not our emotions. When Jesus whispers peace be still all storms must obey. The Bible says this in Psalm 86:10 "For thou art great, and doest wondrous things, thou art God alone". When I look back at what God did that day I stand in awe and praise his Holy name. The Bible says in Psalm 83:18 "That men may know that thou, whose name alone is JEHOVAH, art the most high over all the earth". God wants His children to trust in His ability, not our own. If we keep this in mind our worry and fear will begin to disappear. Praise god for His power that can still any storm.

Scriptures For This Chapter

Psalm 83:18 "That men may know that thou, whose name alone is JEHOVAH, art the most high over all the earth."

Psalm 86:10 "For thou art great, and doest wondrous things: thou art God alone."

Mark 4:39 "And He arose, and rebuked the wind, and said unto the sea, peace be still. And the wind ceased, and there was a great calm."

Chapter 6

Rejoice in the Lord Always, No Matter How Bad You Feel

The Word of God says in Philippians 4:4 "Rejoice in the Lord always: and again I say rejoice". When Paul penned down this wonderful verse he was writing from prison and the conditions were miserable. In Acts ch 16 we find this Paul fella once again bound in prison, singing and praising God along with Silas and enjoying the spirit of the Lord. The great Apostle Paul was showing us through his writing and through the life he lived that Christians can worship no matter what state they find themselves in. The next time you are going through a trail of a storm just start singing and praising the Lord and see what happens. Christians need to learn that God is good all the time and He is worthy to be praised. All throughout the Word of God we find God blessing those that praised Him through the fire. Always remember you cannot be down and rejoice at the same time. Praising the Lord drives away doubt and fear and ushers in the joy of the Lord. The Bible says the joy of the Lord is our strength and God wants us to be strong during the dark times of life. Whenever we are mature enough to worship through our sad times, God will show up and bless us in special ways. The Bible teaches in Psalm 147:3 that God "Healeth the broken in heart, and bindeth up their wounds". Always understand in your heart that no matter how alone you feel God loves you and wants to comfort you. Allow Him to comfort you through worship and the results will be a blessing. Whenever I feel down in the valley I make it a habit to praise His name and when I do the blessings of the Lord always seem to flow. The next story is just an example of the importance of praising God no matter how we feel and the reward that comes because of it. Allow this story to bless your heart.

One morning as I was driving to work I made the mistake of having a pity party and focusing on my storm more than the Savior. The Devil filled my soul with sadness and depression started setting in. My mind was dwelling on the wrong things and I knew I had to turn my focus back on Jesus so I turned on a Gospel CD and began to worship. Almost instantly I sensed God's presence enter my car and I put both hands in the air and rejoiced in His goodness. My heart was revived and I thanked God over and over for His blessings and His mercy upon my life. When I got to work I received a call from a woman who had been praying for my book ministry. She said "Tony, just a few minutes ago you came to my mind and I felt led by God to give you $200 for your ministry". When I looked at my watch I noticed it was around the same time I was praising God through my storms. Always worship God despite how you feel and God will smile down upon you. If you're in the valley encourage yourself in the Lord and God may show up. The Bible says in Psalm 145:2 "Every day will I bless thee, and I will praise thy name forever and ever". Rise up out of the ashes and cry out from your soul "The Lord giveth and the Lord taketh away blessed be the name of the Lord". Worthy is the lamb who was slain.

Scriptures For This Chapter

Psalm 145:2 "Every day will I bless thee: and I will bless thy name for ever and ever."

Psalm 147:3 "He healeth the broken in heart, and bindeth up their wounds."

Job 1:21 "And said, naked came I out of my mother's womb, and naked shall I return thither: the Lord gave, and the Lord hath taken away; blessed be the name of the Lord."

Acts 16:25 "And at midnight Paul and Silas prayed, and sang praises unto God: and the prisoners heard them."

Philippians 4:4 "rejoice in the Lord always: and again I say, rejoice."

Chapter 7

A Friend Like No Other

There is a friend that sticketh closer than a brother and his name is Jesus Christ. So many different people we meet will tell us that they will never leave us and even die for us but when the hard times arrive you can't find those people with the FBI. Folks, there is no man who keeps his word quite like Jesus does. Hebrews 13:5 "Promises that He will never leave us nor forsake us" and throughout the ages of times this has proven to be true in the lives of countless believers. The Bible tells us in John 15:13 "That there is no greater love than this that a man lay down his life for his friends". The Lord proved His love for each and every one of us on a bloody hillside called Calvary, and the Bible teaches that we owe Him everything. The Bible says in Proverbs 17:17 that "a friend loveth at all times" and whenever I think upon this verse I immediately think about our Lord and Savior, Jesus Christ. The great old song describes Him like this "The God of the mountain is still God in the valley". No matter how hard this life becomes we have assurance from the Word of God that we will never walk alone. The great hymn writer penned these wonderful words from the depths of his heart "What a friend we have in Jesus, all our sins and griefs to bear, and what a privilege to carry everything to God in prayer". Whatever pain we feel, no matter what storm comes our way, nothing is too big for Jesus. God loves us with an everlasting love that is beyond human comprehension and he longs to have fellowship with us. The Bible says in I John 1:7 "But if we walk in the light, as He is in the light, we have fellowship one with another, and the blood of Jesus Christ His son cleanseth us from all sins". Many Christians are burdened down with the many care's of life and it's hard to watch them struggle on a daily basis. Jesus offers relief and he stands at the hearts door of man just hoping for that door to swing open wide. The Bible says in Matthew 11:28 "Come unto me all, all ye that labor and are heavy laden, and I will give you rest". We as humans need to give up and let Jesus take over so we can have peace on the inside. Every single day we should have a desire to walk with the master and seek His will. Jesus wants to show us His power through a life yielded to Him. The Lord wants to walk with us and talk with us throughout our time on planet Earth. We should all be able to get a hold of God at any given time and that will never happen if we don't take our walk with Him seriously. We should tell the Lord often how much we love Him, and we should worship Him as much as possible. Whenever we walk close to Jesus, great things will come our way. May this next story capture the importance of walking ever so close to the Savior. I pray this story is a blessing to your soul.

    Early one morning, as I was working at the school, I began telling the Lord how much I appreciate and love Him and I could feel His presence close by me. After a few minutes of singing and worshipping His most holy name, a verse came to my mind and it was a blessing on that cold Monday morning. The Lord directed me to I John 5:14 and this is what it says "And this is the confidence that we have in Him, that if we ask anything according to His will, He heareth us". For the next several minutes my heart and mind dwelt upon this verse and a prayer came to my lips. When my meditation was complete I began to pray to the Lord and beseech Him to answer this prayer from my heart. My prayer to God was simply this "Lord, I know you love me and I love you, I'm asking you right now to place it on someone's heart to give me exactly $100 and I will use it for your will".

When this prayer was over I went back to work with total confidence that God would answer this prayer. As the day unfolded, nothing seemed to happen but I had absolute faith this prayer would come to pass. Praise the Lord, later on that night the prayer came alive and it was a blessing to my soul. As we were going out of the church a man stopped us and said that the Lord placed it upon his heart to give us $100 and he prayed it would be of help. Folks, as I held that $100 the joy bells started ringing in my soul and once again I was praising His precious name. The Word of God tells us this in Psalm 34:15 "The eyes of the Lord are upon the righteous, and His ears are open unto their cry". Christians all across this world are missing out on His power and His blessings because they value something in this life more than their relationship with Jesus.

We will never experience joy unspeakable and full of glory again until we hunger and thirst for a relationship with Him. The old song says it like this "Though I fail the Lord, He has never failed me". This life at its best is sinking sand, but a wise man buildeth his house upon a rock. If you trust in the Lord He will never let you down. What a great friend we have in Jesus.

Scriptures For This Chapter

Psalm 34:15 "The eyes of the Lord are upon the righteous, and His ears are open to their cry."

Proverbs 17:17 "A friend loveth at all times, and a brother is born for adversity."

Jeremiah 31:3 "The Lord hath appeared of old unto me, saying, yea, I have loved thee with an everlasting love: therefore with loving kindness have I drawn thee."

John 15:13 "Greater love hath no man than this; that a man lay down His life for His friends."

Matthew 7:24 "Therefore whosoever heareth these sayings of mine, and doeth them, I will liken unto a wise man, which built his house upon a rock."

Hebrews 13:5 "Let your conversation be without covetousness: and be content with such things as he have: for he hath said, I will never leave thee, nor forsake thee."

I John 1:7 "But if we walk in the light, as He is in the light, we have fellowship one with another, and the blood of Jesus Christ His Son cleanseth us from all sin."

I John 5:14 "And this is the confidence that we have in Him, that if we ask anything according to His will, He heareth us."

Chapter 8

The Stamp of Approval from Almighty God

If you are facing an important decision in your life, please do yourself a favor and wait for direction from Almighty God. Whether you are going to preach a message, or produce a CD, or write a book, or anything else that requires a lot of work, sit down at the feet of Jesus and seek His will in your life. Whenever we try to make things come to pass on our own we will find it failing in a tragic way. Learn how to seek the council of the Lord and make sure His stamp of approval is applied to each and every decision you make. The Bible says this in Isaiah 9:6 "For unto us a child is born, unto us a son is given: and the government shall be upon His shoulder: and His name shall be called wonderful, counselor, the mighty God, the everlasting father, the prince of peace". Without asking council from our everlasting father, every decision we make will be void of peace. Seek His face early and often and wait on His guidance for however long it takes before jumping into a project. Always avoid being in a hurry when making decisions and always ask the Lord if it's His will before doing anything.

The Bible teaches in Psalm 37:23 "The steps of a good man are ordered by the Lord: and he delighteth in his way". Please make sure it's God's will, not yours, and strive to please Him and not your own fleshly desires. We need more ministries directed by Almighty God, and we need far less ministries that operate without the touch of the Lord. The story I will now give is powerful, and a real blessing to this old sinner boy. It's so wonderful to have a ministry directed by God and I'm sure after you read this story you will agree that God is in it. Allow God to bless you through this next story.

Around two years ago the Lord placed a strong burden on my heart to produce a second volume to the book Walking On The Water With Jesus. This burden was strong so I wanted to make sure it was the Lord dealing with me and not my own self ambitions, so I sought out to gain direction from on high. Quickly, I grabbed my Bible, my notes, and a copy of Walking On The Water With Jesus and I went to the back of the house to pray and meditate on this important decision. When I went in the back, I noticed my daughter left the TV on and it happened to be on the Discovery Channel so I just left it on. I remember looking up into Heaven and saying "Lord, if you want me to produce Walking On The Water With Jesus Volume 2, make it very clear to me right now". Immediately after I prayed this prayer I happened to look up at the TV and like a flash of lightening a lizard took off and was running on the water. When this happened it stunned me so I watched for a few minutes to make sure what I just witnessed was real. Sure enough, they were doing a special on a lizard that had the ability to walk on the water and this special lizard is commonly referred to as the Jesus lizard. Never in my life have I seen this lizard before but as I was praying for direction of God he allowed it to go across my TV set. As I viewed this lizard it seemed to run with so much freedom and at the moment the Lord told me to write the book with His approval so we submitted to His will. Folks, ever since this day the Lord has blessed this decision and so many have been touched by that book. It's amazing how God reveals things unto men when we seek His will above anything else. When you have a ministry with God's approval, great things are bound to happen. I'll never forget the power of this moment, and the joy I felt in my heart. We all need to sit at the feet of Jesus and seek His will in every situation we encounter. Let me close out the chapter with this verse Psalm 27:14 "Wait on the Lord: be of good courage, and He shall strengthen thine heart: wait, I say, on the Lord".

Scriptures For This Chapter

Psalm 27:14 "Wait on the Lord: be of good courage, and He shall strengthen thine heart: wait, I say, on the Lord."

Psalm 37:23 "The steps of a good man are ordered by the Lord: and he delighteth in his way."

Chapter 9

If You Will Give God Your Little Lunch, He Can Multiply it for Years to Come

How many times over the years has God directly spoken to us about giving up what we have to help the cause of Christ? If I were to ask for a show of hands on this question, I'm sure all of us could raise our hands and remember times when God pleaded with us about sacrificing for the greater good. God is pleased with those who listen to His voice, not those that ignore it. In the eyes of God, giving is a priceless act and He longs to use your gift of faith to further His wonderful plan in reaching others.

At different times in all of our lives, God tests us to see who will give and who will not. Those who obey receive great blessings and they who refuse fail the test. The Bible says in Matthew 17:20 "If ye have faith as a grain of a mustard seed, ye shall say unto this mountain, remove hence to yonder place;

and it shall remove". God is looking to do great miracles in our life but He is waiting for us to act by faith. In John Ch. 6:9 a boy was willing to give up his little lunch at God's command and as a result, around 25,000 were fed. The most amazing thing about this story is the fact that while the crowd was doubting, the lad was trusting and God performed a supernatural miracle. Jesus is looking for those who will give their little lunch, and when they do, blessings can flow for years to come. The Lord can take your gift of faith and multiply it in ways you have never dreamed. For the rest of this chapter I will list three different times God led me to give my little lunch and because I listened, many were blessed. Allow these three stories to motivate you to do the same.

While serving God in Detroit under the ministry of Dr. Lawrence Mendez, God seemed to move on me in every service. The need in Detroit was great, and the preaching was from the glory world. These two elements together pushed me to limits with God that I've never been before. Over and over again God would say "Give" and I would say "Yes, Lord". One night under Holy Ghost conviction, God spoke to me about buying the church a few buses so without question I acted on faith and gave up my lunch. Little did I know that night that God would allow those two buses to pick up thousands of kids for church for the next 15 years. Jesus took that little lunch and fed the multitudes with it and I give Him all the glory.

Another time God took my lunch and fed others while I was on a visitation night in Detroit. As we were knocking doors one night I overheard a dear lady mentioning that she needed a car or she would not be able to come to church anymore. Without hesitation, I took my check book out and with a heart of faith wrote her a check so she could get a car. This decision not only blessed me, but more importantly it blessed her and her family. She used the money to buy an old beat up car in hopes that it would last a year. My friends, God put His hand on that car and allowed her to bring her family to church for the next 11 years. If I would have not given up my little lunch that day, this woman's life may have ended up very differently. Always do what God tells you and you will never regret it.

The final story I will give concerning this subject is amazing to say the least. Years ago, a dear preacher had a need for a used floor buffer for his hardwood floor business, so I felt led to get it for him. When I got him the machine it was old and used up but I asked God to allow it to be a blessing for years to come. Not long ago I asked this man of God if he still had the floor buffer. To my amazement he said "I still do and for 18 years I've never had one single problem with it". The preacher told me that every morning as he looks at it he remembers my act of kindness and marvels how it lasted so long.

These are just three examples of what God can do if we are willing to give up our lunch for the cause of Christ. God wants to take our gift of faith and feed the world many times over. Just do what God commands and the blessings will last a lifetime. Allow God to do miracles through your life of faith and years down the road you will never regret it.

Scriptures For This Chapter

John 6:9 "There is a lad here, which hath five barley loaves, and two small fishes: but what are they among so many?"

Matthew 17:20 "And Jesus said unto them, because of your unbelief: verily I say unto you, if ye have faith as a grain of a mustard seed, ye shall say unto this mountain, remove hence to yonder place; and it shall remove; and nothing shall be impossible unto you."

Hebrews 11:6 "But without faith it is impossible to please Him: for he that cometh to God must believe that He is, and that He is a rewarder of them that diligently seek Him."

Chapter 10

Feeling God's Angels All Around

I've come to realize more and more as I get older that the angels of God are all around us. There are so many stories throughout the pages of time that reveal to us the powerful encounters of angels showing up on the scene when people needed them most. Seemly, every day I hear a story, or read about angels visiting mankind and it's hard to explain away. Many times throughout my own personal walk with God I've been humbled to sense the presence of angels around me. God has protected and sheltered me and my family on several occasions and we give Him the glory for that. We could probably all tell stories of the mercies of God concerning angels, and the Bible is filled with accounts as well. The following story is powerful, and I pray it will richly bless your heart.

Not long ago, we as a family took a trip to Pigeon Forge, Tennessee, and we had a blast. The trip lasted a week and we had many wonderful moments. As we were packing up to leave the Lord impressed on my heart to pray for safety on our way home so I did just that. My prayer to God was very simple and I asked for Him to send an angel to watch over us as we travelled home. Shortly into our journey back home, a car began to move into our lane and it just kept coming. I remember looking over and watching something hold back that car from completely coming into our lane. Folks, it was a miracle of God that we were not in an accident and I know an angel kept us safe. Around an hour later, we had another close call and we could sense His presence all around, keeping us safe. I often wonder what would have happened if I didn't pray. It is very possible that we would not be here today. The Bible says in Psalm 34:7 "The angel of the Lord encampeth round about them that fear Him, and delivereth Him". Thank God for the many angels that surround us that we cannot see. If God would open our spiritual eyes to how many were near us at any given time it would blow our minds. The Bible says in Hebrews 12:22 that there is an innumerable company of angels. There is no way of knowing how many angels exist today, we are just thankful God sent one to protect us that day. Thank God for His love and watch care over His children, we should never take that for granted.

Scriptures For This Chapter

Psalm 34:7 "The angel of the Lord encampeth round about them that fear Him, and delivereth them."

Hebrews 12:22 "But ye are come unto Mount Zion, and unto the city of the living God, the heavenly Jerusalem, and to an innumerable company of angels."

Chapter 11

Pay It Forward

How often have we all heard this saying "pay it forward"? Nearly every day I hear this saying by somebody, somewhere. The phrase "pay it forward" is basically taken from the Biblical principal of giving and receiving. Seemly, every human has their own wonderful story about how they gave to someone else and God returned a similar blessing later on for them. Folks, I'm no different and I too have a lot of great stories concerning this topic. The Word of God is filled with stories that bless our hearts and that prove that giving and receiving is a powerful thing. People are passionate about paying it forward because there is nothing more powerful than real stories that move the heart. My advice to all mankind is simply this: pay it forward to others and I promise it will come back to you. The Bible says in Ecclesiastes 11:1 "Cast thy bread upon the waters: for thou shalt find it after many days". When the Bible makes statements like this I promise you can go to sleep every night with confidence that it's true. The following story is a blessing and I hope it's a motivation for you to pay it forward every chance you get.

One day while coming out of Taco Bell, the Lord moved on my heart to dump out all my change on the ground to help someone in need. It seemed a bit unusual, but I knew the Lord spoke to me so I emptied out $2.52 on the ground next to my car. The man I was with said to me "what in the world are you doing, are you crazy?" When he said this, I said to him "yes, maybe, but God wants me to pay it forward and He told me to do it". The man said "Are you sure?" and I said "Yes, sir, I am, and I promise He will give it back and much more". The very next day, I was asked by my boss to work a Saturday and that rarely ever happens. As I walked into work the next morning, I could not believe my eyes. My job that day was to pick up trash all around the football field. God allowed me to pick up 38 dollars' worth of pop bottles in one afternoon. He also allowed me to work 3 hours overtime and I found three dollar bills as well. My mind kept flashing back to the day before when God led me to drop my change on the ground with the promise of it coming back.

Sometimes, God will direct us to do unusual things. My advice to you would be to never question His leading and always do what He says. My Bible still says this in John 10:27 "My sheep hear my voice, and I know them, and they follow me". Don't ever question His leading because He will never lead you astray. Pay it forward and God will bless in ways we never imagined.

Scriptures For This Chapter

Ecclesiastes 11:1 "Last thy bread upon the waters: for thou shalt find it after many days."

John 10:27 "My sheep hear my voice, and I know them, and they follow me."

Chapter 12

Getting A Big Surprise While Driving Home One Night

For anyone who knows me well, you understand that I'm a big believer in sowing and reaping. Any time a human being sows seeds, whether good or evil, you can mark it down that seed is coming back later down life's road. The Word of God teaches in Galatians 6:7-8 "That whatsoever a man soweth that shall he also reap". Always be aware of this verse in all decisions that you make. If you want to have a life that is blessed by the hand of Almighty God, make it a habit every day to sow good seeds. Sometimes things we sow in faith during our younger years will spring up in a great fashion years down the road. This next story is an example of that and I pray it encourages you to sow good seeds towards others.

When I was a young man at Open Door Baptist Church, my life was consumed in helping other ministries. Nothing in the world meant more to me than helping some ministry reach its full potential. My heart was fixed on God and every check was gladly going towards the Gospel of Jesus Christ. When I reflect back on those years, great joy fills my soul because I know treasures have been laid up in Heaven and no one can take that away from me. Jesus instructed us in Matthew 6:20 to "Lay up treasures in Heaven" and we will never regret it. When you lay up treasures in Heaven and help others along life's journey, great things will be in your future and God will return the favor. God promises us that if we sow good seeds, we will never go without and He will raise up people to bless us and what I'm about to tell you will prove just that. One night while driving down the road I noticed I was being followed by a vehicle and it lasted all the way until I got home. When I pulled into my driveway, this man pulled right behind me and got out of his car. Honestly, I was a little nervous because I had no idea who it was so I allowed him to approach my vehicle. When the man got to my car, I noticed it was a big man so I reached for any weapon available to defend myself. As I rolled down the window, I quickly noticed that it was a dear brother that I hadn't seen for a long time. This great man told me that from out of nowhere God convicted him about bringing me some money to be a blessing so he followed me to give it to me. He said "Brother, I'm doing this because 10 years ago you helped my family when I was in need so I'm doing the same thing for you". He said "Tony, hold out your hand". So I listened to the man of God. When I reached out my hand he placed $390 in it and he said "I love you Bro". Folks, every time we sow good seeds, God in Heaven takes records. We really needed that money and God's timing was perfect once again.

I want to encourage you to trust God and invest in others and I promise God will respond in a great way. The

Bible says in Psalm 18:25 "With the merciful thou wilt show thyself merciful". Give it a try everyone and see what God can do.

Scriptures For This Chapter

Psalm 18:25 "With the merciful thou wilt show thyself merciful; with an upright man thou wilt show thyself upright."

Galatians 6:8 "For he that soweth to his flesh shall of the flesh reap corruption; but he that soweth to the spirit shall of the spirit reap life everlasting."

Matthew 6:20 "But lay up for yourselves treasures in Heaven, where neither moth nor rust doth corrupt, and where thieves do not break through nor steal."

Chapter 13

Our God Knows What We Have Need Of

So often when the storms of life gather, and the pressures of life flood our soul, we have a tendency to focus on the storm instead of the Savior. When hard times arise and bills come to our mailbox, sadly we allow worry to distress us and fear to grip our hearts. As Christians, we must understand that we serve a God that knows the future and He understands exactly what we are going through. Although we may experience emotions and feelings that feel out of our control, let me remind you that God is not stressed out and He has everything under control. Many times throughout life God has a clear reason why He does things but we as humans cannot see the future so we immediately turn to doubt instead of trust. The Bible says in II Timothy 1:7 "For God hath not given us the spirit of fear; but of power, and of love, and of a sound mind". The Bible also says in I John 4:18 "But perfect love casteth out fear". We as children of God have the victory and may I remind you that I John 5:4 says "and this is the victory that overcometh the world, even our faith". God does not want us to live a life of fear but rather a life of faith, love, and confidence in what He can do through us if we will trust Him. Psalm 62:8 tells us to "trust Him at all times". The Lord is not in Heaven stressing out about our situations like we are and He has a reason for everything He does in our lives. God desires for us to seek His face when problems come, and if we do, great things will happen. The next story will be a blessing to you as it was for us.

A short time ago my wife and I received two different bills in the mail that arrived unexpectedly that totaled $503. My wife looked at me and said "What are we going to do about these bills? What should we do?" My response to Erin was "I don't want to have to borrow the money, but we may have to". Once I made this statement God's spirit showed up and reminded me that prayer is always the answer so I decided to pray about $503 coming in. The Bible says in Jeremiah 33:3 "Call unto me, and I will answer thee, and show thee great and mighty things, which though knowest not" so I clung unto that verse for a few days. When Sunday arrived, a dear woman approached me and said "Tony, God wants me to give you $75, I hope it's a blessing". The gift that the woman gave me was a blessing and I began to seek His face again, trusting Him for the rest of the money. We went home, had a great afternoon, and before church I approached the Throne Room of Grace one final time, trusting that the money would come in. We went back to church, heard some great preaching, and as we went to leave a man of God had a gift he wanted to give us. This man told my wife that God had been dealing with him about giving us some money and he handed my wife a huge pile of cash that she just put in her purse. When we got home, we counted it together and to our amazement it was $432. All in all that day, between the $75 and the $432, our bills were paid with $5 to spare. There is a great lesson we learned from this moment in time, and that is to always make God the first option and things will always turn out right. Let me close this chapter out with Hebrews 4:16 "Let us therefore come boldly unto the Throne of Grace, that we may obtain mercy, and find grace to help in time of need".

Scriptures For This Chapter

Psalm 62:8 "Trust in Him at all times; ye people, pour out your heart before Him: God is a refuge for us. Selah."

Jeremiah 33:3 "Call unto me, and I will answer thee, and show thee great and mighty things, which thou knowest not."

II Timothy 1:7 "For God hath not given us the spirit of fear; but of power, and of love, and of a sound mind."

I John 4:18 "There is not fear in love; but perfect love casteth out fear: because fear hath torment. He that feareth is not made perfect in love."

I John 5:4 "For whatsoever is born of God overcometh the world: and this is the victory that overcometh the world, even our faith."

Chapter 14

There's a Miracle in the Making

When Jesus Christ walked among the crowds during His earthly ministry, people from every walk of life tried to get near Him. Jesus' fame increased more and more with each passing day and that caused many people who were sick and in pain to hunger and thirst after His healing touch even more. The four Gospels are loaded with many different stories of men and women who got to the point of getting completely desperate for a miracle and they clearly knew Jesus was exactly what they needed. Men and women from every country were doing whatever it took to get to Jesus and whenever folks had this mindset, Jesus would have compassion on them and heal them. We as Christians in this day and age need to take a page out of their book and hunger again after healing from the Master. As long as people hold onto their problems and refuse to seek after God, they will remain in their broken state of life; void of any help from on high. When we know we need help, we must swallow our pride and do whatever it takes to draw near to the hem of His garment. Jesus is looking to perform miracles in all of our lives, but it will never happen without brokenness and a hunger for healing. I never want to get to the point where my lack of faith or pride holds back miracles in my life. Every day we should seek the Lord at a deeper level and long for that touch from above. We serve a God of the supernatural and the only thing that limits His power is our lack of faith towards Him. The next story will highlight the ability God has to perform miracles in our lives if we just believe he can. Allow this story to speak to your heart.

Not long ago, the precious Savior opened up a door to get my book Walking On The Water With Jesus to some billionaires from Texas, but I literally had no money to even pay for the shipping costs. A dear woman told me that if I sent the book, she would personally take it to them so I immediately tried to figure out a way to make this happen. I recall sitting down at work and pulling up a song on YouTube called "There's A Miracle In The Making" and the words really began to do wonders for me. Over and over again I replayed that song and really tried to take in the words. On the fourth time of listening to that song, a peace like a dove swept over my soul and I knew my miracle was on the way. After I was done listening to this great song God gave me joy unspeakable that remained for the remainder of that day. Moments later while walking down the road picking up trash a car came towards me at a high speed and stopped right beside me. The window rolled down and a dear lady started throwing money at me under Holy Ghost conviction. The dear woman looked at me and said "While I was sitting at home, God told me very clearly to come up to the school and give you $100 so you must take it". Directly after making this remark, she drove off saying "God Bless You". When my work day was over, I immediately sent a book to the billionaires and now we are friends on Facebook. God is able to perform miracles for all of us but we must believe He can and will. Matthew 15:28 says it like this "Then Jesus answered and said unto her, o woman, great is thy faith: be it unto thee even as thou wilt, and her daughter was made whole from that very hour". Praise God for faith, mercy, and His everlasting compassion towards them that believe He can do the impossible. Let's end this chapter with this great verse Matthew 19:26 "But Jesus beheld them, and said unto them, with men this is impossible: but with God all things are possible".

Scriptures For This Chapter

Matthew 15:28 "Then Jesus answered and said unto her, O woman, great is thy faith: be it unto thee even as thou wilt. And her daughter was made whole from that very hour."

Matthew 19:26 "But Jesus beheld them, and said unto them, with men this is impossible; but with God all things are possible."

Chapter 15

Jesus is Always There When We Need Him

One of my favorite passages in the Bible is found in Isaiah 43:2. This wonderful verse is an encouragement to me and it has been an encouragement to millions down through the years. Whenever you feel down in spirit, run to this verse and verses like it for the comfort that you need. Isaiah 43:2 reads like this "When thou passeth through the waters, I will be with thee; and through the rivers, they shall not overflow thee: when thou walkest through the fire, thou shalt not be burned; neither shall the flame kindle upon thee". According to this verse, no matter how alone we feel, God will be near us. No matter what storm we are encountering, God has promised to walk through the fire with us. Child of God, we are never alone and never allow Satan to convince you that you are. The Devil loves to work overtime to discourage us, but God works overtime to enhance our faith and He uses verses like Isaiah 43:2 to accomplish this in our life. Always trust the purity of God's voice over the lies of the wicked one. Whenever you are going through a battle, understand that your feelings and emotions will try to take over. When this happens, slow yourself down and eliminate your fear by running to the truths from the Word of God. This next story will be a blessing to all of us who feel overwhelmed by the pressures of life. We have a God that wants to help and if you run to Him, He will hear your cry for help. Allow this following story to minister to your soul.

Not long ago on a Tuesday morning at around 7:15 A.M. I received a message from a dear friend of mine and right away I could tell he needed prayer. This wonderful brother started to desire prayer for his finances and he has never been one to ask before. This man has always been a blessing, so immediately I started to pray for my friend. I remember bowing my head right there on the spot and asking God to open up Heaven for this saint and to do something unusual as only He can. When I lifted up my head a peace came over me and a sweet verse swept over my soul. The verse that flooded my soul was Psalm 46:1 which says "God is our refuge and strength, a very present help in trouble". After thinking over this verse for a few minutes, I felt led to go inside the school I was working at and I could feel my steps being ordered by the Lord. When I was walking through the building a woman named Honey stopped me and her news was glorious. She said "Tony, I thought of you this morning and wanted to ask you if you had a need for some free cereal". I looked at her and said "Sure, I have a friend I just prayed for and he needs help". She said "You can have as much as you need". Folks, I walked away with full boxes of mini cereals. Each box contained 96 boxes in it and in total I was able to give this man I prayed for 576 boxes of cocoa puffs for his family to enjoy. After this took place, I looked up into Heaven and said "Yes Lord, that was unusual and I praise you for it". My friends, life may get rough and hope may seem to vanish from view, but I assure you that God has not gone out of business and He loves you very much. We serve a supernatural God. Psalm 46:10 says "Be still and know that I am God. Amen and Amen. O taste and see that the Lord is good".

Scriptures For This Chapter

Psalm 46:1 "God is our refuge and strength, a very present help in trouble."

Psalm 46:10 "Be still, and know that I am God: I will be exalted among the heathen, I will be exalted in the earth."

Psalm 34:8 "O taste and see that the Lord is good: blessed is the man that trusteth in Him."

Isaiah 43:2 "When thou passest through the waters, I will be with thee: and through the rivers, they shall not overflow thee: when thou walkest through the fire, thou shalt not be burned; neither shall the flame kindle upon thee."

Malachi 3:10 "Bring ye all the tithes into the store house, that there may be meat in mine house, and prove me now herewith, saith the Lord of hosts, if I will not open you the windows of heaven, and pour you out a blessing, that there shall not be room enough to receive it."

Chapter 16

The Lord Will Hear When I Call Upon Him

No matter how great the need is, God can meet that need through the avenue of prayer. Jesus declared in Matthew 7:7 "Ask, and it shall be given to you; seek, and ye shall find; knock, and it shall be opened unto you". Jesus also made the statement in Matthew 21:22 "And all things, whatsoever ye shall ask in prayer, believing, ye shall receive". James 4:2 says clearly "Yet ye have not, because ye ask not". Hebrews 4:16 plainly says "Let us come boldly unto the Throne Room of Grace, that we may obtain mercy, and find grace to help in time of need". The Bible teaches that God has all the answers, and without coming to Him through prayer in total faith, we will remain hopeless and searching for the truth. Jesus said in John 14:6 that "I am the way, the truth, and the life, and no man cometh unto the father, but by me". The quicker we understand that God has what we need, the better off we will be. The Lord is the great problem solver, the great burden bearer, and the greatest friend one could ever have. Proverbs 18:24 says "There is a friend that sticketh closer than a brother". Matthew 11:28 says "Come unto me, all ye that labor and are heavy laden, and I will give you rest". People all around this world are tired and weary and little do they know that Jesus has His arms open wide to any and all who will come unto Him. When I find myself in a mess and I don't know what to do, I find myself going to Jesus and I always leave satisfied with that choice. As the famous song says, "Give Up and Let Jesus Take Over". The next story is an example of the benefits of asking God for help and allowing Him to come through. I pray this story will bless you.

One day as I was alone at home, I had a burden heavy on my heart that was weighing me down. After about 10 minutes of trying to figure it out on my own the sweet Holy Spirit whispered in my ear "Why don't you allow me to help?" When I heard this still small voice, I dropped to my knees and said this prayer "Lord, you know this need, please help me if you will". Moments later, there was a knock at my door so I went to answer it. When I opened the door a sweet lady handed me flowers for my wife and a check for $200. As she left that day, a great burden had lifted from my soul, and I wondered why I didn't do that sooner. If you have a burden weighing you down, don't delay, run to Jesus today. Revelation 3:20 says "Behold, I stand at the door, and knock: if any man hear my voice, and open the door, I will come in to Him, and will sup with Him, and He with me".

Scriptures For This Chapter

Proverbs 18:24 "A man that hath friends must show himself friendly: and there is a friend that sticketh closer than a brother."

Matthew 7:7 "Ask, and it shall be given unto you; seek, and ye shall find; knock, and it shall be opened unto you."

Matthew 11:28 "Come unto me, all ye that labor and are heavy laden, and I will give you rest."

Matthew 21:22 "And all things, whatsoever ye shall ask in prayer, believing, ye shall receive."

John 14:6 "Jesus saith unto him, I am the way, the truth, and the life: no man cometh unto the father, but by me."

Hebrews 4:16 "Let us therefore come boldly unto the Throne of Grace; that we may obtain mercy, and find grace to help in time of need."

James 4:2 "Ye lust, and have not: ye kill, and desire to have, and cannot obtain: ye fight and war, yet ye have not, because ye ask not."

Revelation 3:20 "Behold, I stand at the door, and knock: if any man hear my voice, and open the door, I will come in to Him, and will sup with Him, and He with me."

Chapter 17

Call Unto Me and I Will Answer Thee

God in Heaven desires to answer our prayers, but only if we approach Him with a clean heart. David said in Psalm 66:18 "If I regard iniquity in my heart, the Lord will not hear me". The reason we cannot seem to get prayers to go past the ceiling is because we know deep in our hearts that something we are doing is grieving the spirit of God. It is not that God can't answer our prayers, but it's because God refuses to answer our prayers because our sin is standing in the way. Isaiah 59:2 says "But your iniquities have separated between you and your God". People all around this planet refuse to come clean with God and it results in a dead prayer life. Life is too short and God is too good for Christians to live in that way. If Christians would just worry more about impressing God rather than impressing man, our churches could experience revival once again. In Acts 4:31 we read a powerful account of men who had clean lives and could get a hold of God. Acts 4:31 says that "When they had prayed, the place was shaken where they were assembled together; and they were all filled with the Holy

Ghost". Folks, this is what we desperately need again, people that hunger and thirst for the power of God who can pray in the Holy Ghost like Jude talked out. God has not and will not change and He never will. Sadly, we are the ones who changed and it breaks God's heart. The Bible still says that God is able to do exceeding abundantly above all that we can ask or think. This next story will once again prove that God is still on the throne and He still answers prayer.

    Not long ago, I received a text message from a Godly sweet lady that really blessed my heart. In the message, this woman made it clear that she felt God wanted her to give me $60 just to be a blessing and it touched my heart. As fast as I could, I sent her a text back saying that I believe God would give this woman five times the amount she gave me and that I was trusting it would happen. Later that night, the school was having a carnival and they were raffling off prizes worth a lot of money. There were hundreds and hundreds of people there that night, trying to win the prizes that were available. When the numbers were called, this dear precious saint had a winning number and walked away with one of the prizes and it happened to be worth five times the amount she gave me. You see, folks, the power is there, we just are not tapping into it. Elijah prayed just 63 words and the fire of God fell. It's not the length of the prayer that carries the most weight, it's the purity of our hearts that does. Come clean with God and you too can make this statement "In my distress, I called upon the Lord and cried unto my God: He heard my voice out of His temple, and my cry came before Him, even into His ears". God is still able to hear and answer any prayer we have, but we must humbly seek His face in order for this to happen.

Scriptures For This Chapter

Psalm 18:6 "In my distress I called upon the Lord, and cried unto my God: He heard my voice out of His temple, and my cry came before Him, even into His ears."

Psalm 66:18 "If I regard iniquity in my heart, the Lord will not hear me."

Isaiah 59:2 "But your iniquities have separated between you and your God, and your sins have hid His face from you, that He will not hear."

Acts 4:31 "And when they had prayed, the place was shaken where they were assembled together; and they were all filled with the Holy Ghost, and they spoke the Word of God with boldness."

Ephesians 3:20 "Now unto Him that is able to do exceeding abundantly above all that we ask or think, according to the power that worketh in us."

Jude 1:20 "But ye beloved, building up yourselves on your most holy faith, praying in the Holy Ghost."

Chapter 18

The Goodness of God Leadeth Thee to Repentance

The Word of God clearly teaches in Psalm 33:5 that the earth is full of the goodness of the Lord. Folks, there could never be a more truthful statement than that. The goodness of God is overwhelming at times and it should bring us to our knees in total gratitude and worship for what He has done and for what He is doing for us all. The goodness of God ought to lead everyone on Earth to repentance. Psalm 145:2 says that "Every day will I bless thee: and I will praise thy name forever and ever". Psalm 145:8 says that "The Lord is gracious, and full of compassion: slow to anger, and of great mercy". Psalm 34:1 says it like this "I will bless the Lord at all times: His praise shall continually be in my mouth". Psalm 150:6 says "Let everything that hath breath praise the lord. Praise ye the Lord". Far too many Christians fail to notice and fail to focus on God's goodness and it really hampers and effects the way they live. Always remember this verse as you live your daily life: Romans 8:6 says "For to be carnally minded is death; but to be spiritually minded is life and peace". In other words, if you train your mind to be negative, you will always fail as a Christian. However, on the flipside, if you train yourself to think positive, life and peace will always be close by. The Bible still says it like this "And we know that all things work together for good to them that love God, to them who are the called according to His purpose". Every single morning we get out of bed we should allow ourselves to enjoy life, enjoy creation, laugh, love, and walk with God as He has intended us to. We serve a God of love and a God of mercy. The Lord has showered down His blessings on every single one of us and he desires to work on us and conform us into the image of His dear son. Every day I walk planet Earth I want to notice the beauty of creation. I want to bask in the sunshine of His love. I want to cherish every precious moment and live a life that brings honor to His holy name. We are all here for a divine reason and we must sow as many good seed as we can, so later on in life fruit may burst forth because of it. We are bought with a price and we owe Him everything. Whenever we sow good seeds you can mark it down that seed is coming back towards us in the same fashion every time. The following story will prove this is true and it will also show us what a good God we serve.

Many years ago, on a Wednesday night, God suddenly started to convict me about selling my car and giving it to a preacher. Without any hesitation, I surrendered to His voice and gave the preacher my car while knowing that somewhere down the road God would remember this decision and bless me for it. Galatians 6:7 says "For whatsoever a man soweth that shall he also reap" and I've always believed every word of it because God cannot and will not lie. Folks, years went by and nothing ever happened, but God was working behind the scenes on our behalf. One day, my wife made a statement that maybe we shouldn't have given that car away and maybe we should have sold it and paid off some bills. I remember turning to her and saying "Honey, we made the right decision, and God always honors giving and He always returns the favor". Two weeks later, I got a call from my wife that her grandfather felt led to give us his 2007 impala with just 57,000 miles on it. We are still driving this car today, and it is such a blessing.

James 1:17 says that "Every good gift and every perfect gift cometh from above". Every step we take, every move we make, and every gift we enjoy, all comes from the hand of God. We all should realize that our God is good and He works on our behalf on a daily basis. Psalm 68:19 says "Daily the Lord loadeth us up with benefits". It's high time we understand that God is good to all and He is worthy of all praise. Every time we sow good seeds He in return will bless us in the same way, somewhere down life's road. This story is just proof of that statement, and I could give you hundreds more like it. God's goodness is such a beautiful thing.

Scriptures For This Chapter

Psalm 33:5 "He loveth righteousness and judgement: the earth is full of the goodness of the Lord."

Psalm 34:1 "I will bless the Lord at all times: His praise shall continually be in my mouth."

Psalm 145:2 "Every day will I bless thee; and I will praise thy name for ever and ever."

Psalm 68:19 "Blessed be the Lord who loadeth us up with benefits, even the God of our salvation. Selah."

Psalm 145:8 "The Lord is gracious, and full of compassion; slow to anger, and of great mercy."

Psalm 150:6 "Let everything that hath breath praise the Lord. Praise ye the Lord."

Romans 2:4 "Or despisest thou the riches of His goodness and forbearance and long-suffering; not knowing that the goodness of God leadeth thee to repentance?"

Romans 8:6 "For to be carnally minded is death; but to be spiritually minded is life and peace."

Romans 8:28 "And we know that all things work together for good to them that love God, to them who are the called according to His purpose.

Titus 1:2 "In hope of eternal life, which God, that cannot lie, promised before the world began;"

Galatians 6:7 "Be not deceived; God is not mocked: for whatsoever a man soweth, that shall he also reap."

James 1:17 "Every good gift and every perfect gift is from above, and cometh down from the Father of Lights, with whom is no variableness, neither shadow of turning."

Chapter 19

But My God Shall Supply All Your Need

It never ceases to amaze me how God Almighty supplies every need of His children. Time would not permit me to dive into the many stories I've seen through the years concerning this subject. Over and over again, I've watched God bring people to the very limits of their faith only to watch Him step in on His perfect timetable and supply their every need. We serve the God of all power and understanding and we must learn to trust Him no matter how dark our situation may be. By the authority of God's holy word, we can have complete faith that God will come through when we need Him most and He knows exactly what we have need of. There is a quote that helps me so often throughout my life and it helps remind me of the faithfulness of God. This quote is very simple and very profound: "Always trust God's promises that never change over your feelings that change all throughout the day". If we can rest in the fact that the Bible is a solid rock and our feelings are shifting sand, we can stand any raging storm that comes our way. This next story will be just another example of God's mercy in the area of Him supplying every need, whether big or small.

One day, as we were all sitting around eating dinner, my wife said "Honey, isn't it time to get some new shoes?" When she said this, I looked down at my shoes, which looked like they had been through the war, and I knew it was time to consider buying new shoes. My wife said "Let's go to Walmart and get some new shoes" and I said "Alright, we will after dinner". Directly after marking this statement, God started dealing with me about waiting a while and trusting Him so we cancelled our trip to Walmart. The very next day while working at Huron High School, a woman approached me with some wonderful news that blessed my soul. In her hands were red Nike Air shoes and she said "Tony, you were the first one to come to my mind, do you need some shoes?" My response to her was "Yes, what size are they?" She responded by saying they were size 11 and that happened to be my exact size. When she handed me the shoes, I just knew that was an answer to prayer and that God made that happen. God loves to provide for His own and what's even more amazing about this story is the fact that two more pairs of shoes were given to me that same day, and they also were size 11. We serve a loving God that knows what we need before we even ask. Rest in the fact that God will come through every time we place our trust in Him. My Bible still says "But my God shall supply all your need according to His riches in glory by Christ, Jesus". If the blessed holy book says it just believe it, don't doubt it. Always remember that the just shall live by the faith and there is no other way to live if we want to please him.

Scriptures For This Chapter

Philippians 4:19 "But my God shall supply all your need according to His riches in glory by Christ, Jesus."

Romans 1:17 "For therein is the righteousness of God revealed from faith to faith: as it is written, the just shall live by faith."

Chapter 20

Amazing Grace, How Sweet the Sound

The greatest song ever written was penned by one of the worst infidels that has ever lived. The song is Amazing Grace, and the man was John Newton. This song displays the love of God that can reach the vilest of sinners. John Newton invented new curse words, and went to any extreme to rebel against the teachings of his Godly mother. Mr. Newton would drink, smoke, cuss God, steal, lie, cheat, abuse, slander, and run around and laugh at Holy living. He owned slaves, and by his own words was capable of anything. At his lowest point in life, God sent a violent storm his way when he was travelling by way of ship one night. The storm was so fierce that it forced Mr. Newton to realize that he may die, and he knew he was unprepared to meet his maker. Suddenly, versus flooded back to his memory that his mother taught him when he was a child. Deep conviction struck his heart and in the midst of the storm he began to seek after God like never before. The Lord heard his cry, and Mr. John Newton was transformed in a supernatural way. The God he hated was the God he suddenly adored. The song Amazing Grace is his personal testimony of how wonderful the grace of God was for him, and can be for you if you would only receive it. This song has reached the masses for Christ, and has become almost bigger than life.

For the rest of this chapter, I would like to borrow the third verse of this wonderful hymn and apply it to my own life. You will see the mercy and grace of God in the way of divine protection and safety towards me in a breathtaking fashion. God has watched over my life, and sent His angels to protect me over and over again. The third verse of the song Amazing Grace reads like this: "Through many dangers, toils, and snares, I have already come, thus grace has brought me safe thus far, and grace will lead me home". In the next few minutes, I will give you a brief description of many close calls that I have had, and I will show God's hand of safety through all of them. Paul once gave a list in II Corinthians 11:23-28 and showed God's watchful care during His ministry, and that's what I aim to do in this chapter. My desire is to magnify God through these stories, and reveal the fact that He is the potter and I am the clay. Let me start from my beginning and slowly go through my life, bragging on the grace of God.

It all started when my mother was carrying me in her womb. She told me how she was riding a bike one day and fell off that bike on her belly, exactly where my head was located. She told me how she went to the doctors and told them what had took place. The doctors feared that there could be brain damage due to her fall and it was something to be concerned with. Through prayer and God's grace, I turned out fine and my parents thank God for it to this day. Another problem I faced upon being born was a very rare back problem. There was a step in my spine that only 50 people in America had at the time. This problem crippled most who had it, and the situation was very serious. My problem was placed on the prayer list, and within 3 days my back was healed.

When I was around 7 years old, I almost drowned, before my mother saved me. As a child, I remember stepping on some old nasty glass one day that cut my foot wide open and there was blood everywhere. This could have caused disease and infection, but praise God, my foot is fine today. While playing baseball in the yard one day my brother hit a baseball around 100 miles per hour and hit me in the face from about 35 feet away. This could have killed me if it would have been hit just right, but I shook it off and kept playing. Another scary moment took place when my mom hit a deer at around 45 miles per hour and severely damaged her van. My brother Bobby and I were in the van, but walked away with no injury to show for it. I remember while golfing one day as a teenager, on the ninth hole of a course called Harbor Club, lightening hit a tree next to me. At the time when it struck the tree, I had a metal club in my hand.

Another scary incident happened while working on the road one afternoon, driving signs into the ground with a 75 pound jack hammer. I was holding stubs in place while another man used the jack hammer to drive them into the ground. This jack hammer could drive through concrete and was very powerful. As we were working, my hand was too high on the stub, and the man I was working with put the jackhammer right on my thumb and started driving the stub with my thumb caught under it for over 4 seconds before he noticed. The pain was beyond anything I had ever experienced, but I kept my finger, and it has healed up now. Praise God, he spared my finger, and I'm glad it wasn't much worse than it was. I fell off a truck one day, from about 12 feet in the air, and landed on my tail bone. Although it hurt, nothing broke, and I was okay.

One day while working on the freeway, a car crossed the yellow line and almost ran over my foot. Another time at work, the wind caught 14 signs and I found myself under them. Each sign was 108 pounds apiece; totaling over 1400 pounds that fell on me. I should be paralyzed, but I'm still walking fine today, and I returned to work 2 days later.

When you look at my life, I'm almost like a walking miracle.

Many years ago when I was working in Ohio, something happened very early in the morning that woke me up pretty quick. I was setting barrels out to close traffic when, from out of nowhere, a semi-truck took a barrel out of my hand, and took it up the road about half a mile. If I would not have let go of that barrel, I probably would have lost my hand.

To say I've been lucky just isn't good enough, I believe God's hand has protected me all these years.

I still remember the day I was part of a six car accident on Southfield Freeway with multiple spinouts involved. The sight was almost like watching a movie, with all the sights and sounds it produced. No one was seriously hurt, and I was praising God. Another incident that comes to mind is when I fell asleep at the wheel at 3:00 in the morning and almost tipped my S-10 pickup over at 70 miles per hour. God kept me safe and kept that from happening. I also remember getting lost while driving one day and heading towards oncoming traffic. Thank God somehow I avoided an accident, and was able to make it safely to my destination.

Time after time, day after day, God's hand seems to guide me around pitfalls and dangers in my life. Please allow me to give you a few more examples of close calls.

One day while driving in the winter time, I hit black ice and spun out of control. When it was all said and done, I ended up landing in a ditch, face down, a foot from a tree on one side, and 2 feet from a mailbox on the other. My truck was badly damaged, but I was safe and sound. Something else that comes to mind is the time my tire blew out, heading to Cedar Point, and my truck went across lines of traffic, almost hitting cars. It was almost like landing a plane, but after it was over, once again I was safe. A few years back, my car died in a busy intersection and a number of cars almost hit me head on, and if so I would probably be in bad shape today. While playing football one day, I was tossed in the air and landed on my neck. After a few minutes of sitting out of the game, I returned without injury. At a greenhouse one day, while closing an old glass window, I was severely cut on the head and bled for over an hour. I returned to work the next day. Around a month later, at the same greenhouse, my lip was cut open this time, and I bled for around 2 hours.

I have almost been shot twice, been hit by cars, been in more accidents and close calls then I can count. I've almost hit a few deer crossing the road, and nearly got on a ride at Cedar Point in which a man died on 5 minutes later. The list goes on and on, and the fact is, I really should be dead right now. David said it perfectly when he said "There is but a step between me and death". The Bible tells us in Psalms 34:7 that "The angels of God encampeth around them that fear Him". God has sheltered and protected me, and I am forever in debt for His grace in my life. I took a list at home and counted around 43 times where I could have died or been crippled but Gods mercy protected me. The song Amazing Grace is more than just a song, it is a biblical reality. My life has been nothing short of amazing, and his hand of protection has lead me every step of the way. Like Fanny Crosby once wrote "To God be the glory, great things He hath done". The Bible says in Psalms 34:19 that many are the afflictions of the righteous; but the Lord delivereth him out of them all". God deserves all the praise for everything He does, and I hope through this chapter we have seen this. The fourth verse of Amazing Grace reads like this "When we've been there ten thousand years, bright shining as the sun, we've known less days to sing God's praise than when we first begun". Let's end this chapter with Psalm 23:4 "Yea, though I walk through the valley of the shadow of death, I will fear no evil: for thou art with me: thy rod and thy staff they comfort me. Amen and Amen."

Scriptures For This Chapter

Psalm 23:4 "Yea though I walk through the valley of the shadow of death, I will fear no evil; for thou art with me: thy rod and thy staff they comfort me."

Psalm 34:19 "Many are the afflictions of the righteous: but the Lord delivereth Him out of them all."

CONCLUSION

As we conclude this book I want to sincerely thank you all for taking the time to read this feeble effort for the Lord. Lord willing, the stories contained in this book touched your soul and blessed you in various ways. Folks, we serve a supernatural God of mercy who displays His love to mankind on a continual basis. We that know Christ are bought with a price and, if the truth be told, we owe Him everything. We as Christians need to surrender all to the Lord and serve Him with every fiber of our being.

My prayer for this book is that in the years to come, when folks read these stories, it will drive them to the very throne room of God. We need people on the front line for God again, sold out to further the cause of Christ. This world needs us to be the salt of the earth and the light of the world again. Folks, simply put, we need revival and that's my heart's desire. Soaring With Eagles Volume 2 is meant to infuse life and victory in the believer's life again and I pray it has and will in the future.

PUBLISHED by PARABLES
Earthly Stories with a Heavenly Meaning

ANTHONY RITTHALER

CPSIA information can be obtained
at www.ICGtesting.com
Printed in the USA
FFOW02n0054310717
38156FF